What
You Have
Heard
Is True

Also by Carolyn Forché

Poetry

Blue Hour
The Angel of History
The Country Between Us
Gathering the Tribes

Edited by Carolyn Forché

Poetry of Witness: The Tradition in English 1500–2001

Against Forgetting: Twentieth-Century Poetry of Witness

PENGUIN PRESS
New York
2019

*For Julianne,
with best wishes,
Carolyn Forché
1 October 2019*

What
You Have
Heard
Is True

A Memoir of Witness
and Resistance

Carolyn Forché

Carolyn Forché

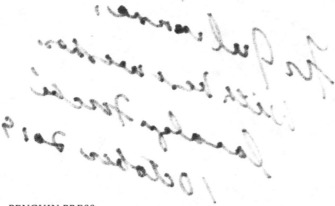

PENGUIN PRESS

An imprint of Penguin Random House LLC
penguinrandomhouse.com

Copyright © 2019 by Carolyn Forché
Penguin supports copyright. Copyright fuels creativity, encourages diverse voices,
promotes free speech, and creates a vibrant culture. Thank you for buying an authorized
edition of this book and for complying with copyright laws by not reproducing, scanning,
or distributing any part of it in any form without permission. You are supporting writers
and allowing Penguin to continue to publish books for every reader.

All photographs, unless credited below, are courtesy of Carolyn Forché.
Photograph on page 201 courtesy of Bruce Forché.
Photographs on pages 333, 336, and 343 by Harry Mattison. Used with permission.
Photograph on page 338 by Benoît Gysembergh, courtesy of *Paris Match* via Getty Images.

ISBN 9780525560371 (hardcover)
ISBN 9780525560388 (ebook)

Printed in the United States of America
10 9 8 7 6 5 4 3 2 1

Set in Dante MT Std
Designed by Cassandra Garruzzo

Penguin is committed to publishing works of quality and integrity.
In that spirit, we are proud to offer this book to our readers;
however, the story, the experiences, and the words are the author's alone.

Some names and identifying characteristics have been changed
to protect the privacy of the individuals involved.

In memory of
Leonel Gómez Vides,
1940–2009

Hope also nourishes us. Not the hope of fools. The other kind. Hope, when everything is clear. Awareness.

—**Manlio Argueta**

For the strangest people in the world
are those people recognized, beneath
one's senses, by one's soul—the people
utterly indispensable for one's journey.

—James Baldwin

No te conoce nadie. No. Pero yo te canto.
Nobody knows you. No. But I sing to
you.

—Federico García Lorca

It is near the end now. We are walking in the rippling heat of a sorghum field: cicadas whirring to an empty sky. A man uncorks a water gourd, another man leans against a spade. There is a woman here too, wearing an aproned skirt over her trousers. Hard light and the dry rattle of sorghum seed heads. I'm holding a spray of seeds. One of the men takes Leonel aside and tells him something—a secret, like everything else. We get into the jeep and without explanation drive to another place, not far from this field. The campesinos, rural peasants, would have walked, measuring distance not in kilometers but in hours or days.

"What are we looking for?" I ask, and as always, he doesn't answer, swearing under his breath through the haze of smoke that hangs in the air where the corn had been growing. We stop near a cluster of *champas,* shacks made of mud and wattle. One of them has collapsed and smoke rises from it.

"Wait here," he tells me, but I don't wait. I had stopped waiting for him months before this, but he can't seem to break this habit of telling me to wait. Smoke is rolling like a shore cloud along the fields just above the blackened stubble. We walk, and when he stops, I stop, and when he continues, I continue. He palms the air to say "Slow down" or "Be quiet." I slow down and am quiet. When we reach the *champas,* no one is in them. No one is home. A large plastic bowl used for making the slurry that becomes tortilla dough is overturned on the ground. There is a child's

T-shirt in the tortilla slurry. Behind one of the *champas* it appears that several hens have been held by their feet and whacked against a stone. They are lying on the ground, one of them still opening and closing its beak.

A HUNDRED OR SO METERS MORE, AND WE HEAR THE WHINE OF FLIES, THE hissing and belching of turkey vultures, a flapping of wings like applause in the maize stalks as the fattened birds try to lift themselves. A flatbed truck follows at a distance behind us, with three campesinos standing in the back. They are calling out to us or to the driver of the truck but I don't understand what they say.

I don't know what I had expected to see, but not the swollen torso of a man with one arm attached to him, a black pool of tar over his crotch. I didn't expect that his head would be by itself some distance away, without eyes or lips. The stench in the air is familiar: a rotting, sweet, sickening smell. Human death. I bend down when I see the head, but I hear Leonel saying, "Don't touch it. Let the others do it."

At first, I thought they were going to find the rest of the man and place his remains in the truck but instead they gather the arms and hands, the legs with their feet attached, and bring them to the torso where it lies on the ground. They set the head on the neck where it once had been, then the three men take off their straw hats and stand in a circle around the man they have reassembled. They stand and one crosses himself lightly. The parts are not quite touching, there is soil between them, especially the head and the rest. No eyes, no lips or tongue, birds nearby hoping we will go away and leave them to this meal. The air hums, we walk. Why doesn't anyone do something? I think I asked.

ON THIS DAY, I WILL LEARN THAT THE HUMAN HEAD WEIGHS ABOUT TWO AND a half kilos.

O ver the years, I have asked myself what would have happened if I hadn't answered the door that morning, if I'd hidden until the stranger was gone. Knowing him as I came to know him, he would have sensed my presence and continued ringing the bell. On that day, I had been at my typewriter, a heavy IBM Selectric that a friend would later complain sounded like a machine gun. There were stacks of papers everywhere: human rights reports, students' essays and poems, unfinished manuscripts, unanswered correspondence. A sea wind passed through the screens, lifting some of these papers into the air and sailing them to the floor. The finches were singing atop their bamboo cage, as its door was usually open, leaving them to fly about the house, perching on ceiling fixtures and open doors. In those days, I could type faster than I could think—my father saw to that when I told him I wanted to be a poet. I would need to be able to "fall back" on something, he'd said. Fall from where? I had wondered to myself at the time. The typewriter was set on the kitchen table, and most days I worked there, the ocean almost audible, the air scented by the fields of nearby flower farms. As it was late morning, the harvesters of Encinitas had already left for lunch, having begun their work at dawn. At first, I might not have noticed the sound of the van pulling into the driveway, but its engine remained idling, so it wasn't simply turning around. Then the engine died and the doors were opening.

It was not my habit to answer the door when I was alone. My mother had been strict about this with her seven children. She couldn't watch all of us at once, she would say, so there were rules. Not opening the door to strangers was one of them.

We had moved to this town house hurriedly, my housemate and I, from an apartment we had also shared, after receiving mail from a town to the north of us, an envelope that contained lewd photographs of a man, with a note telling us that he was "coming to visit" and we were "not to contact the police." The police had said that there was nothing they could do until "something actually happened," and therefore it might be best for us to move somewhere else. So here we were, in a new, unfurnished town-house rental nearer the ocean, as far from the city as we could reasonably live and still commute to the university where I taught and Barbara studied. Twenty-eight miles—far enough.

The vehicle that was not turning around was a white Toyota Hiace. From the window, I could see a man get out and sling a tote bag over his shoulder, with papers escaping from the top. Then the back panel door slid open, and two very young girls climbed down and stood beside him. I remember reassuring myself that an ax murderer probably wouldn't travel with two young girls. When the man looked up at my window, as if he knew I was there, I moved away and cowered against the wall. The dust-covered Hiace had El Salvador license plates.

What I knew of El Salvador, I knew from my Spanish professor in college, himself a Salvadoran, and from stories told during the previous summer when I lived on the island of Mallorca in Spain. I had traveled there with my friend Maya to translate the work of her mother, the expatriated Central American poet Claribel Alegría. The Salvadoran Spanish professor occasionally showed slides to the class, most especially of his family's houses and gardens. Everything I knew about the isthmus of the Americas at that time I knew from Claribel's poetry and the professor's luminous images projected onto a blank wall.

THE DOORBELL RANG, THEN RANG AGAIN.

On the other side of the door, the girls' voices rose in delight, possibly at their first glimpse of the rabbits: does and their young kits leaping in the stubble of garden. The hutch door had been left open. I studied the stranger through the peephole: a tussle of dark wavy hair, a short black beard, heavy eyeglasses. The girls hid behind him, but because they were here too, I opened the door as far as the chain lock would allow.

The man standing on the porch seemed amused by this.

"You are Carolyn Forché," he said through the opening, "and I am Leonel Gómez Vides. These are my daughters, Teresa and Margarita."

"I'm sorry," I said, "just a moment." I closed the door and leaned against it. I had heard this name last summer in Deià. This was Claribel Alegría's cousin. Her mother was the sister of his mother. That summer, Claribel sometimes spoke of this Leonel with great affection, but at other times she seemed not to want to say very much. I sensed admiration, caution, and also a little fear, but I couldn't work out whether it was fear of him or for him.

The name Leonel Gómez was usually mentioned when Claribel and her family were talking about El Salvador, where Claribel had spent her childhood. These conversations concerned people who had been killed there, or who had disappeared, among them their friend the poet Roque Dalton, murdered just two years earlier—the handsome revolutionary who had once escaped from prison, according to the legend, when an earthquake shook his cell walls to the ground just before he was to be executed. In stories like this they often also brought up Leonel but when this happened Claribel quickly changed the subject, especially if I seemed at all curious. When I asked Maya about this secrecy, she waved away my concerns with *Mami's just tired,* or *Mami's still grieving over Roque.* There came to be an unspoken rule: Don't bring up Roque or Leonel around Mami.

Now this mysterious Leonel was standing on my porch in Southern California with his daughters. How was that possible? Wanting to be sure of who he was, I went upstairs for the envelope of snapshots I'd taken in Deià. This seems odd to me now—that I should have required some proof from him, as he did in fact resemble the handsome youth straddling a motorcycle in the photograph that Claribel kept in her study.

When I opened the still-chained door again, I passed the pictures to him, asking that he identify the people turning toward the camera: the wiry, silver-haired man with the cigarette, the woman in a cocktail dress, raising a glass, and the young one, a former ballerina, sitting tall in her chair—my good friend Maya, the poet's daughter. There were others too, a few of the regulars who gathered on the terrace of the poet's house in the afternoons to drink and talk and watch the sun slip behind the peak of the Teix, but I wouldn't have expected him to know who they were.

"This is Claribel," he said, tapping her face with his fingertip. "And there is the husband, Bud. And this?" His voice softened. "This must be Maya. It is Maya, isn't it?"

"Come in, please come in, I'm sorry to keep you waiting, and I'm sorry to have . . ."

"No, it's okay. I like that you checked me out. You were being careful."

The girls were looking around a bit apprehensively. How strange that house must have seemed, so bare walled and empty. Our kitchen table also served as our desk. We used a soup bowl for an ashtray. Our finches flew about the house as they wanted, but mostly they remained on their perches near the cups of millet. There was a small vegetable and herb garden planted on the side of the house. My friend and housemate, Barbara, had taken care of it all summer while I was in Spain. The rabbits were the offspring of Easter bunnies given to us by my students: two females and a male, as it turned out. What were we supposed to have done with them? On this morning, twenty-three rabbits were living in the hutch and garden.

The only furniture was the kitchen table with its four ladder-back chairs, two mattresses on the floors of our upstairs bedrooms, and a single daybed in the living room that we used as a couch. In one corner of the living room, a papier-mâché calliope horse painted red, about four feet high, reared on its hind legs. There were flowers on its rump. Leonel stopped when he saw it, seeming taken aback.

"How long have you had this?" he asked, laughing, shaking his head.

"I don't know. A friend found it in a bin on the street. Why?"

"No, just asking. But it's yours, right? It's *your* horse?"

We had drifted into the kitchen, which must also have seemed odd, with nothing on the countertops, and no sign that food had ever been prepared there. The girls kept close to their father, pinching his shirt to their faces, but slowly they began to steal glimpses of me.

"Do you like rabbits?" I asked, remembering the Spanish word, *conejos*. "They're in the hutch in the garden—do you want to see? There are two mothers, and the babies are a month old. Go ahead, you can play with them."

Leonel bent down for them to whisper in his ear, and he nodded that it was okay for them to go outside.

"Do you have any coffee? I've been driving for three days. I'm dead. And can you clear this stuff off the table? There are some things I need to show you. We have work to do."

Work? I remember thinking then, *What* work? But he was already pushing my papers aside and unpacking his woolen bag, woven with symbols and animals, among them an openmouthed wildcat about to pounce.

———◆———

He began covering the cleared table with white butcher paper cut from a roll he had brought, taping it down, and in the center, he placed what few objects he could find in our cupboards: salt and pepper shakers, a shot glass of toothpicks, a paring knife, matchbooks, and to these he added things taken out of a second, smaller bag: a miniature metal replica of a World War II battleship, a Swiss Army knife, wooden matches and a pouch of Balkan tobacco. Then he set a pack of my cigarettes among these things.

"These cigarettes are now a military garrison. Sit down." And then, "How much do you know about military dictatorship?"

No small talk, no *How is Claribel?* Just *How much do you know?* I didn't know what to make of him.

Leaning over the paper, he began drawing a map of his country, almost without looking, moving the pen in a continuous bleed of ink, traveling in memory from the Guatemalan border south to the Bay of Fonseca, then east toward Honduras, suggesting the volcanic peaks and mountain ranges of El Salvador with a string of chevrons.

"Nothing," I answered. "I know nothing about military dictatorship."

His elbows were on the map, his folded hands pressed against his mouth. I saw myself in his glasses, two of me, and the girls' laughter was sieved through the kitchen screens.

"Good," he said. "At least you know that you know nothing."

He seemed about to say something else, but stopped himself, clamping down on his cold tobacco pipe. His hair fell onto his forehead and against the collar of the plaid shirt that I would later learn was woven in the highlands of Guatemala. Later, I would also learn that his expensive-looking watch was a Rolex, which he wore because, as he said, "such a watch sends a certain signal," but what sort of signal he didn't say. For perhaps the same reason, he wrote with a fountain pen, the first Montblanc I'd ever seen, with a silver-and-gold nib. I wanted to ask him if I might try writing with it, but couldn't bring myself to do it. He drew his illustrations with a different set of pens made especially for drawing.

"Okay. How is your knowledge of history?" And then without pausing for my answer, he said, "Look. There is soon going to be a war in El Salvador. It will begin in three years, maybe five at the most. It might cost tens of thousands of lives, maybe hundreds of thousands."

"How do you know this?"

"Let's talk first about your country—finally, finally, a sitting president of the United States has instituted a human rights policy for his State Department. I'm trying to find out what that means."

"What? What *what* means?"

"This so-called policy on human rights. Okay. Why am I here? Maya wrote to me a few months ago and sent me your book of poetry. You didn't know this? You must have known. You signed it to me 'with warm regards.'" He took his worn copy of my book from his woven bag and slid it across the table.

"How do you think I knew who you were when you opened the door? Your author photo looks just like you, by the way."

"I don't think it does."

On the title page, Maya had added:

Para Leonel, que entenderá por qué le estoy enviando esto, con mucho amor, Maya.

For Leonel, who will understand why I have sent this, with much love, Maya.

"So that is why I'm here. Because of your poetry book, and Maya's letter. She told me all about you."

I didn't tell him that Maya had also told me some things about him. Once, on one of our walks along the beach, barefoot with our jeans rolled up our calves, she had said that her cousin Leonel had given some of his land to the peasants—but who knows? And people say that he sleeps on the ground with his motorcycle in his arms—can you imagine? As she talked, the lace edge of the surf washed over the murmuring stones and the sanderlings hurried across a mirror of water. Gull cries tore at the air above the drying kelp beds and, barely moving their wings, drifted out to sea.

"YOU DROVE ALL THE WAY FROM EL SALVADOR—?"

"Yes, my dear, I did. More than four thousand kilometers. I wanted to talk to you."

"But that's such a long way. What if I hadn't been here? I do go away sometimes, you know."

"Well, I took the chance. And this might also be my last opportunity to spend time with my daughters, maybe the last for a good while, and so I brought them with me on this—this camping trip."

The moment had passed to ask casually what Maya had told him about me, but perhaps I would have another chance.

"Your daughters are beautiful," I said, getting up to turn off a whistling kettle. "What do you want to talk to me about?"

"What I told you. Among other things, I want to talk to you about a certain dead American."

This was his manner—to toss out in a flat voice "dead American," and then refuse to elaborate, as if he were tugging lightly at a fishing line, leaving the lure adrift on the surface.

"What dead American? What do you mean?"

He rose to pace the kitchen, hands thrust in his khaki pockets, pivoting at the end of each sentence to walk a few feet in the other direction, as if tethered to a fixed point.

"Okay. Maybe I should start at the beginning."

"Why don't you tell me why you're here. I don't think it's because of poetry."

He sat down again, studying his own hand-drawn map, picked up his drawing pen, and began a bit wearily, "I'm a coffee farmer from El Salvador. My farm is small but produces high-quality beans. I'm also an inventor, you might say, and a social critic, and a painter, although I no longer have time to paint."

Miniature coffee trees had appeared on the map, drawn as he spoke.

"And a motorcycle racer? And a champion marksman?"

Maya had also told me that Leonel had gone to school for a while somewhere in the United States, a military academy, she thought, she wasn't sure where, and he had been a world champion marksman and racer of motorcycles. There was a wall of trophies in his house, she said, and once, in competition, he had even been awarded a handmade AK-47 assault rifle with a gold-plated inscription. She thought him handsome, and intelligent, but also "too mysterious for most people."

He seemed at once exasperated and pleased by this description.

It was true that Maya had told me these things, but her father had gone further.

"It was possible," Bud said one evening as we sat in the dark on the terrace under the stars, "that he is with the guerrillas, as some people say. *Possible.*" Then, drawing deeply on one of his frequent cigarettes, "it is also possible that he is with the CIA."

In the flaring light between his fingers, his face was entirely visible then, his jaw set, his eyes narrowing, and I heard a sharp intake of breath from Claribel, who spoke her husband's name as if it were a stone cast over a balcony wall.

"She asked me," he'd said evenly. "I'm answering."

Leonel sighed at this and said quietly, "I don't race motorcycles anymore. I do other things."

"And?"

"Well, that's it."

"And why are you here?"

"I already told you—because you are a poet." He stiffened in the chair. "Okay, we're wasting time. *Mirá,* I have about three days here before I have to start back. Three days. And we have a lot to talk about."

He began drawing check marks on the paper: birds flying in a child's sky and, with a few quick strokes, what appeared to be a brigantine at full sail, with a few smaller ships receding to the edge of the paper.

"You wanted me to begin at the beginning, he said, dropping his pen down among the ships. "This is the beginning."

I studied his drawing. "Pirates?"

He thought I had deliberately made a joke. "You might say so, but no. I was trying to draw the Spanish galleons of the conquistadores. Do you see? A brigantine would carry both oars and sails, but the galleon is entirely under sail. The brigantine would have two masts. The galleon, as you see, has three or four."

"Mr. Gómez?"

"Call me Leonel. A brigantine would have greater maneuverability. But I was about to tell you about Pedro de Alvarado. Do you know who he is?" And without waiting for what would have been my no, he held forth for an hour or so about Alvarado, sent by Cortés to conquer the isthmus of the Americas, Alvarado whom the Indians called The Sun, not (as the red-haired Alvarado thought) because they considered him a god but because they thought his head looked as if it were on fire.

"He was brutal toward Indians," Leonel said, "and did all the things you might expect: ordering them flayed alive, roasting them over fires on spits."

The girls had come in with furry rabbits cupped in their hands, whispering to their father again, who laughed and shook his head at whatever they were saying. Then he might have told them to go play, because the rabbits were set loose on the kitchen floor, and the girls followed them on hands and knees around the house and up the carpeted stairs to the two bedrooms.

Arrows appeared on the map indicating the route Alvarado's soldiers had taken inland. I would learn that Leonel was particularly interested in military history, logistics, weaponry, strategy, and tactics, beginning with the ancient world's bowmen, slingers, and hoplites, their infantries, and cavalries of archers mounted on horseback, and later in Genghis Khan's supply routes, military intelligence, and the art of feigned retreats. In the woolen bag woven with a pouncing jaguar, he kept, bound together, a worn copy of Sun Tzu's *The Art of War,* Carl von Clausewitz's *On War,* and Machiavelli's *The Prince,* all of them falling apart and rubber banded, with marginalia in the tiniest script I had ever seen. In the seemingly bottomless bag, he also had the transcript of American congressional hearings and other "documents," as he called them, but first he led me into his dream narrative of the Americas before the conquest, most especially of the isthmus connecting the two continents: a starlit world whose civilization began, according to the Mayan Long Count calendar, on August 11, 3114 B.C.E.

He began with the Pipil Maya, as he called them, artists of milpa cultivation, descendants of astronomers and poets who fled their ancient cities after some catastrophe, possibly having to do with drought. Or cannibalism. It was a world, he said, lit at night only by fire, and they were a people who mapped the stars, for galaxies beyond our own, without the aid of telescopes.

I asked why he was telling me about these things.

"I thought it might interest you—as a poet, I mean—the history from the beginning. Surely poets are interested in this? But we can start somewhere else, anywhere you wish," he said, pulling more papers and pamphlets from his bag and stacking them on the table.

"Let's start with two dead priests and some deported nuns, or with three hundred dead campesinos. Here—these are the proceedings of your own congressional Subcommittee on Inter-American Relations. Read them. I have underlined the relevant passages for you. When you're finished, we can talk about the dead American."

Was he angry? I wondered. What had I done to anger him? But he seemed calm, steel voiced, matter-of-fact. He could have been telling me about scientific research or the history of the Goths and Visigoths.

"Leonel, I'm sorry, but you say you're here because I'm a poet. What does this have to do with poetry?"

"Maybe nothing. I don't know yet. This is what I'm trying to find out. But let's go eat first. I'm starving. Do you know a place where we can get hamburgers?"

"Hamburgers? That's what you want?"

"Yes. Hamburgers and also ice cream."

The waters of the Pacific resembled hammered silver under that cloudless noon as he drove us north in the Hiace, the girls in the back with all the windows open, the music of Peruvian pan flutes floating from the dashboard. This was a drive we would take several times over the next three days, up the road and a little inland, and each time I would run inside with his money and the order—burgers and Cokes, always the same—and other than these trips, and errands to buy what he described as "supplies," we mostly talked at the kitchen table, or rather, he mostly talked while I listened and smoked. Early in the evenings, I would run a bath for the girls and then he'd tuck them into my absent housemate's bed. Sometime after midnight, when I couldn't listen or think any longer, I would go up to my room and shut the door. He would take care of himself, he said, and the house went quiet.

———◆———

I lay awake, drifting in and out of my journey that past summer, when I was twenty-seven years old and in Europe for the first time.

"Come with me," Maya had pleaded. "Come to Deià. Why not? You can work on the translations in the mornings while Mami is writing, and after siesta you can show your work to her and ask questions. She'll help you. And you'll love Deià. It's the most beautiful village on Mallorca. And you'll be happy to know that your English poet Robert Graves lives there, just down the road from C'an Blau. He wrote I, Claudius there—do you know that novel? Surely. Robert is a friend of Mami's. We're all friends there. And if you insist upon being serious, well, most evenings Mami and Daddy hold a salon on the terrace where people talk about all sorts of things:

books, politics. We could also hike to the peak of the Teix one afternoon. You like hiking. And we could go to Soller and Palma and—wait—we could take the trip I've always wanted to take, through Andalusia by train, to Granada, where Lorca lived. The Sacromonte. The Alhambra. Do you know *Tales of the Alhambra*? Surely. We'll go there, and to Sevilla for the flamenco. And . . ."

"Maya? This all sounds beautiful, but no."

"What?"

"I don't think so. It would be expensive."

"Don't be ridiculous! If you are going to be a poet, you must see the world. This is what your poet Rilke wrote, wasn't it? *In order to write a single poem, one must see many cities, and people, and things; one must get to know animals and the flight of birds.* Many cities, Carolyn, and fountains and cathedrals and paintings! How are you going to write if you don't know these things? You have enough saved for a ticket and that's all you need. It will cost you less to live there than to stay at home. And as you said yourself, you can't translate Mami's poems without help. If you don't want to go, fine, but don't say you never had the chance. Here is your chance."

Maya shook her head, loosening her long, dark hair and, pushing her chair away from the table, rested her case. Someone was singing on the record player in the other room, not Edith Piaf regretting nothing, not Mercedes Sosa being grateful for life, someone else. On the table before us there was a bowl of lemons. My cup of coffee was going cold.

Come with me.

———◆———

When I came out of my room in the morning, Leonel was at the kitchen table in his same clothes, reading one of the books or magazines he'd brought with him, including, I noted, *The Prison Notebooks* by Antonio Gramsci, the political philosopher imprisoned by Mussolini, and a magazine about Formula One racing cars, but he didn't look up right away from whatever he happened to be reading—which was a relief, as I preferred to have coffee alone before engaging the world. I usually drank it while standing on our small porch, from a spot where the ocean was visible on clear mornings. When asked if he wanted coffee, he would reply *No thank you, not yet, I don't usually drink it this early in the day,* and then as I headed toward the door: *Hurry back, we don't have much time.*

By then, it seemed that I had implicitly agreed to host him for a few days along with his girls, as he could stay only that long he repeatedly said, a few days, and then they would drive back—a round trip of more than eight thousand kilometers for a visit of a few days. I don't know why I didn't question what sort of sense this made.

It seemed that the work we had to do involved me sitting opposite him at the table as I attempted to follow his braided monologues, while the diagrams, stick figures, and other illustrations flowed from his special pen until there was almost no space on the butcher paper for the helicopters he drew meticulously near the end, resembling an armada of dragonflies in the sky above his sketched hills. On this day, we were somewhere in the midst of the conquest of Mesoamerica, with emphasis upon the military maneuvers of the Spanish, and the ways in which the Indians resisted them, by coincidence using some of the tactics developed five hundred years earlier and a world away by Genghis Khan.

He had read the experts on the great pre-Columbian civilizations of Mexico and the isthmus, he said, and while he found some of the material "useful" on the subject of armed resistance, it was "useless" on matters concerning the consciousness of these peoples, their views of the cosmos, their science, and their art. Nothing is known about them, he insisted several times, especially about the Mayans—for example, why they invented the wheel but used it only for toys, or why they abandoned their vast cities, which he believed now to be hidden in the cloud forests of the highlands. But most important, they were "farmers," he said, "excellent farmers," and the crop they developed in all its varieties was maize, "the greatest cereal crop in the world," Leonel said. When maize is grown in a cornfield they call a milpa, it is grown along with beans, sweet potatoes, tomatoes, chilies, avocados, amaranth, and jicama, so the soil is never depleted, he said. There have been milpas under cultivation "for thousands of years, thousands," he said, as he drew beans climbing maize stalks, squash blossoming along the ground, and beside the stalks, a cartoon man in a straw hat and an avocado tree heavy with fruit.

"If you're interested," he was now almost whispering, "beans and maize form a complete protein for the human diet. Neither is sufficient alone. The Indians also learned that something had to be done to the maize if they were to prevent pellagra, a disease caused by niacin deficiency. Before modern medicine, a thousand years before Christ, they developed nixtamalization, as we call it, from their word, *nixtamal,* a Nahua word for their method of soaking maize before grinding it in a water bath of ashes and lime. The alkaline wood ash releases niacin into the maize. It also softens the hull. *Ingenious!* They understood the value of sweet potatoes and amaranth. They were brilliant nutritionists, and so it went for thousands of years, until their lands were confiscated by the Europeans to establish the great haciendas, first for the cultivation of indigo and cacao, for the raising of cattle, and then," he said, moving his pen to the other side of his map, "when the demand for indigo plummeted, the lands onto which the Indians had been pushed—the blue volcanic highlands—were discovered to be excellent for the cultivation of coffee, and their remaining lands were taken in an inexorable process of theft."

He set the drawing pen on the paper.

"Here is a pamphlet on the subject. Today, there isn't much land left for the milpas. A small family requires ten hectares of land to grow enough food to feed itself, but if you have too many people on too small a land, the milpas will not produce enough and the people will starve."

There were maize stalks inked all the way to the edge of the paper.

"My grandmother did that, and so did my father," I told him. "They planted corn in the same hole as the beans so the beans could climb the cornstalks as they grew. They spread the very same carpet of squash along the ground. I remember picking the yellow blossoms." I seemed not to be at the table any longer with this strange visitor, but was moving down the row again after years, dropping two kernels of corn and two mottled beans into each hole scooped from the tilled row, as beside me my grandmother's pronged hoe covered them over one by one, quickly because of the crows cawing above us, all the while whispering prayers.

"Anna taught you that?"

"Wait. How do you know her name was Anna?"

"You wrote a poem about her, remember? Why don't you read it to me?"

"I thought we had work to do. If talking like this is what you mean by work."

"We do. The grandmother was from Czechoslovakia, right? They make high-quality weapons. The assault rifle, for example, the Vz.58, which you might mistake at first for a Soviet AK-47, but the Vz.58 has an entirely different internal design. The Czechs also make fine revolvers and machine guns, like the CZW-762, which is fed from thirty-round AK magazines."

Well, I thought, they did say that he was a champion marksman, and perhaps this accounted for his encyclopedic knowledge of firearms, but to move so quickly from prehistoric maize cultivation to poetry to weapons?

"Tell me about the grandmother."

He didn't say *your* grandmother, but I would become used to this quirk of his speech. He rarely used possessive pronouns in English. What did he want? I wondered. Why was he interested in me? No one in the world beyond my childhood had ever seemed this curious about my life. Leonel was asking about my own past, my own family. So I talked to him for a while about Anna, about the rosaries prayed before the plaster madonna on Chalfonte Street in Detroit, the women gathered in the small living room for the joyful and sorrowful mysteries, Anna among them when she wasn't disappearing for weeks at a time, driving her Ford Mercury through Pennsylvania and Ohio, staying with relatives and the friends she had made, Slovaks and Mennonites, Hungarians, Native Americans, some of whom, long after her death, would show up on the doorsteps of her descendants, stopping to see her again as they passed through, even after no one passed any longer through the neighborhood in Detroit where her eldest daughter still lived. Anna's friends usually arrived with gifts, and expressions of gratitude for some kind of help she had given, but the Anna they spoke of did not have many traits in common with our Anna, about whom most people in the family had mixed feelings, believing that she had the Gypsy spirit in her as they would say then, that she couldn't somehow settle down, that she was headstrong and did whatever she pleased, and when I was a girl, I told Leonel, my mother warned me that I was in danger of being like her, "and I will not have this," my mother had said, "I will get Anna out of you if it's the last thing I do."

"And *are* you like her?" Leonel asked. "Because that would be helpful."

"I don't know. I can't seem to stay in one place— But helpful? For what?"

"Oh, nothing. I'm getting a bit ahead of myself."

And so as not to get ahead, he reached back and took up where he had left off, with the ships on the butcher paper, sailing from Spain through the Caribbean to the isthmus, going into some detail about how such ships were rigged and supplied, with what weaponry and provisions, and for the next hours he bent over the Spanish galleons and caravels crossing their sea of paper.

THAT NIGHT, IN THE GROWING DARKNESS, HAVING NOT THOUGHT OF MY GRAND-mother in some time, I saw Anna's face in her casket: her waxen skin, her lips sealed, a black rosary wound around her hands. Anna's not here, I had told myself then, leaning to kiss this wax Anna on its cheek. The replica wore Anna's dress, with a broach pinned to the bodice, and gold wire-rimmed glasses, although the eyes were closed behind them. The corpse was asleep with its glasses on. If this had been Anna, I would have reached in and removed her glasses and set them on a night table beside the water glass holding her teeth, the prayer book and crochet hook, and the photograph of herself with my grandfather and one of their infant children that she kept on the bedside table, even throughout her second marriage.

When he asked about Anna again, it was night, the second night, and I was tiring of history lessons.

"I don't know what to tell you," I said. "I don't know what you want to know."

"You said that she prayed while she planted seeds. The descendants of the Mayans also pray, not only when they plant, but when they till, when they harvest, even when they catch birds, they pray. To whom, I don't know. They can tell one parrot's voice apart from another's, and they know how old are the jaguar tracks in the mud, how long a time has passed since the jaguar made the tracks, and how long it has been since the jaguar clawed the bark from the fruit trees. They know which special leaf can be boiled to cure fever. That would be the leaf from the cinchona tree, by the way."

I was lying on the carpet now in the path of the rearing calliope horse, as if I were about to be trampled. Leonel was pacing the room.

"From your book, I learned that you spent time with Native Americans. In several of your poems, I read—"

"Yes. I lived for a short winter with an elderly Pueblo Indian couple in New Mexico when I was twenty-three years old. I had been planning to hike in the Sangre de Cristo Mountains because I was trying to get over something, and they invited me to stay with them instead of hiking."

He looked at me quizzically.

"A death. I was trying to get over the death of a close friend."

"Get over? You don't get over these things," he said gently.

I didn't want to say more, but found myself telling him the story of how I had accepted a writing residency in Taos, but had felt uneasy in the house assigned to me, so I decided instead to hike into the mountains and camp there, leaving the house to its ghosts. I was buying supplies in the plaza when I met the man I now called Grandpa Goodmorning. He saw that I was wearing a backpack and started a conversation, asking where I was going. When I told him that I planned to go hiking in the mountains, he suggested I speak first with his wife.

Teles Goodmorning wore his hair in two long silver-dark braids and held a blanket around his shoulders, as did the other Tewa elders who gathered in the plaza most afternoons. He pointed to his truck and said he could take me to her. The truck had once belonged to the postal service, so the steering wheel was on the vehicle's right side. He'd bought it used, he'd said, and later, when I knew him better, he enjoyed joking that he was an Englishman because he drove on the other side of the front seat.

I wanted to meet a woman elder and he seemed kind, so I went with him to his house: a small adobe to the left of the entrance to the pueblo, but outside the pueblo wall. His wife, Ya-Kwana, listened to my plan and asked me why I wanted to hike by myself. I told her the truth: that a boy-friend of mine had committed suicide a few months earlier in Denver, that I'd met his other friends at the funeral, and joined them for the summer at their house in Seattle. There, I hiked in the Olympic Peninsula and the north Cascades, through high snows and dark, sun-wanded rain forest, where I had slowly begun to emerge from the haze of mourning. I'd come now to New Mexico on a writing fellowship, and thought hiking through the Sangre de Cristos would afford the same relief.

"Maybe you don't want to do this hike," Ya-Kwana said. "It is dangerous—not because of animals but because of men."

Instead, she suggested that I should stay with them for a while. They had a spare bed. I could help them with drawing water from the well and bringing in firewood. And because we were outside the pueblo wall, it was all right for me to stay there, even though I was Anglo. She did ask that I keep this arrangement to myself, and especially not speak with anyone outside the pueblo about it, particularly the anthropologist who showed up there regularly. So I stayed with them, but went back sometimes during the day to the writer's residency, pretending still to live there but never again staying the night.

"Well, that's it," I said. "I was with them until spring, and I even learned a little of their language. In Tewa, the same object might be known by different names, depending on circumstances. For example, the word for wood changes if the wood is growing, as in a tree, or burning, as in a fire."

After a time, he asked if I had been given a name in their language.

"Yes."

"What name?"

I thought it might be all right to tell him.

"Well, Grandpa Goodmorning was Tiem-goo, 'Good Morning' in Tewa, I think, and so he called me Tiem-papu, or 'Morning Flower,' but mostly they shortened it to Papu. I think Ya-Kwana came up with that."

She had also taught me to bake bread in the *horno* and to cook a *pozole* with chilies and pork. She reminded me a lot of Anna. She kneaded her dough the same way, and she had the same hands. She used to bring blankets to me at night, as Anna had done. I'd feel them land on me. As it got colder, more blankets, until by morning I was under a pile of them. I remember how stiff they were, how icy the air, and I was always grateful that they woke before me and got the fire started in the *fogón*.

Leonel seemed more interested in this story than in anything else I had told him, so I went upstairs to get one of the few things I had in my room in those days: a photograph of me with Grandpa Goodmorning. I'm wearing one of those embroidered Afghan sheepskin coats, with a pink-and-green babushka on my head. Grandpa is wearing one of his western string ties. We're both smiling.

"Do you ever see them now?"

"I drive back to New Mexico when I can, and I'm planning to bring Grandpa here for a powwow soon. The Native American Studies program at our university is sponsoring a ceremony, and they want him to be its ceremonial chief. He accepted because he wants to see the ocean and get some cowrie shells from the beach, which he needs because there has been no rain in New Mexico, and he also wants me to take him to the zoo."

"The zoo?"

"He would like to see animals from other continents and offer prayers for them."

I didn't tell Leonel that night about the ritual of burning cedar on live coals, the eagle feather that carries the smoke, the blessing of cedar smoke from head to toe before embarking on a journey, and I didn't tell him about the deerskin dress or the jimson berries or the morning they buried an elder below the bright snow. Later I might tell him. Maybe.

"What else would you like to know?" I asked instead.

"That's good, that you stayed with them. You're lucky. They gave you a rare gift."

"They saved me from falling into a mountain crevasse."

"Not only that," he said. "You ask me what else I want to know? I want to know who you are," he said matter-of-factly, as if wondering about the contents of a package, as he stretched out on the carpet and closed his eyes.

"But we can talk tomorrow. I have to get some sleep. Go to bed."

"Leonel? Why don't you use the daybed?"

"No, thank you. I prefer the floor."

———◆———

He lit his pipe and picked up a drawing pen. His hair was now wet, slicked back, and he offered that he had washed it in the kitchen sink. There was no gray in it then, and he wasn't yet more than a little overweight. I thought he was much older, but that was because I was young and the distance between ages twenty-seven and thirty-seven seemed great. His black horn-rimmed glasses made him look studious, as did the pipe he usually held with his right hand. I didn't know this then, but he had dressed himself to visit a professor in a university, which is what he had been told I was.

"Okay. El Salvador is 160 miles long from east to west and 60 miles wide."

He drew a compass with arrow tips east to west, north to south.

"It is the most densely populated country in the isthmus and among the poorest in the hemisphere. They call it the Tom Thumb of the Americas, who, as you know, was a character from the very first fairy tale printed in English. Tom Thumb was this tiny man, no bigger than his father's thumb. One of Tom Thumb's escapades involved being swallowed by a cow, but never mind. We'll get to the subject of cows later. In *this* Tom Thumb—the country—one in five children die before the age of five, and eighty percent of people have no running water, electricity, or sanitation. What does this mean?"

He had drawn a stick figure trapped inside a cow.

"For many, there is only a trench in the ground with a board over the trench. The chief cause of death is amoebic dysentery and the second, among children, is measles: entirely preventable, entirely curable, but most rural people have never seen a doctor. And what else? Ninety percent of people in the rural areas are malnourished. Ninety percent. They live on beans and tortillas. Whatever else they manage to grow, they sell. In the countryside, seventy percent cannot read or write, and of the rest, the command is very basic. They make their living harvesting coffee and cotton and cutting cane, moving from harvest to harvest. On average, they are paid a dollar a day. To give you the idea: A Coke is fifty cents. Okay? How did it come to this?"

In ink on paper and with both Spanish and English painted in the air between us, he brought us back before the conquest, before Alvarado and his flaming hair, to the time when the lands were held in common by the Lenca and Pipil.

"Very little is known about them, but it is my belief that they abandoned their ancient cities in a time of crisis to settle in smaller villages and carry on the art of the milpa. Some academics think they were closer to Olmecs and to Aztec culture. I have no opinion about that. I only know what *I* think."

He was searching through the bag with a pouncing jaguar on both sides.

"Here," he said, "I brought these books for you, and some monographs. Take a look. Maybe you, as a poet, can imagine what life in that time might have been like. I am not a poet, but the more I study the culture of the Mayans, the more I am in awe. Papu?"—calling me that for the first time, which I wasn't sure was right to do—"I am asking you to imagine it."

Only the Goodmornings had ever called me Papu. It was their name for me in their language. It was private. A secret. I wanted to tell him not to use this name for me, but I thought doing so might hurt his feelings, so I didn't, and instead tried to do as he asked.

CONSIDERING WINTER AT THE PUEBLO, LIFE AT THAT TIME WOULD HAVE BEEN quiet at night, the stars like crushed glass and in that darkness, the Milky Way would have almost appeared to spin, a silver platter tipped into the heavens, sending its outer stars into empty space. The moons would be named for seasons and planting. Many of the plants would be known, along with their properties, including what would heal what, and the Earth itself was considered a being, sleeping in winter because she was pregnant during the cold season. The elders didn't have to talk much. Conversation floated silently among them, and what was heard was the crackling of the fire.

It wasn't possible to think about this without dreaming back to Grandpa Goodmorning getting up from his stool at night to take a coal from the *fogón,* a burning coal rimmed with light, and lift it with a small shovel, dropping a handful of dried cedar onto it until smoke rose up, and then he'd ask me to stand, and with a feather he brushed the smoke up along my body to my head. And if Ya-Kwana or anyone else was there he also did this for her, and then he carried the smoking shovel around the room, to the entranceways, smoke rising in the kitchen where the unplugged refrigerator was, where Ya-Kwana kept her flour and other dried goods to preserve them from pests. He carried the smoke to the beds and walked around them, whispering in Tewa. The house was blessed in this manner almost every night, as was the well outside, and especially the front door. Ya-Kwana's hands became Anna's hands, the scarves they wore were the same and also their eyes, with light always in them, almost like candle flames. If I cupped my hands over my ears, Tewa sounded like Slovak. I sometimes made believe it was. Anna prayed too, every night, but her prayers were whispered into a book she held, or while rosary beads ran through her fingers, and sometimes she also listened to a radio station that broadcast prayers in Polish, Slovak, Hungarian, or Czech. The radio was covered in brown leather, with tubes visible inside it like a miniature city glowing with orange lights, and as she turned the dial, the voices changed, and because they were in different languages, and I was a child, I imagined that the radio was a city of voices from all over the world.

A short while after this request for imagining, Leonel said he wanted to tell me a story about a Catholic priest.

"You are a Catholic, aren't you?"

No one had asked me this question for a long time, and I wasn't sure of the answer.

THE GIRL I ONCE WAS, WHO HAD BEEN A CATHOLIC, WOKE FOR THE BELLS OF the Angelus at six in the morning. *Angelus Domini*, I sang to myself as I walked to morning Mass under a canopy of maples, through a wetland of swamp cabbage and red-winged blackbirds, the quiet, low Mass where it was possible to pray in peace, with the Latin liturgy a murmur in the air. The neighbor boy Joseph also attended this Mass daily before school and I was always aware of him, of where he knelt in relation to me. When he turned twelve, he left to study in a seminary, and I decided that if he was going to become a priest, I would be a nun in his parish.

Six years later, Joseph went to Vietnam, and later returned as a different Joseph, one who would move back and forth between monastic life and the streets. I would not become a nun, although I considered that vocation. As a child, I had even imagined that I saw the Blessed Mother in the clouds above the roof of my house one summer night after dark. If she was real, this was what the nuns of Our Lady of Sorrows called a vision, so I must not have seen her. Brighter than the moon with her arms open. I still have my satin First Communion purse, the Sunday Missal with its pearl cover, and rosary beads of aurora borealis crystals my mother strung for me, all wrapped in a foiled box not unlike the silver Christmas box where my mother kept the poems she had written in her own girlhood.

I felt at peace in the church, on the padded kneeler near the stained-glass windows depicting the seven sorrows along the west wall, the seven joys along the east. These windows had been made in Chartres, France, and brought to our parish by ship. As a child, I had imagined the slabs of glass crossing the sea, rising and falling in the breaking waves. The nuns told us that there were precious jewels hidden in these windows. When I knelt beside them, the floor, the pews, and my own body were quilted in colored light.

"I was born Catholic, yes," I said. "I attended Catholic school for twelve years. But those of us who no longer attend Mass are called fallen or fallen away. I'm fallen."

My school was run by the Sisters of St. Dominic, Order of Preachers, in the parish of Our Lady of Sorrows, in a church shepherded by an old Irish monsignor who, for some reason, was an admirer of a man he called Generalissimo Franco of Spain, and Franco, we were told as children, led the forces of the Church faithful to victory over the enemies of God in the Spanish Civil War. He was the leader by the grace of God, we were taught.

Thoughts of Generalissimo Franco marched through my childhood and came to a halt that summer in Spain with Claribel, especially as Franco was newly dead, and Spain was said to be "awakening" from nearly forty years of dictatorship. Posters in the public squares urged the people to *Vota* for this or *Vota* for that. These posters were works of art, and many people were seen peeling them from the walls before the election. Poster collectors, I thought at the time, somewhat naïvely.

———◆———

"Let me tell you about a priest," Leonel said, "Padre Rutilio Grande—did Claribel happen to mention him?"

"No, I don't remember her talking about any priest."

"Really? Interesting. Well, he was a Jesuit, and last spring he was murdered in the village of Aguilares along with an old man and a young boy. They were traveling by truck through the cane fields to Mass when they were stopped and machine-gunned to death. Three children in the back of the truck managed to escape. They ran to the village El Paisnal and told the people what had happened. The children said that when Padre Grande saw the soldiers on both sides of the road he said, 'We must do God's will.'

"But this is a God," Leonel went on, jabbing the air with the pipe, "that Padre Grande taught was not up in the sky lying in some damn cloud hammock. This was a God who expected us to be brothers and sisters, and to make of Earth a just place. What I know, although this is not in many of the reports, is that the soldiers then went to Padre Grande's church and ransacked it. They even crushed the Communion hosts into the ground. A few months later, a death squad they call Mano Blanca killed another priest, this time in the city, for the crime of saying a Mass in protest against fraud in the elections. A young boy was killed with him too. Just for being there. Leaflets flew around the city: *Be a Patriot! Kill a priest!* And a short while after that, the army launched a siege on Aguilares. Three Jesuit priests and three campesinos were inside the church, one of them grabbing the rope in the bell tower and ringing the bell hard for the village. He was shot down from the rope, then they shot at the altar, tied up the priests, and the next thing anyone knew these priests were in prison in Guatemala. And that is the situation as it stands now."

I imagined the young boy rising and falling in the tower, using all of his weight to rock the bell, ringing its clapper through the clouds as if this were a wedding or a war was over, and then letting go.

"What are you thinking, Papu? You have a tendency to drift off. You have to learn to pay attention."

———◆———

That summer, Maya and I had gone on a journey together through Andalusia, hoping to find the grave of the poet Federico García Lorca, who was said to have been murdered on the 17th or 18th of August 1936, in the first year of the Spanish Civil War. The soldiers of General Franco had taken the poet to "visit" his dead brother-in-law, the former socialist mayor of the city. After beating Lorca with their rifle butts and calling him a faggot, they filled him with bullets. The grave, sought by many, has never been found. Claribel herself had made this search when she was younger, and wrote a poem about failing to find the grave.

We were young and determined enough to imagine that we might succeed in finding it. After all, Franco had been dead for two years, and surely someone would come forward now and guide us to the poet's secret resting place. We hiked into the foothills of the Sierra Nevada, following the instructions in Claribel's poem, looking where she said to look, and what we found was a wooden cross, pounded into a hollow of earth at the side of the road some distance from La Fuente Grande. The grave might have been where the instructions in her poem suggested, but it was a bit farther along the road, and nearly unmarked but for the rough-hewn cross. We walked a short distance from the road and were told by two young men from the Sacromonte that we were standing over the remains of Lorca. Around the cross, near a stone between two olive trees, sardine tins and bottle caps were scattered, little bits of chewing-gum wrapper and broken glass. I cleared these, putting some of the garbage in my purse, and discovered that violets were also growing there beneath the debris. We said a prayer by reciting a few lines from his poems, and then I scooped some of the earth into a 35mm film container. I picked one violet and pressed it between the pages of my notebook. This was or was not Lorca's grave. But it had been visited in the past, as was apparent from the litter, so someone was buried there. When we told this story to Claribel, I couldn't tell whether she believed us or not.

During the journey through Andalusia I wrote in my notebook of a road awash in light, and the Alhambra, a ghost ship in the distance, of starlight salting the night sky, of vigil lamps where there is no Christ and shrines where there is no memory, of Spanish brandy and black tobacco and a dictator dead but yet still awake in the minds of people. I was at the time quite young, with a romantic view of the world, and I was also an American, which made this worse.

AFTER WE RETURNED FROM OUR ANDALUSIAN JOURNEY, SOMETHING BEGAN TO change within me. I was still translating in the morning and in the evening bringing the English versions of the poems first to Maya, and then to Claribel. Sometimes they seemed pleased with what I'd done, but at other times my versions baffled them as I didn't seem to understand their political and historical context, or, as Claribel would say, "the conditions from which the poems arose." I confided to Maya that the dictionary was of little use, the problem seemed to lie with me. I couldn't distinguish between literal and figurative language: Were the guitar player's hands, mangled by an ax, a metaphor? What about wingless birds, and the dead waving their arms? I puzzled over phrases having to do with the dead eating their dead, and words written with *tears, fingernails, and coal*. What, I wondered, was a *smoking heart*? Why did this poet believe herself to be a cemetery, and why does she imagine herself walking arm in arm with ghosts?

After dark, I read by flashlight, as I had under the blankets as a child, its light brushing across the poetry as if along a path leading into a forest at night or another unknown place. The olive and lemon groves had by now grown familiar, as had the light on the ocher walls at certain hours. The widows in black walking down the roads were now nodding in an almost friendly way when they passed me. I no longer heard the goat bells clanking on the slopes, or the waters of the *torrente* rushing beside the walls, or the Libyan winds unless I listened especially for them. Deià was becoming a place I knew and where, for that summer, I lived.

One afternoon in August, a young woman arrived for Claribel's late-afternoon salon. She was about my age. No, she was exactly my age, and was accompanying the poet Cristina Peri Rossi from Uruguay, who had come for a visit. This younger woman was very thin, and didn't look directly at anyone. It's strange to me now, but I can't remember her first name. Her face is clear. She was on the edge of the circle where I usually sat, so she was next to me. Cristina began to speak. By this time, I understood most of what was said in Spanish, but this Spanish, hurried, hushed, ruptured, and coded, was more difficult. Cristina was urging the younger woman to share her story with the group. Staring down at the cold stone floor, she began to speak in broken phrases: *My name is—I'm from—*. Her eyes darted around the circle to see how well this was going. I wanted to reach out to touch her arm but somehow couldn't. She told us that she had been held in a clandestine prison in Uruguay, where she was tortured for seventeen days, and forced to stand naked and barefoot on a block of ice. She was beaten intermittently throughout that time. When one ice block melted beneath her, they brought another.

With trembling fingers, she kept touching her face, and then tucked her hands under her thighs to hold them still. She didn't know why they had let her go, she said. No one else was let go. Her interrogators told her to shut up about everything, and one of the guards said that if she stayed in the country she would soon be arrested again, and this time there would be no getting out.

"The feet aren't right anymore," she whispered.

———◆———

It was late afternoon, and the harvesters were boarding their trucks to go home. After they left, I sometimes went out to gather broken flowers from the side of the road, especially if they were carnations. There were always some lying there with bent stems or crushed heads. These I put into water glasses around the house. They seemed still alive.

Leonel was at the table, looking through his papers for something that he said was important. But everything was important. The girls were coloring on the floor, where he had spread white butcher paper torn from the roll. At that time of day, I watered and fed the finches and put carrots and lettuce in the hutch. Still he didn't seem to find this important thing for which he searched, and so I sat down across from him to wait. He licked his thumb to leaf through the onion-skin pages of a congressional committee report, muttering something in Spanish under his breath. I saw that he had highlighted whole blocks of type in neon yellow and, also written in the margins, mostly question marks and exclamation points, sometimes both.

"I highlight what is important," he would tell me one day. "I question-mark the lies, and I exclaim at the stupidity. Don't you ever read these things, Papu? You should. They're from your own goddamn government."

But he wasn't talking to me this way yet. Instead, he lit his pipe, drew a little smoke into his mouth, and prepared to hold forth or, as he would say, continue his days-long "briefing." I sometimes wonder why I let this go on when I had so much else to do. Student papers. Correspondence. Laundry. For some reason, I dropped everything to listen to him. I thought it might have had to do with those months of feeling ignorant in Spain, and also with the realization that, although I had a college education, I knew very little about the rest of the world.

"These death squads," I said, "I'd like to know more about them. What you call Mano Blanca. White Hand?"

"Who told you about this?"

"You did. Also Claribel and Bud, last summer. *Escuadrón de la muerte.* I heard it at first as death squadron. I thought they were airplanes, but then . . ."

"No, my dear, they are not airplanes, but we'll get to that. First, you must understand something about the military." To illustrate, he drew what looked like a family tree. The girls had left the door open, and one of the finches flew outside and disappeared into the eucalyptus. I got up to close the door, and when I returned to the table, he had filled his tree with names.

"You know how, when you are in school, there's a certain group of kids who sort of take over? Not bullies exactly, but you know, the kids who try to dominate everyone else." He laughed. "Maybe *some* of them really are bullies."

"We called them the in-crowd. Or the clique. We had a group like that, yes."

"Clique, okay, so this will be useful to you as a way of understanding what I'm about to tell you. In a military academy, for example in El Salvador, there are also cliques, but the stakes are much higher because the rewards are greater. It might work the same way with every military. I'm not sure. But let's just say."

And then he stopped, just like that, lost in thought or searching the air for the words, or as if he didn't know how much to tell me and how much to withhold. At the time, I didn't think about the fact that he wasn't a native speaker of English. I didn't yet know to take into account that he might be translating, not only between languages, but also from one constellation of understanding and perception to another.

I was impatient with this from the beginning. I wish now that I had not been.

Just as suddenly, he resumed.

"First, you must understand how the Salvadoran military is structured, how it works, and why. There are reasons for everything. You see, Salvadoran military officers, during their training, form these groups called *tandas,* and by the time of graduation from the military academy, the most powerful *tanda* is in line for the highest offices of the government. These are, shall we say, like the cool kids in a high school. The other groups fall in line behind this *tanda,* and its leader eventually becomes president of the country, and all wealth and power follow from that fact. Every four years elections are held, but the military candidate wins *every time,* regardless of how the ballots are cast. The ballot boxes are stuffed with illegal votes. They call this sugaring the ballot boxes. Sweetening them up. If you rise in the military, the sky is the limit, financially speaking. Or rather, I suppose you could say the generosity of the U.S. government is the limit, along with how much money can be stolen from international bank loans and things like that."

"What do you mean 'generosity of the U.S. government'?"

"A little attempt at irony, my dear. Where are you going?"

"The bathroom? I have to go to the bathroom."

At least he didn't say again "Hurry up, we have work to do!" Instead, he asked how I trained the little birds to live in their cage, even though the door was open.

"I didn't have to train them," I said, shaking my hands dry. "That's where the food is. Speaking of that, do you think the girls are hungry? I know I am."

"You want to eat something? Me, I always want to eat something. Do you know a place where we might get some grilled shrimp?"

"You want grilled shrimp?"

"If it's possible."

"Of course it's possible."

So that is how we wound up in a fancy restaurant on the water, where, at high tide, the ocean waves spray the windows. The girls sipped Shirley Temples and picked at their salads, while their father worked his way through a specially ordered platter of shrimp. I don't remember what I had, but I remember watching him eat with gusto, licking his fingers and thumbs as he told a strange story having to do with weapons, undercover detectives, a car dealership, and a sting operation in Mount Kisco, New York.

"Do you know where is Mount Kisco?" he asked.

What, I thought, does this have to do with *milpa* cultivation, dead priests, infant mortality rates, and everything else he's been telling me? I shook my head no.

The restaurant was very nice, but I noticed that the waiters began slowing down during service to our table as Leonel talked excitedly, occasionally waving his hands, about undercover policemen pretending to be mafiosos in Mount Kisco.

"I mean, *goddamn* it," he said, as he started the story again.

Apparently, there had been an arrest in Mount Kisco that exposed a plot by Salvadoran military officers to sell ten thousand machine guns and more than a million rounds of ammunition to men he thought were members of the Mafia.

"And where do you think this hardware came from, my dear? Take a guess."

Without stopping to let me guess, he bellowed: "The United States! *Thirty million dollars* in U.S. military aid provided by U.S. American taxpayers. And what do you suppose these officers were going to do with the proceeds from the sale? Put it in their pockets, of course! The offer included missiles and aircraft equipped with heavy armament. So what happened? The undercover detectives created a sting operation. Did you see that movie with Paul Newman and Robert Redford? *The Sting*? You should see it. Anyway, they posed as gangsters and rented Cadillac sedans from the local Cadillac dealership. Then they set up a meeting in some goddamn motel or something and those sons of bitches walked right into it."

By now, it seemed to me, the diners nearest us were also listening. Ocean water crashed against the windows but Leonel seemed not to appreciate this very experience for which the restaurant was famous.

"So," he said with some satisfaction, taking his napkin out of his collar where he'd tucked it, "who do you think was trying to sell these weapons? None other than the chief of staff of the Salvadoran armed forces, Colonel Manuel Alfonso Rodríguez. The son of a bitch was arrested and held until he could raise and post bail of three million dollars. This happened just a year ago. And it's very unusual, you know, that a high-ranking officer would actually be arrested for something like this, which is why it interests me. I expect," he went on, studying the dessert menu, "Colonel Rodríguez won't stay in prison very long."

"I'll have the sorbet, please." I always order sorbet, and the girls joined me in this.

"And I'll have, let me see, is there any way to have ice cream with whipped cream and hot fudge sauce?"

"We'll see what we can do, sir."

———◆———

When we were back at the house, he talked for a few more hours about corruption, and the ways in which the highest ministers of the military government, and especially the president, made money through kickbacks and theft of American aid, and through various concessions they controlled at the airport, the post office, and other places. He didn't have a better word than "concession" and I wasn't sure what this meant, but he said that they also controlled customs and immigration, and the corruption was such that these ministers, who were not themselves from rich families, were able to retire with millions on deposit in U.S. banks, even though the salary of a colonel was, in colones, then about two hundred U.S. dollars a month.

"Doesn't the U.S. government know about this?"

"What do you think? Of course they do!" he shouted almost gleefully, then lowered his voice and said as if to himself: "They know."

Searching his papers again, he found the document he had wanted to show me. Case File No. S-124, the Mount Kisco detectives' report and, clipped to it, a short local newspaper article about the arrest, not more than three column inches.

"You'll get a kick out of this," he said, just the way an American would say it. He barely gave me time to glance at the documents before he began talking again.

"Can you imagine? And the Salvadoran military, by the way, is beginning to be interested in cocaine, but we can talk about that later. Right now, I need to tell you about something else. Remember the dead American? Last year, an American citizen was murdered while in the custody of the Salvadoran government. His name was Ronald Richardson, or James Ronald Richardson, or something like that. He was a black man from Philadelphia. He's in Guatemala and he gets picked up for staying too long on a tourist visa. He tells the Guatemalan authorities that he's a Vietnam veteran and would like to offer his services to them as a military mercenary. This wasn't of interest at the time to the Guatemalans, so they decided to deport him. Richardson pleaded, for some reason, not to be deported back to the United States. He clearly did not wish to go there. Okay. So, the Guatemalans decide to send him to El Salvador or Honduras, you know, pass the problem along to someone else? Maybe they needed military mercenaries in Honduras or Salvador, I don't know."

Leonel often finished his explanations of things with the phrase *I don't know,* offered dismissively. At such times as this, he could talk without stopping, pacing about the room, marking off his paragraphs by retracing his steps.

"The American embassy in Guatemala then sends the American embassy in El Salvador a cable marked ACTION CONSULATE as this was a matter concerning the whereabouts of a presumed American citizen. Okay. Soon after that, the consular office of the American embassy in San Salvador receives a report from the Salvadoran government that a person claiming to be an American citizen named Richardson had been picked up for nonpayment of hotel bills or something like that and was being held, once again it seemed, pending deportation. Are you following this? The American embassy gets asked to verify that Richardson is an American citizen, so some American consular officer interviews Richardson and fills out a report that is sent to the United States, while Richardson remains in custody and the whole thing lands in somebody's inbox in Washington. That's the word, isn't it? 'Inbox'?"

Leonel sat down, but quickly got up from the table to pace the room again.

"So, what do we have so far?" he asks. "By way of review—we have an American citizen waiting in a Salvadoran jail for American paperwork. Let's rest. Let's go to the beach."

———◆———

We walked in a cloud of ground fog, the girls running ahead, gulls hovering, taut winged and crying out as the surf heaved to the sand and withdrew. Pebbles murmured beneath us as the water pulled back its sheet of light. There were dried kelp beds and piles of bladder wrack here, stinking under swarms of sand flies.

"Richardson, the man I was telling you about? He ran out of time. Maybe he'd been in prison in the States, I don't know, or maybe he had watched too much television, but when his offer to become a mercenary didn't work, he decided to tell the Salvadoran authorities that he knew something about cocaine—that he was, in fact, part of some cartel, and he was prepared to give these authorities information about this cocaine, in exchange, of course, for his freedom. To understand what happened next, you have to know something about a certain Salvadoran colonel, who was the director of immigration at that time, but also chief of the military regime's intelligence operations."

The girls had returned to Leonel, one on each side, holding him by the hands, showing him cowrie shells, part of a dried gull wing, and the carapace of a sand crab. He spoke softly with them, pocketed their shells, pushed a gull quill into the sand, and rose, continuing in English with me.

"This man's name was Colonel José Francisco René Chacón, director of immigration, chief of ANSESA, the Salvadoran national security agency."

Then, nodding toward his daughters, and with a knowing look, he whispered, "To be continued."

We climbed the sand steps carved into the embankment. The fog had lifted, and behind us the beach was bathed in sun. Leonel toweled the sand from his daughters' feet, then from his own while I did the same with a separate towel he had given me. He shook the towels out, folded them carefully, wrapped them in a garbage sack, and laid them in the back of the Hiace, neatly beside some black metal footlockers. He took a canteen from the back and poured water over the cowries in his palm, then put them in an empty film container and snapped the lid shut.

ON THE WAY HOME, WHEN HE SAW IN THE REARVIEW MIRROR THAT THE GIRLS had fallen asleep, he began again.

"In order to understand the significance of Richardson's error in saying that he knew about drugs, you have to know something about what happened a month prior to Richardson's arrival in El Salvador. The first ever cocaine bust in Central America was accomplished at the Camino Real Hotel in San Salvador during an operation orchestrated by the Drug Enforcement Administration of the United States. Two Peruvian women were arrested, a mother and her daughter, carrying ten kilos of pure cocaine. They were what they call mules. That operation was a success, except that within days the police had been paid off, the judges had been paid off, and the women were released to return to Peru. The cocaine, however, had already been delivered to the American embassy, where the political officer of the time burned it in a fifty-five-gallon drum. The story made the papers, of course, and it was widely reported that the cocaine that was burned in the drum had an estimated street value of up to two hundred million dollars. *Two hundred million,"* Leonel repeated, nodding on each word. "That's a lot of money. And in El Salvador, when anything is worth that much money, certain people get interested. Colonel Chacón, for example, informed the American embassy that he would be happy to assist in future drug enforcement operations, as did several other so-called civic-minded senior-ranking officers."

We had reached the house. He lifted the younger one from the backseat into his arms, the older girl following, holding a corner of his shirt, rubbing her eyes. He whispered endearments to the sleeping child, stroking her back as he walked to the front door, standing aside as I unlocked it. He then carried the child up the stairs, the other walking behind, and I left them alone.

I don't remember what I thought about any of this at the time. I only remember what happened and what was said. At that time of day, if I wanted to work on poems, I would have made coffee, as I was still young enough to be a late-night writer. I would have gotten out pens and paper and stared into space. Our table, however, was now covered with butcher paper thick with diagrams and drawings, maps and charts, figures, arrows, x's. There were also the objects Leonel had gathered, and the documents stacked on the place where he'd drawn waves to suggest the Pacific Ocean. Where Mexico would have been, there were the books he'd brought along to show me or to read. I would have sat at the table with my coffee and would also have lit another cigarette.

Huffing down the stairs, he continued. "Meanwhile, Richardson is in the custody of Colonel Chacón, who is now quite interested in whatever information he can supply regarding drug operations. So he lets Richardson go, and even has him put up in a hotel at the colonel's expense, where Richardson begins to run up another bill, charging women and drinks to his room and generally enjoying himself while he pretends to wait for word from his Panamanian contacts, and Chacón begins to make arrangements for Richardson to leave for Panama. But when the hotel bill comes due, the fool Richardson has it sent to Chacón himself for payment, Chacón, whom he now imagines as his patron. *Mirá,* Carolina, if you are going to smoke another cigarette, I'm going to light my pipe if you don't mind."

He took a pinch of tobacco from the pouch and packed it into the bowl, then held a struck match over the bowl and puffed, drawing the flame several times into the bowl.

"After a while," he went on, shaking out the match, "Chacón begins to suspect that Richardson doesn't know anything about the cocaine trade, and so he has him taken into custody again. *Also,* meanwhile, the American embassy learns that the addresses Richardson supplied are all false. There are no relatives in Philadelphia, and there are no friends. There is no record of a Ronald James or James Ronald Richardson's having served in the American military at that time. He is not a veteran of the American war in Vietnam. No one knows who he is, or anything about him, only that he appeared to be an American, as he claimed, when the consular officer visited him in jail. And his face was on an expired driver's license issued by the state of Hawaii. The political officer of the time thought that Richardson was, and I quote, 'a lone drifter with mental problems, a small-time con man, perhaps fleeing a real or imagined legal problem, a nobody.' An American nobody," Leonel repeated, crossing out the word ~~Richardson~~ on his drawing.

We sat in silence for a while, Leonel tapping the table with a pencil.

"And then?"

"And then, under orders of Colonel Chacón, Richardson was taken, along with a few political prisoners, for a short helicopter ride over the Pacific, and they were tossed alive into the sea."

"Why not just give him back to the Americans? This doesn't make sense."

Leonel shrugged, removed his glasses, and rubbed his face with his palms, then, after wiping the lenses on his shirt, put the glasses back on.

"I was told," he said, "that Chacón gave the order dispassionately, that he was simply cleaning out his inbox, as they say, taking care of routine matters, and now it seems to be routine to dump political prisoners into the sea. I know that this is true because some of the bodies of the disappeared have washed up on our beaches. But Richardson? No. There's been no sign of him."

His pencil rolled toward me, and the refrigerator hummed and went quiet.

IN THE DARKNESS OF MY ROOM, IN HALF SLEEP, THE HELICOPTER LIFTS, THEN HOVers, a long green military gunship, and on the bedroom ceiling, whitewashed by headlights from passing cars, the rotor blades flicker and in the open door of the chopper, one man after another appears and is pushed into the air, with hands tied behind their backs, legs pumping as if they were riding bicycles, until even the legs are still, and, like corpses wrapped in cloth, they enter the water. The helicopter hovers awhile longer. A soldier in the doorway trains binoculars on the surface. When nothing is seen, he motions with his free hand and the chopper tilts back toward land. The rotors flap like playing cards clipped to the blades of a fan.

———◆———

It was morning when I opened my eyes to the sound of the front door's opening, closing, opening, closing again. I seemed to have fallen asleep in my clothes, so I leaped from the bed and hurried downstairs, nearly bumping into him.

"Good morning, my dear!"

He was now speaking in a feigned German accent.

"It's about time you got out of bed. First of all, I'm about to starve to death, and second, we have work to do."

He set a grocery bag on the counter and began unpacking bananas, a carton of eggs, milk, Cheerios, cheese, and a few jars.

"I'm going to make breakfast," he bellowed. "Do you have a small pan?"

"Leonel."

"I've been out, as you see."

"Where are the girls?"

"They're with the rabbits. Do you have a spatula? I'm going to prepare one of my famous omelets. How do you work this thing?"

"You have to turn the knob and listen for the clicks."

"Self-igniting. Very interesting."

The girls were again in the kitchen, holding the rabbits. I stood near the butcher-paper mural taped to the table and lit a cigarette.

"You don't make coffee by any chance, do you?" I asked him.

"I could make you some. But not with this fancy coffeemaker. Sit down."

He sent the girls to return the rabbits to the hutch, and then set places for them on the mural and served them cereal and oranges before turning his attention to the butter foaming in the shallow pan and the beaten eggs. The girls returned and ate the cereal quickly, taking the oranges with them as they ran back outside.

"We have to talk more about the Richardson case. There are things I haven't told you."

From then on, he would refer to this story as the "Richardson case."

"Leonel, why do you care so much about this one American? You spend more time talking about him than anyone else, more than the priests, why do you care?"

He set the omelet before me, perfectly folded, a delicate wallet of egg and melted cheese with a twist of pepper, and then returned to the stove to make another.

"Interesting," he said, with his back turned. "You're not the first American who has asked me that." Then, bringing his own plate to the table, and setting it on a drawing of a military base, he said, "Because of Chacón."

Perhaps, as was often the case, I looked puzzled to him, a bit blank or tired. Again, I wasn't listening well enough, or couldn't put the pieces together. Later he would learn the expression "Connect the dots" and we would do a great deal of dot connecting. So, by way of an explanation, he let fall to the table a few more pieces of his puzzle as he paced back and forth, perhaps to see if I was capable of assembling it myself:

"Batalla de Girón. Bay of Pigs, 1961. The failed invasion of Cuba. CIA-trained mercenaries out in the cold. Soldiers of fortune, mobsters, gangsters, and guns for hire. Enter Chacón, one of the most corrupt senior officers in Salvadoran history. Chacón organizes his own paramilitary forces throughout the isthmus. The so-called Chacón Group. The White Warriors Union. Mano Blanca. Are you listening, Papu? You asked me to tell you about them. Chacón has those he kills butchered, ground up, and kept in a freezer to feed to his dogs. And he does other things. The U.S. government turns a blind eye as Chacón and his fellow officers steal American aid. They call this the cost of doing business. They say clichéd things like 'He might be a bastard but he's our bastard.' Then something strange happens, a thing I hadn't seen before . . ."

He let this hang in the air or, rather, waited for all he had said to sink in, and as I started to gather the empty plates, he motioned for me to sit back down, then he carried the dishes to the sink, running them under water, reaching into the cupboard below for the soap, spreading a dish towel on the counter. He tucked in the flap at the top of the Cheerios, wrapped the cheese, and put it, along with the eggs, in the nearly empty fridge, then polished the counter with a dishcloth the same way I had seen him polish his van, circling methodically, ". . . and the strange thing was," he said, "that I was able to get the American embassy interested in the Richardson case—I mean, beyond the consular section. They were willing to go beyond the usual pro forma—is that how you say it?—response. Maybe, I thought, it was because of this new human rights policy coming out of the White House, or the State Department—which I can tell you really pissed off the Salvadoran military. I don't know, but that's what I thought at first, that this was going to be a new day in American foreign policy. That we were going to be seeing a different kind of American animal."

He paused, seeming to realize that he was still wiping the counter. "Even I thought this. And I'm not a man easily fooled."

The phone might have rung, in my memory it is ringing, and it is Barbara, telling me that she will be back in two days, and how is everything? I wove the phone cord through my fingers and found myself trying to sound casual, as if I had been all this time alone grading papers, trying to write, and eating Cantonese takeout from paper cartons, but getting something done, and yes, everything is fine, yes, I'll see you then. As for the books, the soup bowl filled with cigarette butts, the paper-covered table, the van in the driveway with its hood open and Leonel now bent over its engine, and as for the girls who had built a house for the rabbits under the table, covering the dining chairs with bath towels, perhaps the less said. I would tell her about it when I saw her, and if she arrived while they were still here, well, she would see for herself. I hoped that they'd be gone. I didn't want to have to explain what had transpired during the past few days.

"Okay," she said. "You sound a little strange. Are you feeling all right?"

"I've been grading papers."

"Get some sleep," she said.

Leonel had spread a chamois at the edge of the raised hood and laid a small, open toolbox there. The tools were arranged by size, tucked into their respective slots. Most toolboxes I had seen in my life, my father's, for example, were gaping, tiered, and jumbled collections of screwdrivers, monkey wrenches, and pliers through which one rummaged for something not usually found.

"Well," he went on from beneath the hood, "both the American ambassador and the political officer tried to find out what had happened to Richardson and to get the State Department to push the issue with the Salvadoran government. They really tried," he said, pressing a metric wrench into its slot. "Or I think they did. The ambassador at that time was a Republican newspaper publisher, appointed to his post by your President Ford. The political officer was a career foreign service man—one of those best and brightest types, as you people say, one who joined during the Kennedy administration and thought he was going to do something good with his life. Well. Guess what happened? Take a guess."

"Nothing?"

"Very good. That's right. Nothing. Do you happen to have a rag or piece of cloth I can ruin? A paper napkin would be good."

He wiped the dipstick across the rag I found for him in the garage, left there by the previous tenant.

"Nothing. Yes. Carter gets into office, and you know, every new president has the right to make his own diplomatic appointments, so when Carter is inaugurated, the ambassadors from all over the world automatically submit their resignations. Some of these aren't accepted, and those ambassadors continue in place. But some of the resignations are picked up, and in those instances, the ambassador is out. Gone. Replaced. Guess who was among the first of the ambassadors to have his resignation accepted by Carter, even though the administration knew, and of course the State Department knew, that the Richardson case was active, and they knew why? Guess."

"The ambassador to El Salvador?"

"That's right, my dear, you are correct."

He closed the box, took the chamois away, and shut the hood, pushing down to make sure the latch caught.

"Out of all the goddamn embassies in the world! And I'm not blaming Carter himself, mind you. I have no idea whose bright idea it was to pull the rug out from under the Richardson investigation."

He put the toolbox in the back of the Hiace, then poked a bit among his things, rearranging the lockers, duffels, and rolls of topographical maps and, as my father would say, "neatening" his provisions, and then he headed again toward my front door with me trailing behind.

"I can't stay here too much longer. We have to leave tomorrow. But let's take this a little further. What message do you suppose is sent when the ambassador who has been asking questions about Richardson's disappearance is suddenly no longer the ambassador? Let's say you are Chacón. What is Washington telling you?"

"I'm sorry—message? What do you mean?"

"How will Chacón interpret the ambassador's departure?"

"I suppose he would be relieved."

"Close, but he would not merely be relieved, my dear, he would be reassured that nothing has changed, that he is free to kill people with impunity, even American citizens, and if you can kill American citizens, so they reason, you can kill anyone. Do you understand what it means for a man like Chacón to receive such a message?"

We had reached the door, had gone through it, and were back in the empty living room with the papier-mâché horse.

"It means the butchery will continue and many more people will die. It means that the military will believe that they are safe, and that they have nothing to fear from this new human rights policy. It's a show intended only for the Soviets."

"What do you mean?"

"Never mind. We can talk about it later. Right now, we have to have a serious conversation. We have run out of time. Sit down. I'm going to ask you some questions. Think about your answers carefully. Think about all that I have told you."

He moved the salt and pepper shakers into position on the table, and also the toothpick holder. He pushed a miniature metal ship into the Pacific. The card deck was in place where he said the garrison would be. "Okay," he kept saying as each object took its place. "Okay."

I noticed that his glasses were smudged again. How could he possibly see through them? I had never met anyone so focused, obsessed really, or anyone whose children were this compliant and well behaved. At their age, I wouldn't have played with rabbits for three days, as they did, or lie on the kitchen floor making drawings, which were, come to think of it, not unlike those their father made, but these girls did so happily, and seemed accustomed to waiting for him.

Leonel then asked me what I remembered about the confiscation of the common lands, first for the planting of indigo crops, then the cultivation of sugarcane and cotton, and then, on the volcano's slopes that were all that were left to the Pipil and Nahua people, the planting of coffee, the most lucrative export crop of them all. He asked me questions about wages, plots of land, milpas, labor unions, life expectancy, and malnutrition. The last questions concerned the uprising of 1932 and its aftermath, about the volcano's erupting as the uprising began, the mysterious appearance of U.S. and Canadian gunships in the harbor. Thirty thousand or eighty thousand people were massacred in the following days, no one knows how many, but it was always given as a round number.

"Allow me to present a scenario. You are a colonel in the generation about to take power."

He moved the toothpick holder into place. "You are disillusioned. Your superiors have engaged in unprecedented levels of corruption. Papu? Are you listening to me? Okay. Several other younger officers share your concerns. What do you do?"

"A coup d'état?"

"No, not yet, but you are thinking along the right lines. You would assess the conditions and determine whether the time was right. Let's try another. You hear that the embassy—always the U.S. embassy in cases such as this—isn't happy with the general your *tanda* has chosen to be president."

He moved the pepper shaker into place near the pack of cigarettes he called the Other Garrison.

"There is a possibility that the U.S. will back a different *tanda*."

He pushed the saltshaker toward this garrison like a chess piece.

"What do you do? Think," he said, "like a colonel."

I gave an answer, many answers, all of them guesses: I would maneuver within the *tanda* to push the leader aside. I'd go behind their backs to the Americans and make some sort of deal, promising them influence and intelligence. That is, if I was a colonel. Or—I'd do nothing.

I had no idea how to think like a colonel.

After a long silence, he leaned back in his chair. The sun shone on the paper over the house the girls had drawn. The doves were on their perch outside, leaning into one another. The sea was bright through the window.

"Forché, I award you a Ph.D. in Salvadoran studies."

I hadn't slept well and had smoked too much, judging from the bowl of stubs and the rawness in my throat. I had to know then why he was telling me all of this. It was interesting, yes, but why? No one had ever, in truth, spent so much time talking to me about important things, and with such patient urgency, certainly no man, and never had I met anyone who took poetry this seriously who was not himself a poet.

"Thank you. Now why don't you tell me what you want." There was an edge in my voice that surprised me.

He leaned forward again, put his hands together making a church steeple with his forefingers, and he shrugged.

"What are you going to do, Papu? Write poetry about yourself for the rest of your life? And if you're going to translate our poets, don't you think you should know something about Central America?"

There was a flapping of doves taking flight, and children running outside and closing the door behind them.

"What do you mean?"

"What I just said. Are you going to write poetry about yourself for the rest of your life?" And then he sighed and acknowledged that this might not have been fair.

"I'm sorry. Let me put this a different way. What are you going to do with the poetry fellowship you recently received?"

"Fellowship? Oh yes. I don't know yet. I didn't think I would get one, so I don't have a plan. I'll think of something."

"Well, I have a proposition for you. Not that kind of proposition, a more interesting one. I assure you, my intentions are honorable."

"Wait. How did you know about the fellowship?"

He didn't answer.

"No, really, how did you know?"

"I don't know. I can't remember how I found out."

Then, changing the subject, he asked if I knew how my benefactors had made their money.

"Lead, copper, and silver mines," he said. "They once controlled all mining and smelting in the United States, but they also operated in Mexico. They owned a smelter in Monterrey, where they employed thugs to force workers at gunpoint into the blazing heat. I just thought this might interest you as some of this money will soon be yours."

"My grandfather worked at a blast furnace, in a coke oven . . ."

"Then maybe you are collecting his just wages. Here is my proposal: Why not come to El Salvador? You've already spent a summer with Claribel. You've translated her poetry. Now write your own. It might be interesting, and you could improve your Spanish. I can make arrangements for you to work with some good women—doctors and social workers. You could call this my reverse Peace Corps. You would be coming to our country not to help us, but so that we can help you. I want to give you a bit of the education that you missed in your U.S. schools. And to be honest, war is coming, and the United States is going to play a pivotal role, as it always does in our region, and what the United States decides will determine how long the war will have to be fought. You will be, by the way, my second reverse Peace Corps volunteer, not the first."

"I don't think Americans are interested in getting involved in any more wars, Leonel. We just left Vietnam."

"Yes, you just left Vietnam. Did you, by the way, understand why your country was at war there?"

He was sucking on that cold tobacco pipe again.

"Let me guess not. Would you like to see one from the beginning?"

"One what?"

"Vietnam, from the beginning."

He has no idea what he's saying to me, I thought. Yes, I would like to see—for myself, from the beginning, but I wouldn't tell him anything about my personal history having to do with the war in Vietnam. This was all none of his business, I thought at the time.

I went down to walk on the beach alone, the sanderlings running, my tracks filling with water behind me. For a moment, I worried that when I returned to the house I would find him gone. He might leave his drawings taped to the table, but otherwise it would be as if he hadn't been there and I had imagined this whole thing. I decided not to stay long at the water, but I wanted to think. I was twenty-seven years old, too young to have thought very much about the whole of my life, its shape and purpose. The only consistencies were menial labor and poetry and, more recently, translating and teaching. There was always a book on the bedside table. That November it was the poetry of Nâzim Hikmet, a Turkish poet translated into English. His poem titled "Autobiography" was dated the 11th of September 1961, East Berlin. I would have been eleven years old. The poem begins with the year of the poet's birth and goes on to list all that the poet had seen and done until then in the course of his life. It was at once a list of autobiographical facts but also an inventory and a confession. I tried several times to write a poem like it, but failed, and decided that I hadn't lived long enough or interestingly enough, but this didn't entirely account for the failure. When I wrote about the places I had been and the things I'd done, there was no thread of purpose or commitment, as there was in the life of Hikmet. Maybe Leonel was right to say that my poems were about myself, even if they were also about others, even such important others as Grandpa Goodmorning and Ya-Kwana.

Still, there were lines and images that surprised me to have come from my hand: phrases such as the *hollow crackle of hatching snakes* and *if the whisper was in your mouth*.

Why did it seem that, during these past few days, time had slowed, even the ocean was taking longer to heave itself onto the beach, longer to withdraw, and what should I do? What did this man want? There was a word for it, wasn't there? The music the stones make as the water passes over them? Like the sound that dried beans make when they strike against the thorns in a rain stick? I wanted one word for that. Murmur. I wanted to know what to do.

Leonel did not seem then to be a dangerous person and, in fact, no one in Deià had described him that way. What they said was that he was "playing a very dangerous game." What game that was they wouldn't say, and otherwise they had great admiration for him. The El Salvador he described was not at war, although he did say its peace was "the silence of misery endured." Those were his words. The war, then, was next door, against the dictator Somoza in Nicaragua. But war was coming, he had said, in three to five years. So it was still far off. There was nothing keeping me here, in this empty house by the water. And yes, I wanted, for personal reasons, to know something more about Vietnam, "from the beginning," as Leonel said.

WHEN I REACHED THE HOUSE, HE WAS STILL THERE, AND AS I'D IMAGINED, ALL but his drawings had been packed into the Hiace. The mural was still taped to the table. Later I would understand why he drew diagrams and stick figures as he talked, but at the time I just thought he was a bit like me, needing a pen in his hand all the time, unable to think without it.

"Well?"

The girls were saying good-bye to the rabbits, holding them up to their cheeks.

"I'm not sure. What would I do there?"

"Well, you could see quite a bit of the country, I think, and you could learn about the situation, and then you could come back here, and when the war begins, you would be in a position to explain it to the Americans. I could make you an expert, and that is something the Americans can never have enough of—experts."

"Leonel? I think you want someone else, a journalist maybe, someone with the credibility to do this—whatever it is you have in mind."

"I've thought about that, and I don't want a journalist. I want a poet. Why do you think I came all this way?"

"So, this wasn't a family camping trip?"

"Yes, it is also that. But I came here so that I could talk to you. And this might be my last chance."

"Last chance? You know, Leonel, your relatives in Deià are a little puzzled by you. They aren't sure who you are."

"They don't know who I am? I see. What difference does it make who I am? I'm not important."

"It doesn't, then. Make a difference. I guess."

"Good. You can tell them to come back to El Salvador. Tell Bud and Claribel to come back."

"But they'd be in danger there, wouldn't they? Especially Claribel."

"Come on, everyone is in danger there. Tell them to come back. We could use some help, and what are they going to do, spend the rest of their lives in Mallorca drinking cognac? I think not. You can't make a difference in the world by going to parties." He went back to sit in front of his drawings, and when I challenged his attitude toward Claribel and Bud, he admitted that he wasn't being fair to them.

"I don't think you understand, Leonel. I'm a poet. Do you know how poets are viewed here? We're seen as bohemian, or romantics, or crazy. Among the poets I admire, there is one who waved good-bye before jumping from a bridge, another who put on a fur coat and gassed herself in her garage. Great American poets die broke in bad hotels. We have no credibility. Although this isn't true of every poet, and I'm giving you the dramatic examples, when poetry is mentioned in the American press, if it *is* mentioned, the story begins with 'Poetry doesn't matter,' or 'No one reads poetry.' No matter what else is said. It doesn't matter."

He appeared surprised. "Well, you'll have to change that. In my country, and in the rest of Latin America, poets are taken seriously. They're appointed to diplomatic posts, or they're assassinated, or put into prison but, one way or the other, taken seriously."

The entire table was covered now with garrisons, volcanoes, milpas and crosshatched villages, coffee trees, and cotton bolls, and in the paper sky, a squadron of American gunships hovering, and from the ground, bursts of fire inked from the barrels of antiaircraft guns. The soldiers were drawn as stick figures with helmets, but the campesinos wore straw hats and trousers, had water gourds slung over their shoulders, and carried machetes—the whole of it a mural of the country at that time, and I knew that if I didn't accept his invitation, I could never live as if I would have been willing to do something, should an opportunity have presented itself. I could never say to myself: If only I'd had the chance. This was, I knew, my chance.

"Here's an address," he said, jotting something on a slip of paper torn from a corner of the mural. "I want you to write to this man, my first reverse Peace Corps volunteer. He's a historian. His name is Tom Anderson, and he wrote a book about that massacre in El Salvador in 1932. Ask him to tell you about me, and also about the situation. He can help you. Think of this as checking my references, as you people say."

He was now gathering his books and pamphlets from the table, his special pens and pouch of pipe tobacco, all of it back into the woven bag.

"Come in early January, right after the holidays. I'll send you a ticket for a flight on our national airline. It will be cheaper than anything you could buy here. And by the way, you don't need much. Bring a toothbrush. Get a gamma globulin shot and maybe something for yellow fever and oh, malaria pills, don't forget those. I'll take care of everything else."

"I won't be able to stay more than a month then."

"That will get us started." He gave me a quick tap on the shoulder. "Ciao."

The girls got into the washed Hiace after dutifully kissing me on both cheeks, as someone had taught them, their mother I guessed, who was from one of the wealthy families, and from whom he was separated, saying something about how impossible domestic life had become under his circumstances.

Everything was loaded into the van.

"Ciao!" he called through the window as he backed out of the driveway.

I waved to the back of the Hiace as he drove downhill toward the glittering water, Andean flute music fluttering into the air. He put his head out the window and called back, "See you in January!" And as the van disappeared behind the hill I shouted back, "I didn't say yet I was coming!"

———◆———

You don't know this man, my friends will say. This isn't a good idea. You're going to get malaria or even worse. So what if he's a relative of Claribel Alegría's? According to you, even *she* claims not to know who he really is.

No one thought I should accept the invitation to go to El Salvador, and of course I didn't talk about it with my parents, who in any case lived thousands of miles away, because I knew what they would say. But I kept talking about the visit and invitation, and everyone dissuaded me until an old friend from Michigan, passing through on his way to Mexico, stopped for coffee and listened to the story. We were at the table, the same table, the finches all in their cage, quiet beneath the kitchen towel that allowed them to sleep, and I told him everything because why not? What did it matter? I asked myself. He would say no like everyone else, and I would stay here for what seemed the rest of my life.

"How many opinions have you gotten so far? You're going to ask people whether to do this or not until someone tells you to go," he said. "It is what you seem to want to do, so let me be that person. Go."

From childhood, I had experienced bouts of depression, and my mother had also suffered this during her child-raising years. I would find her in her room sometimes, crying and staring at nothing. She told me that I would understand when I was older, something she said about many things. In my own life, this darkness descended always unexpectedly. That is, it did not seem caused by particular events. The sadness arrived, stayed for a while, and just as unexpectedly lifted.

Something could, at times, push against it. Work did, and also the urge to do something in the face of some wrongdoing or injustice inflicted against another, and this urge swelled during the conversations on the terrace in Mallorca that summer, as I sat on the edge of the circle taking things in, until, toward the end, I also worked at being invisible, because it seemed, from what I understood from these conversations, that injustices of a political nature were not historical accidents, and that most injustices in Latin America were supported or made possible by the United States, or that was my impression. One of the visiting writers had even responded to my plaintive question regarding ways I might get involved with something like: *There is nothing you can do, my dear. Change your government. Enjoy your summer.*

When I finally decided to go to El Salvador, I wrote to Professor Tom Anderson, as Leonel had suggested I do, asking about the invitation to

come to El Salvador, and received the following reply, which was somewhat encouraging:

October 20, 1977

Dear Ms. Forché,

I'm delighted to do anything I can for a friend of Leonel, but I don't
imagine there is much I can tell you about the country that Leonel
hasn't. I take it you are interested in the politics and the people rather
than the scenery. What everyone thinks of, of course, is the political
terrorism which has been going on for some time. . . . There is a school
of thought which holds that it is all (even the left-wing violence) a
product of the National Police. I don't buy that, though there may be
some truth in it. . . . There is also, as I'm sure you know, an Unión
Guerrera Blanca operating on the right. They are indeed linked to
retired, and perhaps active, officers of the Policía and the Guardia. There
is an extraordinary document that surfaced two months ago in Miami,
apparently leaked by the CIA, which links right-wing terrorism and
pseudo-left-wing terrorism to Col. José Francisco René Chacón, former
counter-intelligence chief. Chacón, in turn, is linked to Guatemalan
gangsters of Lebanese origins . . . if one can believe any of this! Chacón,
at any rate, is a well-known psychopath who was responsible for the
murder in prison of the black North American soldier of fortune and
petty thief James Ronald Richardson. I am sure you know of this
incident. This is by no means Chacón's only murder. He is out of
government, but there are plenty left of his stripe.

The letter went on to describe the persecution of Jesuits and the deaths of
the priests, and then:

Leonel can tell you more about the peasant movement than I can,
as he is closely involved. How he escapes assassination is a perpetual
mystery to me and I think of him as an endangered species. I am afraid I

have made it all sound very cloak and daggerish, but it isn't, unless you want to get involved. The streets are peaceful. The Guardia Nacional is less evident now than it was in the high-handed days of Chele Medrano. The press is not censored (why should it be? It is owned by people the government can trust) and you can talk to the opposition leaders at the Catholic university, where most of them work. The Rector there, by the way, Román Mayorga, is well worth meeting. In all, you should enjoy it in El Salvador. The seafood is terrific!

Sincerely,
Tom Anderson

The ticket arrived in the mail some weeks later, booked for January 4, 1978. As Leonel had suggested, I went to a tropical disease specialist for a gamma globulin shot and quinine pills, but they didn't think I needed a vaccination against yellow fever. Later that day, an older woman friend, who had enrolled in one of my writing classes at the university, and who had lived in Latin America for fourteen years, asked me if I knew what I was doing.

"We'll talk when you get back," she said. "You're going to need to talk then."

Qué te he dado, lo sé. Qué has recibido,
no lo sé.
I know what I have given you. I do not
know what you have received.

—Antonio Porchia

When I arrived at Ilopango International Airport on a still night in the dry season, Leonel Gómez Vides was nowhere to be seen. The darkened clamshell terminal was crowded with soldiers, and as there were only a few passengers on the flight, and no other foreigners, I was alone as I retrieved my bag from the broken conveyor and carried it through customs. Two armed guards asked me to open the bag. They went through my clothes, opened the toiletry case, sniffed the talcum powder, and when I was at last cleared and my passport stamped, I stood in a small parking lot, surrounded by men who casually shouldered automatic weapons. After too long, a tall young man walked toward me, asking if I was Carolyn.

"I'm John Taylor. I'm with the Peace Corps," he said, extending his hand, then swinging my bag into the back of his truck. "I'll bring you to Leonel. He's sorry that he couldn't be here himself, but something came up, as something always does. You know him."

We drove the unlit streets of the barrios, past clusters of shacks built at the roadsides, mud shacks roofed by sheets of corrugated steel weighted by rubber tires. Truck lights washed the shacks white.

"So," he asked cheerfully, "how long have you known Leonel?"

It sounded strange even as I said it. "Three days."

"He gave me the impression that you two were old friends. So—you don't know him very well, either, eh?"

Either. We were now in a business district.

"He's a pretty strange guy," John said, downshifting and glancing at me.

"What do you mean?"

"Oh, I don't know, I guess you'll see. We're friends, but I can't say I know him well. We've been in some interesting situations together. Sometimes too interesting."

He was pulling into the parking lot of Benihana of Tokyo, San Salvador.

"Leonel chose this place, so don't blame me. He's inside with a group of people. I'm a vegetarian myself, but I'll be joining you. There's always rice."

Leonel rose as I walked toward the square of tables surrounding a hot steel grill, where a Salvadoran chef, dressed in a Japanese yukata, was tossing sprouts, shrimp, and shredded vegetables into spitting oil, juggling knives and pepper grinders, expertly sending a splash of soy sauce skittering across the grill's surface.

Motioning for me to sit on the stool beside him, Leonel introduced the others, all of them men: two campesino union leaders, some kind of businessman, someone from a "nongovernmental organization," a nervous university student, and John, the Peace Corps volunteer. Japanese koto music played above the chef as he performed, and Salvadoran women floated past wearing kimonos, their coiled hair held in place by ornate chopsticks. After smiling and nodding at me, the men resumed their conversations and Leonel whispered in my ear: "Where do you suppose you are?"

"Benihana of Tokyo?"

For some reason, he thought this was amusing.

"Let's say this is Vietnam," he said, and after a pause, "it is 1959."

I remember thinking that there was a good chance I had made a mistake, and if so, it could be rectified quite easily by taking a cab back to the airport in the morning. I didn't, however, rectify it. I had just arrived, and no matter how surreal my welcoming was, it was possible that, for once, first impressions weren't entirely reliable. Leonel talked to me at dinner, I don't remember about what—something having to do with the calm before the storm, or standing at the edge of a precipice. After dinner, he took me to his friend Blanca's house, where the former dictator had once lived: General Maximiliano Hernández Martínez, ruler during the violent 1930s.

"This was his very house," Leonel called out, hoisting my suitcase up the stairs. "I thought it would be interesting for you to stay here first, to begin in 1932, because you will find your way in El Salvador by the light of the volcano Izalco erupting on the night of the massacre. Who knows? Maybe Martínez saw it through these very windows."

The house was dark and spacious but not especially grand, a colonial house with shuttered windows and mahogany wainscoting, a house for a dictator, Leonel said. Blanca, who lived here now, was the sister of a Catholic priest, and I would meet this priest later. This is where I would stay for the time being, he said, and then: "I have to leave now but first let me tell you a little about the man in whose bedroom you will be sleeping. He was president from 1931 until 1944."

I reminded him that Claribel and Bud had written a novel about this period, *Ashes from Izalco,* and that I had read it.

"Yes. Well, your bed belonged to the man responsible for those thirty thousand dead. Or eighty thousand, depending on your source."

He walked around the room, opening and closing the doors of the armoire, then pulling the drape across the window.

"By the way, Martínez used to hold séances in this house, probably not in this room but in the parlor. He was a recluse who didn't drink or smoke, but for some reason he was always trying to talk to the dead, not those he had butchered, mind you, but those he thought might guide him from the beyond into higher realms. He believed in reincarnation, and even claimed that if some of the peasants he killed were innocent of being subversives, nevertheless he had done them the favor of sending them to their next, possibly better, life. Martínez also said, and I quote, 'It is a greater crime to kill an ant than a man, for when a man dies he becomes reincarnated, while an ant dies forever.' He once tried to cure smallpox by having Christmas lights strung throughout the city. He wrote his speeches while sitting in the bathtub. So. Maybe you can write a poem about sleeping in the dictator's bed? That would make a good poem, don't you think?"

"Leonel, that isn't how I write poems."

"Don't worry. I'll see you tomorrow. Sleep well. And by the way, he was a vegetarian. I thought you might like that."

———◆———

I seemed to be alone in the dictator's house when I woke that first morning. I saw myself unexpectedly reflected in a mirror as I entered the hallway, but then I heard dishes clattering in a far room and found Blanca downstairs, setting the table for a Salvadoran breakfast of beans with cream, white cheese and tortillas, and if there were eggs, there would be eggs, and also papayas with limes. She came to greet me in a flutter of Spanish and then put her hands on my shoulders, looked into my eyes, and warmly said, *Bienvenida, Carolina, y mil gracias.*

A thousand thanks? I had only just arrived. For what was I being thanked?

We talked simply then in Spanglish as my conversation skills were still limited, and her English had been learned from American television shows. From what I could gather, she was worried about her brother the priest. Two other priests had already been killed, but I knew that, yes? More than forty foreign nuns had been deported.

She began reciting something that sounded almost like litany: Aguilares, Padre Grande, Padre Navarro, *aquí en San Salvador y en Aguilares y campesinos,* "hundreds, three hundreds, all dead, even *niños* dead."

She folded and refolded her napkin. Her eyes searched mine and held my gaze. She shook her head, then poured more coffee for us both.

"Some whole villages—Leonel will take you."

She drew a sharp breath.

"Blanca, *gracias,* yes. *No, no más café, gracias.* Blanca, when is Leonel coming?"

"Who knows? We never know when he will come."

———◆———

The following day, or the day after, he arrived in time for breakfast. I came down to the kitchen still half asleep, and tried to hide my irritation at being left on my own with nothing to do except make notes about the dictator's house, and as the house now belonged to Blanca, the taking of an inventory of objects in the house might not serve to illuminate anything about him. I had paced and fretted while Leonel was away, and again made plans to go home.

"Good morning!" he sang out, apparently having arrived before I woke up, as he was already well into breakfast.

"Go and get dressed, we have work to do—and wear something nice and bring a bag with you in case we don't come back here tonight."

Blanca had been talking with Leonel, but she stood and poured coffee for me, then sat back down with her head in her hands.

"Blanca, your brother knows what he's doing, he knows how to watch out for himself," then to me: "I'm sorry I'm late, but I had to take care of a few things. Go get ready."

This is what he would often say, not always, but often, and in the beginning, he let these so-called things he was taking care of remain vague.

A whole day and night late, I thought.

"Where have you been?" I asked as lightly as I could as I climbed into the Hiace, smoothing my skirt beneath me, my "something nice." Maybe he would tell me where he had been, I thought, if I didn't seem too interested in the answer.

"Something has come up."

We were weaving through traffic in San Salvador on a cloudless day with the radio blaring "*Domingo, Domingo, Domingo,*" passing buses painted blue with bright flowers, black smoke belching from their pipes, bundles strapped to the roof, arms hanging from the windows, and as I would discover, Leonel was driving just as Salvadorans did in those days—glancing often in the rearview mirror. There was an international issue of *Time* magazine between us and as I reached for it, Leonel stopped my hand.

"Don't touch that."

Something bulky had been tucked into the magazine. He lifted half the pages to reveal a handgun.

"It's dangerous here right now," he said, "very dangerous. A lot has happened in the last few months."

I had never been around weapons, although I competed as a girl in archery tournaments and once, in the hay-stubbled snow of a friend's farm, had shot at tin cans with a .22 caliber rifle, mostly to please the boy who reached from behind to hold my arms in the correct position.

"*Mirá*," Leonel was saying, a word that began many of his sentences, look. "As I said, something has come up."

I reached to turn off the radio so I could hear him better and he stopped me again.

"Leave it on. It's better if you leave it on."

The jingle on the radio gave way to a Swedish pop song that seemed to be the song of the season.

"*Mirá*, it seems there is a delegation coming here in a few days from the United States, a human rights delegation, and it's going to be headed by a U.S. congressman. And that congressman, who is from Massachusetts by the way, is also a Catholic priest. A Jesuit. And this Jesuit is going to be asking questions, and we have to make sure that our question is among the ones he asks."

"And what is our question?"

"That's what I'm about to tell you, but first we have to find some place where we can talk. And eat. I'm hungry."

"But we just had breakfast."

"Well, I have to have breakfast number two."

We were in traffic, but the street was also crowded with people on foot, including many children, women balancing basins, urns, and baskets on their heads. A boy whizzed past on a bicycle, striking our vehicle twice with his fist, and Leonel said something like *He's just letting me know he's there,* and then we stopped in front of a shop with a CLOSED sign, and after sliding the gun into his rucksack, he went up to the door anyway and knocked a few times.

"I think they're closed, Leonel."

"Yes, they're closed. That's why we're here. A friend of mine owns this place."

Over his breakfast number two of eggs, beans, and *crema*, brought to him after coffee was brought to me, in a café opened especially for him, he would, he said, explain everything having to do with our question.

"Our question," he said, "concerns the Richardson case. You remember? The dead American? If they won't take up the case of the dead American, then we'll know who they are."

He broke the yolk with his fork and pushed it onto a tortilla.

"The congressman? But you know who . . ."

"No, not the congressman."

He appeared somewhat irritated, pushing himself away from the table, and seeming to ponder what, or how much, to say next.

"The congressman's *handlers,* and the new people in the embassy—we'll know who this new ambassador is, and the new political officer. Are they going to push the Richardson case as hard as their predecessors did? I don't think so, but that's just a guess."

"What if they're just not interested in Richardson?" I asked. It seemed a reasonable question.

"Not interested? Okay. That would mean they're only interested in human rights when it suits them."

He bent over his eggs again, wiping the yolk from the plate with the last of his tortilla.

"Which," he said, licking his fingers, "is what I think, but we have to be fair. We have to give them the chance to ask about Richardson when they meet with the president of the republic. Besides, the Richardson case has become, for me, a good litmus test."

"Litmus test of what?"

I heard the little bell on the door. The woman who had let us in was turning the CLOSED sign to OPEN. While we'd been talking, she'd set the other tables and stroked the floor with a cloth mop so that it now shone gray in the light coming through the window. When she came to our table, answering Leonel's raised finger, he gave her some money and she beamed at him, covering her toothless mouth with her palm, then he whispered something to her that I didn't understand.

"Litmus test of what?"

"I'm also going to ask if you can accompany the delegation, but I think they'll say no, which is too bad because you'd really learn something—and not," he added cryptically, "about El Salvador."

Back in the hot Hiace, he placed the gun between our seats, covered it with the magazine, then started the engine and turned up the radio.

"First, however, we have to decide who you are. I have thought about this, and I think the truth is best, that you are a poet. You work in a university. Sometimes you write for newspapers maybe, or magazines, which would make you also a journalist."

We were in thick, slow traffic now, the air suffused with the smell of decay and exhaust.

"What is that?"

"The smell? Oh. Rotting coffee husks. I don't smell it anymore."

"I'm not a journalist."

"I know that. You know that. They don't know that. So, when necessary, we tell them you're writing an article about the country. You can be vague. In fact, it's usually best to be vague. But mostly you're here on a fellowship from the United States, and you are a poet."

He continued talking almost to himself through the barrios and *colonias* of San Salvador, glancing from mirror to windshield, from the street and the truck ahead to the stucco walls, searching the buildings as if he were looking for an address, but there were no addresses here. There were gates and walls. He pulled over and stopped, yanking on the emergency brake. A tiny woman in a white apron darted behind a gate that swung open to the walkway.

"Well, we're here," and once again sliding the gun into the rucksack, he said, "Let's go," with a slip of resignation in his voice.

"Where are we?"

He paused with his hand on the door handle.

"I wasn't going to begin this way but we don't have much time, so I don't have any choice. I'm going to introduce you to someone. You don't have to say too much, just listen. This is a little bit of a risk, Papu, so be careful."

"Be careful in what way?"

"His name is General José Alberto 'Chele' Medrano, founder of one of the largest paramilitary organizations in the country and the former director of military intelligence. He's retired now, but he is still a very dangerous man. Not without reason do they still call him *jefe*. Be careful."

I remembered this name, Medrano, from Tom Anderson's letter: *The Guardia Nacional is less evident now than it was in the high-handed days of Chele Medrano.*

"Be careful how?"

"Just—listen to what I'm saying."

"Why am I meeting him?"

"I told you."

"No, actually you didn't."

"He's a man who . . ." He seemed to catch himself, and turned to look behind us, first in the rearview mirror and then in the back window. I turned too. No one was there.

"*Mirá,* do you want to learn about this place or not?" And in the silence that hung between us he said: "Okay, then. Let's go."

———◆———

This was one of the better *colonias,* where appearances were deceptive. Such houses as belonged to General Chele Medrano were set back from the street and surrounded by walls and security gates. Armed and half-uniformed men usually stood watch. After sounding the buzzer, the guard would be told to admit the visitor. Sometimes there was no buzzer, or it wasn't used. The guard communicated with the house via two-way radio. Chele seemed to have no guard but the timid maid who had already slipped away. Tropical foliage bordered the narrow path that led to the door. Once inside the gate, and only then, the maid appeared holding the door open and shyly waving us toward a side table in the front hallway where the visitors' bags were to be left: Leonel's rucksack, my rucksack and purse. We were shown to the room where we were to sit and wait. The maid brought coffee cups, a bowl of sugar cubes, a small pitcher of milk, and glasses of water. This was always the ritual, although in the afternoons, we were sometimes offered Coca-Cola or orange soda, with lemon wafers or some other cookie. For a short time, I would have the chance to study the room for clues as to the owner's tastes and interests. General Medrano's sitting room was dimmed by wide, gray Venetian blinds coated with dust. There were framed prints on the walls and porcelain curios on the side tables. The old television's dead green tube reflected the stuffed sofa and the blinded window.

Leonel stood as Medrano came into the room wearing a white guayabera and trousers belted just below his chest. I remember the house slippers on his blue-veined feet, his faint gray mustache and dancing eyebrows, one arched higher than the other, his bulbous nose, and rheumy eyes. His gravelly voice was hard for me to understand. He nodded to each of us in turn but did not offer his hand. As he lowered himself into his chair, assisted by the same maid, we took our seats facing him in a small circle.

In the beginning, I didn't really understand the conversations that took place between Leonel and men such as Medrano. Their rapid, mysterious, obscenity-strewn Salvadoran Spanish was more revealing of mood than substance, and the moods swung from jovial to menacing. When my turn came to be included, the Spanish slowed or Leonel interpreted.

This time, Leonel began with pleasantries, as if this were a social call, asking after the general's family and health, but then the conversation hardened. Medrano was furious about something. Leonel listened intently and nodded from time to time, so I also listened to what seemed a fierce and incomprehensible debate. I heard: *subversivos, mierda, a la gran puta, cabrón, las fuerzas armadas, los gringos,* and *comunistas.* Most of the foul language came from Leonel while the retired general was a little more reserved. As they talked, I turned toward one and then the other. Leonel later said that the expression on my face was serious and intent, as if I were recording every word, and that my silence, in his opinion, had therefore been "perfect." But during the meeting I felt hopelessly lost, and so imagined that I was watching a play, until Leonel interrupted in slow Spanish, repeating in English: "She is interested to know your current impressions of General Romero's *tanda.*"

With this, Medrano gave me his full attention for the first time.

"This crop?" he asked.

I didn't know quite what Leonel was talking about, but I pretended yes, "this crop."

"Well, as you know, our group had a lot of problems and perhaps we dealt with people a bit harshly back then, but of course we played the game as it is played, and mostly we did well. There was corruption, yes. There is always corruption. There is always money to be made and what choice really do we have? *You* understand this, of course. But these *cabrones* in power now? The worst thieves I have ever seen, *historically* the worst. And that, as you must know, is saying something."

He smiled and I nodded, ever so slightly.

"There is something else," Leonel said. "What about Richardson? The dead American? They still have a dead American on their hands."

The retired general looked at his watch, then at me.

"I'm no longer in charge of these matters," he said.

Then, as a way of ending the meeting, he asked if I had further questions. For some reason I said no, nothing else, and thanked him for his time.

"Perfect!" Leonel blurted as he started the engine. "You were very good."

"What does that mean?"

I was trying not to sound irritated, but I honestly didn't know what he was talking about.

"Oh, God, Carolina, do I have to explain everything to you? Just take the compliment. I don't give many, as you might have noticed. Look, you were serious and you were not very forthcoming. You were paying attention. And you thanked him. That's important. I think he formed a good first impression. And we managed to ask about Richardson. It couldn't have gone better."

I folded my arms and turned to watch the street through the side window.

"What's wrong?"

I didn't know what to say at that moment.

"Nothing. Nothing's wrong."

"Papu . . ."

"Why did you drag me in there? There was no reason for me . . ."

"Oh yes, there was. You have no idea."

"Well, that's a problem, isn't it? It's a problem for me."

"All right, then, let's review. You just arrived in the country, an American with no known affiliations, and suddenly you are asking to meet with Chele Medrano of all people."

"But I didn't ask to meet with him."

"Yes, you did. Because I told him you wanted to see him and that's how we got into his goddamn house in the first place. He might have met with me alone but I don't think so. Why should he? And we planted a good seed, and, as they say, it fell on fertile ground."

"But you used me, and I don't even know for what."

"Lesson number one: I did not use you, I gave you a rare opportunity. And we accomplished many things, more than I'd hoped. You are now a mysterious person of some importance, and that might save your life."

He reached over and patted my thigh. "Come on, Forché, cheer up."

———◆———

The human rights team headed by the congressman did its work. Tom Anderson, Leonel's first reverse Peace Corps volunteer, accompanied the group as record keeper. During this time, Leonel rented two rooms in the hotel where the group was staying—to save time, "to keep an eye on developments," and, most important, to seize upon any opportunity to ask about the dead American. As he predicted, I wouldn't be joining the group as an observer, a decision not taken by the congressman himself but by his handler, a man from a vaguely religious but, in practice, secular organization dedicated to service, one of the many people whom Leonel came to call kumbayas, in honor of the American campfire song.

"He is who he is," Leonel said of this man, as he would come to say about many people.

Later, he explained that there were many ways to find out who people really are, behind the personas they present to the world. There are also ways of learning, in a relatively short period of time, if a person can be trusted.

"For example," he said, "you might give someone a bit of harmless or even false information and see where it travels and how long it takes to come back to you, and if, after several such tests, the information fails to come back, you might have a person you can more or less trust."

We were in the hotel coffee shop, waiting for Tom to join us. It was Tom who had delivered, by telephone, the bad news, which wasn't so much that I couldn't join the group but that the delegation clearly had no interest in asking the Salvadoran military government about the Richardson case, and this meant they had no interest in stirring matters up regarding the murderousness of such men as Chacón.

"Maybe he doesn't understand how important this is," I suggested, trying to distract myself from smoking another cigarette by toying with the sugar packets.

"Come on, Papu. He knows. Anyone who has been paying attention to El Salvador knows. Listen, I'm not asking them to spend a lot of time, I'm just asking for one little"—holding his index finger a half inch from his thumb for emphasis—"one *little* mention of a dead man's name in at least one official meeting. That's it. And they can't even do that."

"Don't get up," a cheerful voice boomed, but Leonel was already on his feet, embracing Anderson, the two taking turns patting each other on the shoulder, asking after families, marveling at how long it had been, then turning to me, Tom extended his hand.

"You must be Carolyn. Delighted. Sorry I'm late. What a day!" He asked if we'd like coffee, adding that he wished he could join us for dinner but, apparently, they were scheduled to dine with the embassy people later in the evening.

"And I'm sorry you won't be with us in Aguilares," he added. "I tried, but it seems they have a set agenda, and they're quite nervous about this whole thing, as you might expect. Ever since Father Grande's murder, Aguilares has been off-limits. The plan to go there has the embassy in a tizzy. Two coffees, please. Leonel, what are you having?"

"Nothing," he said, "water's fine. Tizzy?"

"I think they would rather we skipped Aguilares altogether, but the congressman won't have it. One can imagine how he feels, a fellow Jesuit . . ."

And again, he apologized.

"Don't worry about it, Tom," Leonel said gently. "Forché will get her opportunity to go to Aguilares. But about this dinner tonight? I do have a small favor to ask of you. If the moment is right, would you mind trying to find out what this new ambassador thinks about the Richardson case?"

Leonel seemed to be choosing his words carefully, his tone almost professorial, mirroring Tom's manner of speaking.

"Sure. I doubt he'll have anything to say to me, but of course I will. You know, Leonel, you should try to get a meeting with him yourself. I'm sure he'd see you."

"I have no interest, Tom. How long has he been here? Long enough, I would think, that he should at least have read his predecessor's notes."

As was often the case, I felt myself withdraw as the two men talked, into a familiar state that allowed for writing in my stenographer's pad: the same green, oblong notebook, spiral bound at the top, that I had begun using while in high school, available on the supply cart for the girls studying shorthand, the lost art of taking notes rapidly in an abbreviated symbolic language illegible to anyone else. I wrote in pencil, then as now, to keep the writing light and erasable. Mostly I wrote descriptions of things—images, lines, and other notes toward future poems, but with a little practice, I realized I could also probably get back up to speed "taking dictation," as we called it in the past, transcribing conversations so they could be read back nearly verbatim.

"Carolyn?" Leonel was speaking to me now, prompting me to tell Tom about the military officer I had met a few days earlier, smiling as if he were proud of me or of himself.

"General Chele Medrano," I offered, feeling a bit embarrassed to have been put on the spot.

"Really? Very interesting. Was he forthcoming?"

I didn't understand the question.

"Not much," Leonel answered for me. "But it was a good meeting. She did well."

"You're not going to put her through too much, are you, Leonel?" Tom was smiling as he said this, then to me: "Be careful with this guy. You never know what he's going to get you into—no, seriously though," he added, patting Leonel's shoulder again, "you're lucky to have him as a friend, and you'll learn a great deal from him. I know I did."

We were all standing now, Leonel whispering, "Wait here," before the two men walked a short way off, then turned toward each other and had a brief, earnest conversation. It was around that time that I remembered something from Tom's letter: that he was afraid that he had made it all *sound very cloak and daggerish, but it isn't, unless you want to get involved.*

We were in the hotel lobby the next day as the congressman swept through, shaking my hand among many, while his handler marched around the periphery of the group, striding to the hotel desk and back, and once or twice I thought I saw him casting a wary eye on Leonel.

The group left suddenly, climbing into two embassy vehicles that had pulled in front of the hotel, leaving its gleaming lobby empty, like a flock of crows that had suddenly flown from a field, flapping into the air for reasons known only to themselves. It was quiet again, except that I thought I heard the scratch of a two-way radio, a voice crackling through white noise, then clicking off. Leonel was wearing a fresh guayabera—his equivalent, he told me, of a business suit. This is the best I have, he said, and in a falsetto voice added: *my formal wear.* Later he would joke that if he died, they'd better not put him "in a jacket and tie, the standard uniform of corpses" for men of his class. He shrugged and turned away, motioning me to follow with a flick of his hand, and all the way to the van he was quiet.

"Well," he said finally, "well, we tried."

IT WAS THEN THAT HE DECIDED TO TAKE ME TO THE *CAMPO*, OR THAT HAD BEEN the plan all along, but we were driving away from the city, and not in the Hiace but in an open jeep, my hair whipping around my face, the mountains amber through my sunglasses, and fields of corn and cane and cotton crops broken by bony, pastured cattle, and along the road, walking the shoulders on both sides, women with clay water urns balanced on their heads, barefoot children following behind them, men leading burros loaded down with kindling and bundles, and every so often we would pull up behind a slow, coughing bus, and Leonel would downshift and slide into the left lane, racing toward oncoming traffic before slipping back in front of the bus just in time. When he did this, I squeezed my eyes shut and braced my feet on the floor.

"What?" he would ask, and then to my silence, answer, "Don't worry. I'm an expert driver."

The highlands were fog wrapped from a distance, and as it was January, the coffee harvest was still in progress, although coming to an end. Harvesters were among the coffee trees, pulling the last of the coffee cherries into the canastas tied at their waists. When these canastas were filled, these cherries were poured into a sack that the harvester dragged behind her, and when the sack was full, the coffee would be weighed and the harvester paid so many centavos for each *tarea* of coffee, almost nothing, Leonel explained, downshifting around a curve, filling the silence that still hung between us.

"It has always been almost nothing—nothing and a tortilla. Maybe. And you know, it wouldn't have gone as well if you had known any more than you did," referring to our visit with Medrano. And then he asked if I knew when coffee consumption had begun, and for a moment I saw the Leonel who had visited me in California.

Without waiting for an answer, he shouted over the engine: "In the fifteenth century in the Sufi shrines of Yemen."

"No, I didn't know that."

"Well, then, there might be other things you don't know. Such as when these sons of bitches interrogate someone, they tie the man to a chair, put his hand on a table, cut off one of his fingers, and they flush it down a toilet before asking the first question."

He glanced at me, barely taking his eyes from the road. I tried not to react.

"And our Colonel Chacón has a friend he works with, and this friend claims to be a doctor but I don't know. The doctor injects the spine of a victim with anesthetic, then he slices through the person's abdomen with a scalpel, reaches in, and starts pulling out guts while the person is conscious and can see what is happening. And then the colonel gets to his first question."

"All right," I said. "All right."

Pushing a cassette into the player, he asked if I minded music.

"This is Silvio Rodríguez," he said. "In one of these songs he is singing to poets from a fishing boat named after the landing place for the Bay of Pigs invasion of Cuba in 1961. Playa Girón, Bahía de Cochinos. As I told you in San Diego, the CIA sent fifteen hundred armed Cuban exiles to fight against the new regime of Fidel Castro. That little war lasted seventy-two hours—what?"

"I'm not sure I'm following you."

"Chacón! The man I'm telling you about, who chops off fingers and has people disemboweled? Where do you think he gets his foot soldiers? It has been sixteen years since the Bay of Pigs and those Cubans are still angry, and if they can't overthrow Fidel, they'll work for any *hijo de la gran puta* who hates Communists." Any son of a whore.

Silvio Rodríguez sang plaintively from the dashboard. One thing did not have much to do with another at this moment. I didn't fully understand the lyrics, but in this song Rodríguez seemed to be asking poets how to write about a fishing boat named *Playa Girón,* without sounding sentimental or political. To be fair, he seemed also to be asking musicians and historians how they would sing about such a boat or write the history of the men who defended Cuba at Playa Girón. The music went well with the wind, the afternoon light, and Leonel's angry history lesson—Leonel whose single refrain had been, until now, that war is coming. It was much like riding in an open convertible with someone close on a cloudless day, wrapped in wind and music, except that I was with a near stranger in a jeep listening to a revolutionary song, with a gun in the well of the gear shift.

"Where are we going?" I asked, raising my voice above the wind.

"I'm taking you to see how most people live. Most people in the world."

He coasted to a stop along the gravel shoulder toward a roadside stand and when he returned, he was carrying what appeared to be two wooden balls with straws stuck into them.

"Peace offering, Forché," he said, handing me one. "Coconut milk. Why don't you get out and stretch your legs? We still have a way to go."

He was talking to the coconut vendor, as he seemed to talk with people almost everywhere he went. The coconuts were not the hairy kinds one sees in supermarkets in California—they were pale and smooth like wood, piled into pyramids beside the stand. The vendor was a small man, almost skeletal. He took off his straw hat as I approached, then opened another coconut with his machete in one slice of the blade and handed it to Leonel. He took mine and hacked it into a few pieces.

"So you can get at the meat," Leonel offered. "Try it."

"*Yo no sé,*" the man was saying, "*ha sido muy tranquilo.*" It's been quiet.

"*Gracias, compa,*" Leonel said, tapping the vendor's shoulder. To call someone *compa*, or the longer form *compañero*, meant something, I would later learn.

"Who was that? You seemed to know each other."

"Oh, just someone. A friend."

"Why be so mysterious? You always seem to be hiding something, even when it's as simple as buying a coconut. Why don't you answer questions?"

We had turned onto a dirt road and I had to hang on to the side bar as we rocked into deep grooves and swerved to avoid protruding boulders.

"Maybe we should have lesson number two. Please don't ask me who people are. They wouldn't want me to tell you."

"Lesson number three," I said, "you don't have to condescend. I'm not stupid."

"That isn't lesson three. Lesson three has nothing to do with you."

———◆———

Thickets of banana palm, bamboo, and ceiba walled the roadside, and a hard white sun wetted the leaves. The jeep engine was the only sound, and there was no wind. We went on and on, bouncing, downshifting, lunging from side to side to avoid the deepest holes. The silence between us was coming now from me. There's something wrong here, I remember thinking. I thought this often in those first days. I was guessing that it was Leonel's reticence and seeming dishonesty. Where was the affable man who had taken such pains to describe things, the man who had bent over butcher paper for hours, illustrating his monologues with pen sketches? Now, he seemed to be hiding something.

He stopped the jeep in the middle of the road.

"Papu, what are you seeing?"

"What do you mean? A road. Trees."

He put the jeep into reverse and began backing up.

"What are you doing?"

He kept backing up.

"No, really, Leonel, did we miss a turn?"

His arm was around the back of my seat, and he was facing behind us into the wedge of dust that followed the jeep as would the wake of a ship. Then he stopped, just like that, in the middle of nowhere.

"Okay, we will try this again. When you see something besides trees, tell me and I'll stop."

We drove slowly forward, so slowly that the jeep seemed to be struggling.

Then I saw, through a sparse stand of corn stalks, a glint of metal, and what appeared to be a rubber tire, and finally a shack with walls made from the corrugated metal used for security gates. "Lámina," I would learn it was called, a beautiful word I would write in my notebook, perhaps someday to use in a poem. Farther along, there was a cluster of shacks that appeared to have walls made from newspaper, could that be so? Palm leaves hung over the other shacks that were made of woven twigs. Then, although I hadn't seen them the first time we drove up the road, the shacks were everywhere among the trees.

"Wait. I see dwellings, I think."

"Dwellings," he repeated, as if this word were new to him. "Those are *champas*. Okay. What else? Maybe we should get out and walk a little, don't you think? I know someone in this *caserío*."

"Walk?"

There was no place to pull over, and perhaps it didn't matter as there was no one else here, or so I thought. He took a canteen out of the back and motioned for me to follow him. Now I saw a little path leading from the ditch into the trees. He pushed the palms aside, ducked under a branch, and went in, with me following behind. I smelled smoke and thought I heard chickens. The water swished as the canteen banged against his hip. A twig or something on the path snapped, and we were in a little clearing. A mud-splotched child with a ballooned belly was peeking out from the opening of one of the shacks, but quickly darted back inside, and an old woman emerged, wiping her hands on her apron. I didn't see anyone else, but I did hear another child's voice. The woman nodded at Leonel but her expression was solemn, not so much afraid as wary. He was speaking with her and gesturing toward me, but I wasn't close enough to hear, and their voices were low. She nodded again and he called out: "It's okay, you can go inside. Josita invites you."

The woman was going through the opening in the *champa,* her house, turning to see if I was following behind her.

"She invites you," he repeated.

I entered the small, mud-walled room, where she offered me a stool and a metal cup of water, smiling, her hair tied back, her eyes bathed in a light that had no source other than within her.

Gracias, I whispered, thanking her for the cup, but I didn't want to drink this water.

A packed mud floor, I later wrote, *well swept.* Two walls made of twigs, two of mud bricks, a roof half lámina, half open to the air where clothes are hung to dry. Against the far wall, a grate with an open wood fire, a winding scarf of smoke rising to a hole in the ceiling, pots hanging on the walls and stacked beside the pit, a broom, a big flat stone, light coming through the twigs and pooling down through the hanging clothes, a basin filled with some kind of whitish-yellow mush on the floor.

She sat next to me on another low stool. Light also fell onto the floor between us from a hole in the lámina roof. She rested her blue-rivered hands on her apron.

"*Pues . . . ,*" she began, and told me some kind of story in a soft-pebbled Spanish, something I didn't understand but for a few words: *hijo, muerto, esposo, montaña, Dios mío.* These were all the puzzle pieces she gave: son, dead, husband, mountain, my God. She took from her apron pocket a small card on which was printed a replica of a painted portrait of Jesus as a fair-skinned young man with long, dark-blond hair. *Señor,* she whispered, *Señor, Señor.* This is what she called Jesus. Then she let silence take the place of everything, setting her dark eyes upon mine for a good while without letting go, her blazing eyes. After a few moments of this she smiled again, revealing that she had no upper teeth and, still holding my gaze, nodded that she was finished. I nodded back.

"*¡Vaya con Dios!*" she said as I ducked through the doorway. I didn't know what to say back, so I turned to her and touched my heart with the fingers of my right hand.

"*Por favor,*" Leonel said, and then seemed to be telling the woman that I had to relieve myself. To me he said: "Go to the toilet. Josita will show you."

"But I don't have to," I said in English.

"You'd better. You won't get another chance for a while. Go ahead."

I followed her through the trees. The stench reached me before the sight of two boards placed over a pit. The woman showed me that I was to put one foot on each board, squat down and, when I felt steady, relieve myself in the opening. She pointed to a stack of dry leaves, smiled encouragingly, and left. The waste in the pit was jeweled with green flies and I found myself unable to stand on the boards, but neither could I take my eyes from the pit, as I was far off, again in my own childhood in Michigan, having gone to play where it was forbidden to play, with the children who lived behind the scrim of poplar and birch that marked our property line, where the Joneses and the Keens lived in their tar-paper and cinder-block shacks, and behind those shacks, there were dollhouses or playhouses, as we called them, and in fact we used to play in them, but they were also called half-moon houses—outhouses—benches with oval holes sawn into them, covered by wooden lids that when raised revealed deep wells of feces and paper, lye and darkness, but there were benches, and the hole was deep, and it was possible to sit down rather than squat while balancing on wooden planks, listening to the drone of flies, and I remember as a child wondering if the flies ate the feces, and if not, why were they hovering so attentively over the pit? I stepped back and stood in the dead air. My mother was not calling me. It was Leonel.

"Papu? Is everything okay?"

He was somewhere behind me.

I don't think I answered him then but remember turning around and finding him back in the clearing when again he asked if I was okay.

"I'm fine."

"Okay, then, listen to me. There's a young man who lives here sometimes. He's Josita's nephew. Anyway, this young man hasn't been seen for a while and it seems that people here are worried, so we are going to see what we can find out. I'm going to do what I can, but I also have to get back to San Salvador."

"Okay," I said, wondering what this had to do with me.

"Which means we have to stay until tomorrow."

"Here?"

"No. Somewhere else. Nearby."

Josita came out of a *champa,* holding a naked toddler on her hip. Was she the grandmother? He said no, she was the grandmother's mother. The grandmother is about thirty-five years old, he said, and the mother is fifteen. He's known this family for a long time, and the missing boy too, he's known him since before he was born, since he was in his mother's womb, he said. "We have to help."

When had he begun to say "we"? I couldn't remember another time, so as part of this "we," I asked where everyone else was, as there seemed to be no one here but the elderly and the babies.

"The others had to go to another place to sleep, up the mountain. It isn't safe here for them."

"What do you mean?"

"Just that it isn't safe. And I'm tired," he said. "I shouldn't be tired so early. I need to eat something. And I need to think."

He unscrewed the canteen's cap, took a long drink, wiped the opening on his sleeve, and handed it to me. The water was surprisingly cold.

Again we drove, and for a long way, until a glittering lake appeared on my side of the road and then I think we were in the town of Chalatenango.

"I have a doctor friend," he said. "She works in the hospital here, and it was always part of my plan that you should spend some time with her. She's a good woman, and you wouldn't believe the conditions under which she practices medicine. By the way, would you like to go for *pupusas*? I'm so hungry I could eat a goddamn goat."

In the bluish light of a crowded *pupusería*, a stack of *pupusas* with the slaw called *curtido* was set down on a platter between us. I ate one *pupusa*, and Leonel the rest. We both drank orange sodas after he told me that it was not that he didn't like beer, but he couldn't afford to drink alcohol of any kind, as he had to keep his wits about him.

"I don't mind it for others," he said, "but I can't work with people who drink. I cannot trust them."

"And cigarettes?" I asked. "What about those?"

"That's up to you. They're bad for your health, but the only time they present danger here is when there is a need to be invisible in the dark."

"Tell me about Josita's nephew."

He looked puzzled for a moment.

"Oh," he said. "That's not her real name. I didn't realize who it was you were asking me about."

"The missing boy."

"Yes, well, several things could have happened. He might have been captured. He might have gone up to the mountain. He might have run off with some girlfriend, I don't know."

Something prompted him to say: "I don't think it's about the girlfriend. We'll see. I just hope he's not dead. I hope they didn't kill him. And if they did, I hope it was quick."

"They?"

"*Mirá,* it is dangerous here, very dangerous, especially in this region, but also in other areas. About the only place it isn't so dangerous right now is in La Unión. We'll be going there because there is something I want you to see, but for the moment we have to focus on this so-called human rights visit."

"Why 'so-called'?"

"Because I'm not sure, as I told you before, about these people, and I'm not sure that the outcome will have anything to do with human rights. By the way, what did you see in that village where we stopped?"

"What do you mean?"

"I'm asking you what you saw, your observations."

"The people seemed very poor. The houses were made of mud and twigs, and things you would find in a dump. The woman's *champa* was kept clean and orderly, given the circumstances. The child appeared to be malnourished. And the pit . . ." I stopped. I had torn the Styrofoam water cup into little scraps.

"At this moment," he said, taking up where I left off, "eighty percent of the country lives that way, without a decent place to take a shit. The small amount of land they might once have had has been carved up over generations. They don't have enough to feed themselves. They are forced into illiteracy by lack of education. Their life expectancy is about forty-seven years for the men, slightly more for the women. I told you that one in five children dies before the age of five, mostly of dehydration caused by dysentery and also by diseases like measles. These kids don't get vaccinated for anything. Their drinking water is polluted. Average household income is about four hundred dollars a year. A year. And one more thing: Most of them work from dawn to dusk."

I might have been looking around the *pupusería* because he added: "You won't see many campesinos in here. They can't afford this. The people in here work in machine shops or some other goddamn thing. These are urban people, the luckier ones. Barrio people."

"Leonel? Do you mind if I smoke?"

"Go ahead. It won't help."

"Is this a lecture?" I asked, pulling one of my last cigarettes from the pack.

"I would call it a briefing. I prefer that you find things out for yourself, but sometimes it's just more efficient if I give you the context. The people in your embassy will tell you, when you meet them, that you must view conditions here in a context. What they mean is that poverty in countries such as this should be considered to be normal, the way of the world, something that cannot be helped. They will ask you how many so-called Third World countries you have visited, so as to suggest that there is nothing special about this one, and also to imply that you are naïve. They will tell you to view the situation of El Salvador in context, so that is what I hope I have provided."

Although I hadn't noticed before, the fluorescent lights were humming overhead, flickering on and off.

"My Spanish is bad. The great-grandmother told me a story that I didn't understand."

"How do you know, then, that she told you a story?"

"I don't know. The rhythm of her voice, I guess. It sounded like a story. I made out a few words. It was something about a mountain and someone dead, a son or a husband . . ."

"Then you did understand. Good."

"What are you talking about? I don't think I understood much of anything."

The buzzing from the fluorescent lights grew louder, like the distant sound of a drill.

"Are you tired, Papu? Do you want to sleep? This has been a long day and tomorrow we have work to do."

"Sleep, yes, I would."

And that is how I found myself in a small back room of a house with walls the pink of stomach medicine, the house of a woman I didn't know, with Leonel's promising to pick me up early in the morning, and then, having slept in my clothes, I was already dressed when he came cheerily to the doorway, rucksack over one shoulder, hair slicked back from a fresh shower, singing out in a fake German accent, *"Jawohl, mein General!"*

The unknown owner of the house, a woman I had met briefly the night before, seemed already to have left, so I hadn't been able to ask if it was all right to brush my teeth with the tap water. The bathroom shower appeared to be disconnected, and I went to the toilet before discovering that the flusher wasn't attached to anything in the tank, so I put the lid down, thought to leave a note, and then realized that she must already know that it's broken. I saw the plastic bucket near the toilet but didn't yet know what it was for and hadn't yet learned to flush by pouring water from the bucket into the bowl.

After splashing my face and drying off with her towel, I joined Leonel, who was standing in the middle of the only other room, impatient to get going because "we have work to do."

"Who is she?" I asked as we left, meaning the woman whose house it was.

———◆———

It was late in the day when we arrived at the hospital, a low concrete building tucked among ragged banana palms. There was no parking lot, as no one who came to this hospital, patient or visitor, arrived in automobiles then. We parked on the road, half on the shoulder, the jeep tilting a little, and that was when Leonel told me we would be meeting Dr. Vicky, and that I was to stay with her for a few days because it was important for me to see this and he had something he had to do alone.

"This woman is a saint," he said. "The best we have. She stops only to sleep. She went to medical school in Mexico, and she could have done what the rest of them do—set up a nice practice in the city—but she came here to care for the poorest of the poor. Wait till you see the so-called hospital. Don't get your hopes up."

A campesina too young to be a nurse recognized Leonel and ran to get Dr. Vicky, his friend of many years, the only doctor here, the only doctor for the hundred thousand or so people who lived within walking distance, which was considered to be a day's walk. It took a while for Dr. Vicky to come, so we waited in the entrance, standing in a smear of light across the tiles, listening to various sounds in this otherwise quiet place, Leonel as usual walking around with his hands in his pockets. There was a voice or two, water being spilled out, a door swinging on a hinge. She arrived in a white lab coat, with another lab coat in her hand and a stethoscope slung over her shoulders. They kissed on the cheek and she turned to me.

"*Gusto en conorcerle,*" then she kissed me too, and handed me the lab coat to put on.

"How much medical experience do you have?" she asked.

"A little. I was a nurse's aide."

"Well, while you are here you are a medical doctor visiting from the United States."

"But what if—?"

"It's better," Leonel said again. "She's right. I'll see you in a few days, and if for some reason I don't come, stay with Vicky."

———◆———

As a teenager, I had worked after school and summers as a nurse's aide in two hospitals, a nursing home, and a clinic, where a doctor taught me to give injections and draw blood, take an EKG, assist with suturing, and even take and develop simple X-rays of the chest, limbs, and spine. For X-rays, I wore a heavy rubber apron lined with lead and hid behind a leaden door to set the X-ray controls, all the while calling out "Hold still" or "Hold your breath," then "Breathe," feeling that I was doing something important, helping people, and believing that I was competent even though I was nothing of the kind. I pushed only the buttons I had been taught to push, then locked myself in the darkroom to clip the films into metal frames and set them into bins of developer and fixative, then hang them to dry until they could be fastened to a box of light, where the bones would appear white in the shadowy flesh and the lungs looked like clouds.

The darkroom was my refuge, with its dim orange safelight and ticking timer. I cherished my time there, daydreaming and composing poems in my mind until the timer rang and I had to see to other matters.

While the nurses sat smoking cigarettes at their station, I would go from room to room and bed to bed, checking on the patients, many of them strangely awake while others slept with their mouths open. If I thought one of them looked dead, I would feel for a pulse. Only once did I find a dead person, and having touched her stiff and cooling wrist, I stood rigid beside her in disbelief for a few moments, then pressed the call button. It took a good while before the nurse came and pushed me aside.

ONE SUMMER, I WORKED AT A CLINIC, AND THE PHYSICIAN, KNOWING THAT I wanted to go to medical school, let me assist him with procedures such as dilation and curettage. One day, we were removing beer-bottle glass from a young man's forearm. The doctor turned to me midway through a suture and told me to finish closing up, and he winked. The patient, I remember, winced and looked fearfully about the room. My hand shook. I was okay with tying the knot, but I didn't want to push the curved needle into flesh. The doctor then covered my hand with his thin glove, took the needle from me, and finished the work himself, later saying that my hesitancy was a bad sign if I intended to become a physician. I had seen him suture hundreds of times and surely knew how by now. He added that he had also noticed that I couldn't stand the sight of a scalpel's cutting into flesh, that I always looked away—another bad sign. He did not approve of women entering medicine.

—◆—

After waiting an hour more or so for Dr. Vicky to finish what she had been doing, Leonel dropped us at her apartment, where we spent the night. We might have eaten something, and talked a little, but what I remember is lying in the dark, the lab coat slung over a nearby chair, lit by the moon.

In the morning, Dr. Vicky pulled curlers from her hair and dropped them into a plastic bucket, ran a comb through the curls, asked if I would like to take a shower or drink some coffee.

"Yes, both if possible. If there is time."

"I'll get us some breakfast. You like eggs?"

I held cold water to my face and listened to the clink of silver and cups. The bathroom was draped with damp towels, and there were American cosmetics on the back of the toilet, little pots of blush and shadow, almost-empty bottles of cologne. She lived in two rooms. There was a double mattress on the floor beside two smaller ones, a sofa, and a table.

We ate sausage, fried platanos, and tortillas. She joked a bit. Her Spanish was rapid, so she repeated her words slowly, and talked about maybe dyeing her hair red. There were blue pouches under her eyes. Later she would confess that she suffered from a bit of insomnia.

"I don't know how to prepare you for this," she said, and I assured her that I had worked in hospitals many summers as a teenager and after school.

She looked at me, and after a time said, "Well, let's go, then."

An hour later we stood at the edge of a dry potted road, waiting for the first bus, which was hot and crowded but we found a seat together. She talked about Mexico and her work among the street prostitutes: curing their syphilis, delivering their babies, the thirteen-year-olds who came to her when they were too far along to work, wanting to know where the baby would come out, thinking maybe their navels would open, but not really sure. Many girls, she said, were pregnant before their organs were fully mature.

The campesinas on the bus had lowered their baskets and *cántaros* (urns) of water from their heads into their arms, and the women sitting offered to hold them for the women who stood in the aisles. I made a gesture and a relieved young girl placed a basket of *zapotes* in my lap. It must have weighed fifty pounds.

That day we worked in the government-run rural hospital for nine hours, walking through swarms of flies over floors swabbed with a bucket of gray water, tracking through it, ward after ward. Dr. Vicky talked about how the campesina in El Salvador lives, waking before dawn, husking and grinding the maize on the *metate,* setting the mash to boil over the fire, and this before anyone else is up. Then she'll wake her husband if she has one, and the children she almost always has, before working through the morning, slapping wet clothes on rocks, hauling water, taking fruit or grain to market, bringing her husband's food to the fields. She'll bend over his hoe to continue the work while he eats, and then, when she returns to the *champa,* she eats if there is anything left. She works until after dark, sleeps a few hours, and begins again.

Dr. Vicky ran her hands along the body of a naked little girl whose chest and back were bruised, but she seemed more interested in the rash on the girl's inner thighs.

"When I worked in another village, I found quite a few vaginal infections in very young girls," she said. "I thought their fathers were violating them. Then a campesina finally told me that when the girls are little, the mothers in that village take a razor blade and make the sign of the cross on the clitoris. They say it makes them better workers. They don't get ideas."

She lifted the girl to the scale. "She is nine," she said. "She has the weight of a healthy six-year-old."

We sat in the hospital kitchen: an open-pit fire with a pot of coffee balanced on the coals, the walls blackened by wood smoke. Dr. Vicky sipped her coffee, then rubbed her face with her hands and looked at me.

"So you see how it is? I have no lab, no X-ray machine, no supplies of whole blood, plasma, or antibiotics, no anesthesia or medicines, no autoclave for sterilizing instruments. I have to boil them. The forceps are rusted. I have had to perform emergency caesarean sections without anesthesia. Come with me, I will show you."

We went into the operating room: a table with stirrups, another with a bright lamp, glass louvered windows without screens. Flies studded the walls, and there was a whirring in the room as they rose and fell.

Dr. Vicky sent me with Ana through the wards, the young campesina who "had no medical training but whose heart was good," the girl hired to swish the flies with a newspaper from the newborn's head as it crowns, to give sitz baths, as I had learned to do at her age, to diaper the babies, swab the sores, strip and refresh the sheets. We moved together from bed to bed, and she combed the patients' hair while I took pulses and temperatures, startled at how bright and yet blank the patients' eyes were, how the light fell on their bony faces, these nearly skeletal workers from the *campo,* who lived on daily tortillas with a lump of beans and drank boiled sorghum instead of coffee. One woman's feet had swollen to twice their size but the rest of her body seemed made of bones and cloth. A man had suffered a machete wound that had not been closed in time, and the burning gash across his thigh had become infected. Another woman had lain so long on her cot that bedsores had opened on her buttocks, such as I remembered from the convalescent home. There, we would pull the dead flesh away with a large tweezers, then pour a little peroxide over the wound until the bubbling stopped. This woman was lying on her stomach, legs splayed awkwardly under her gown, clutching the bars of the headboard. When Ana lifted the gown, I saw that maggots were feeding on the sore, rising up, falling back, so that the wound itself appeared to be alive. Ana took a teaspoon from her apron pocket.

"We can take them out now," she whispered. "They are finished."

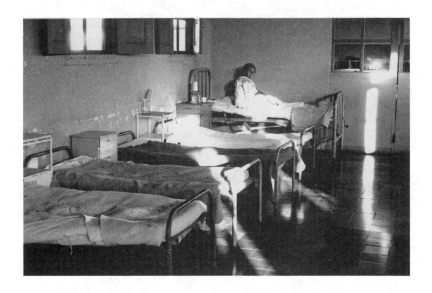

When Leonel finally came for me, we spent a day like many others, with much driving around, but fewer questions about what I was seeing. We stopped several places for brief conversations with various people, and sometimes I was asked to join, and sometimes he made the sign that I should wait in the open jeep. He had brought that morning's *El Diario de Hoy,* and when the sun bore down, I sat with a page tented over my hair until he returned from one of his meetings. He talked to two men leaning on their spades in a field, an old woman in the market, and even a secretary in an auto-body repair shop. She was the only one I met who seemed not to want to talk in front of me. At the end of the day, he told me that it was all right, the boy we had been searching for had "gone up the mountain," which meant that he would no longer sleep at his house, but he was safer there, sleeping under the stars with others who had also had to leave their homes to keep from being captured. By nightfall we were in the city again, and Leonel was letting me off at the former dictator's house, where I would once again spend the night in the squealing four-poster with a mattress that sank beneath me like a hammock. In the mirrored armoire not far from the foot of the bed I could see myself when I raised my head from the pillow, even in the dark.

Leonel had promised, as usual, that he would come for me in the morning. Lying in bed, I thought how surprised Claribel and her family would be if they knew where I was at this moment. But they didn't know. Almost no one knew, not even the man with whom I'd been having a long-distance relationship off and on for a year, and whose letters had slowed in the autumn and had stopped coming just before Christmas. I hadn't written to him yet about Leonel's visit, his invitation, or my trip here, and I wondered to myself why not. I suppose that I didn't think he would approve. I imagined him standing at his open kitchen window in upstate New York, taking a baseball bat to the icicles that hung from his eaves before returning to his desk. He would think this was a dangerous thing for a young woman to be doing, traveling to a country in such turmoil and on the verge of war. He had done his research on the prisons of the Soviet gulag and the Nazi death camps, focusing on the altruism of survivors and on poets who had borne witness to suffering. Later I would tell him something of what I had seen here, and he would argue against my going back. I countered by reminding him of his own writings, quoting him back to himself. This is different, he said, contending that I had a choice while others did not, reminding me that my passport wouldn't protect me, that I wasn't old enough or experienced enough, and I could just as well write my poetry from the quiet of my own study, but I had known since childhood that human suffering demanded a response, everywhere and always, and I wondered: What would I do? I also knew that what I wanted most at that moment was to tell someone where I was, just in case. I couldn't frighten my parents, but someone should know, other than my friend Barbara, who shouldn't have to shoulder this by herself, in case anything happened. When I told Leonel later about this desire, while he was eating his breakfast, he shook his head and smiled.

"What are you going to do, send a postcard? I don't think there's much of a market here for postcards at this moment, Papu."

He was pinching up the last of some black beans with a bit of tortilla, and I was having coffee, followed by a cigarette.

"It's a bad habit," he said and, after a long pause, added, "skipping breakfast."

"I'm okay."

"Papu, regarding communications with the United States—just know that every piece of mail going out of the country, every phone call, is subject to scrutiny by security forces. They take note of the numbers you call as well as your number, and if they want to read your mail, they read it, and if they want to listen, they listen."

"So what are you saying? That I shouldn't . . ."

"No," he said lightly, "make your own decisions."

After breakfast, he said he needed to take a trip back to his coffee farm so he could check on the trees. As I followed him through the coffee, I asked him again where, exactly, he lived.

"You see, Papu," he said, ignoring my question, "this is *Coffea arabica,* so it is susceptible to rust blight. I wish the Peace Corps would send someone here who knows something about rust blight. Instead they send us anthropology majors."

"Do you live here?"

"No," he answered, seeming preoccupied. "No, I don't. This is just my farm."

He was examining the undersides of the dark, glossy leaves, lifting them, rubbing them, moving among the trees while I followed until, emerging from the low forest of coffee, we came to a long cinder-block building. He held the door open for me to see that inside there were metal cots with mattresses, footlockers, and hooks on the walls, some with towels hanging from them.

"I was supposed to stick with hammocks," he said softly. "They really hated me for these cots, probably more than for anything else I have done."

He seemed to be talking to himself.

"Hated you? Who hated you?"

"Let's go out. We probably shouldn't have come inside. This place belongs to the campesinos who work here."

I hurried after him. "Who hated you?"

"Oh, the other coffee farmers, growers in the area—they accused me of setting a precedent, those were their words. Can you imagine? Being threatened by mattresses?"

On the other side of the building, men standing at an outdoor workbench smiled as we approached, and there was a bit of back-and-forth and joking before one of them bent over a scrap of metal and fired up a blowtorch.

"I'll show you what we're doing here. Follow me. It's interesting."

"I don't understand about the mattresses."

"I wanted the workers on this farm to sleep on real beds when they were here. That's all. I wasn't supposed to provide for them real beds. This was almost worse than paying them at a higher wage. Those goddamn beds represented something, I don't know what. It's crazy when you think about it."

We had come to a stand of trees called *pepetos*. People were watering them with hoses attached to odd-looking metal backpacks. There were valves on the hoses hooked up to these packs for turning the water on and off. Leonel knelt to examine one of the seedlings planted beneath these taller trees.

"This is how coffee was traditionally grown, under the protection of forest shade."

He stood up, brushing his palms on his thighs.

"If you're going to grow coffee in full sun, without this canopy, you have to use fertilizer, which is not only expensive but also damaging to the soil and the water table."

Again, he sounded professorial, walking among the trees and talking to himself.

"Of course, you get higher yields with sun and fertilizer, but you get better coffee this way, and without damage to the environment, except of course for the water use."

He suddenly turned to face me, coming out of a reverie. "Well, what do you think?"

Not sure what he was asking, I waited to answer, knowing that if I was quiet, he would resume his monologue.

"The problem is finding a way to get water to these seedlings, lots of water, without having to carry it in the traditional way, which, by the way, compresses the vertebrae in the spine. Those *cántaros* they carry on their heads? They are heavier than you might think. I call this low technology. No bank credits required. No debt, no service contracts, no electric utilities, and," he added, "no problems with vertebrae."

Women, mostly, were moving among the trees with the metal packs, nodding as they passed, but intent on the task at hand. Their children hid behind the trees.

"The staff is talented. We were talking one day and together came up with this idea. We made a few drawings and the next thing I knew, we had these packs. I got the metal at a salvage yard. Wait until you see how the water is drawn from the earth. Come, I'll show you another of our low technologies."

As with the dwellings along the roadside, when I looked now among the coffee trees and buildings, I saw that there were many people moving about, hard at work.

"We have turned this into an experimental farm," Leonel was saying, "it is soon to be organic. We're growing a special coffee here. The soil, the altitude, the climate, the amount of moisture in the air, all make this coffee possible, but the people I have working here make the difference between failure and success.

"Here," he said, "here is what I wanted to show you."

A boy was riding an old bicycle on the edge of the seedling field. The bike seemed to be stationary and had a crank that turned as he pedaled, lowering an oil drum into an opening in the ground and lifting it out again, heavy with water, yet the boy didn't seem to exert himself while pedaling. The metal backpacks were then filled with water from a hose fastened to the drum. The cyclist grinned at me. Other boys had formed a line behind him, jostling each other for a turn on the bike.

"Let the girls have a chance," Leonel said. The girls laughed with their hands over their mouths.

"We needed a way to operate the well without electricity. I have power here, of course, but we're working on systems that most people would be able to use, including the kids. This bicycle contraption could be set up in every village if we had enough bicycles. And oil drums," he added.

"May I try?"

The boys looked at each other, but the one pedaling dismounted and let me take the seat. The pedals turned almost by themselves, and if I closed my eyes, I could well have been riding slightly downhill toward my own house. I felt a tap on my shoulder. Leonel was signaling me to stop. The oil drum was high out of the well, and it was time to distribute the water.

That afternoon he had one more thing, he said, to show me. We drove a short distance from the farm, then pulled onto a dirt road that wound through some avocado trees. There was a bit of chaos to the place: two modest houses and a flock of hens. We circled to the back and a much larger building came into view that seemed to be attached to the larger of the two houses. It was a cross between a small factory and a barn, with columns of sunlit dust dropping from the high windows inside, where a strange machine with chutes, funnels, and a motor such as might come from an old car or washing machine. Valves and wheels for opening and shutting the chutes and conveyors took up half the floor and rose two stories to the lámina roof.

A man came out from somewhere behind it, greeting Leonel with *"Hermano!"*

They talked for a while, pointing at the machine. The motor was running, so I couldn't hear anything. Leonel motioned for me to join them and, after introducing us, announced that I was going to see something that I, no doubt, had never seen, as practically no one had, and at that moment, he sounded like a much younger man, almost a boy, as he shouted over the din. The campesino beside him was quieter, but I could see that he was also proud of whatever this was.

"Wait! He's going to demonstrate for you. It's like something Rube Goldberg would design."

"Who?" I shouted, but a louder motor roared over my voice and the machine began to move its gears and pulleys and shake as coffee beans flowed through the chutes, spilling into other chutes, coursing through the machine that shook until the walls were also shaking, and the metal roof banged into itself with the sound of metal garbage pails struck by baseball bats, and the house to which the machine was attached rattled as if in a strong wind.

"It is dancing with the house!" Leonel shouted.

"What is it?" I yelled back through the coffee-bean dust, just as the other man began to shut it down, and so my voice was louder than it should have been, with one after another part of the machine slowing to a stop and the house itself settling back into place.

"Another original invention, my dear! This contraption is a coffee processor. It removes the husks from the beans. This one can be made with parts that lie around any scrapyard. We made it ourselves, so anyone can do it. Cooperatives growing coffee could process their own beans and save a hell of a lot of money, not to mention avoiding dependency on the crooked processing companies."

The campesino was running around the machine now, adjusting valves and shaking the chutes to empty them of beans as Leonel nodded proudly.

"It still needs to be perfected, of course. But if we get it to work . . ."

"Then what?"

"Then this machine will make them even angrier than the mattresses did."

"You mentioned someone—Rube Goldberg?"

"You don't know who Rube Goldberg is? What kind of education do they give you in the United States? Goldberg was a great artist and cartoonist. One of the characters in his cartoons was Professor Lucifer Gorgonzola Butts, who drew plans for inventions and machines that would accomplish something simple through complicated means, like our machine here. Haven't you ever seen the movie *Soup to Nuts*? The Three Stooges! That was written by Rube Goldberg. You need to work on your cultural formation, my dear. Poets should know these things."

Later I would read about Goldberg and discover, among other things, a drawing of a machine for bringing a diner's spoon to his mouth. It involved a parrot, a clock, a duster, and a small rocket. The diner in the drawing looked a lot like Leonel: black haired, mustached, staring in disbelief at the spoonful of soup rising to his lips.

"And that is what we must do here in this moment, but in reverse. Accomplish complicated things by simple means. Next, we have to figure out how to make a portable bridge that will bear the weight of a jeep or a small truck. I have to find someone who can make that. And also, you said something about your brother's being an engineer . . ."

"He's an engineer, yes. Electrical."

"Oh. Well, I'm looking for someone who can make a small listening device. It should be no bigger than a piece of chocolate."

The sudden mention of my brother in this context jolted me. For some reason, it seemed important to keep this "work," if that is what it was, separate from the rest of my life. "My brother can't do that. That's not what my brother does. Why would you want such a thing?"

The house with its dancing contraption had disappeared behind us in a cloud of road.

———◆———

Leonel slapped a manila folder down on Blanca's breakfast table in the dictator's former kitchen.

"Here, Papu, is the report from the congressman's trip. The official version hasn't been approved for release, so this is the unofficial version. You can read it to me on the way because we have to go."

As usual, we were getting an early start and as usual, I had no idea where we were going.

"Well," I began, holding the pages tightly in the wind, and flipping them over their stapled left corner, "it says that the congressman's group spent their first night at the Catholic seminary, meeting with prominent churchmen, parish priests, and Jesuits to discuss religious persecution and the terrors inflicted by the paramilitary group ORDEN—isn't that the group Chele Medrano founded?"

"That's the group. He founded that with American help, you know."

"Then there was a concelebrated Mass in the cathedral, followed by meetings with families of the disappeared. The report notes that the testimonies were tape-recorded. The next day they met with the American ambassador and his staff to be briefed on social and economic conditions, followed by lunch at the ambassador's residence."

"Chicken," Leonel interrupted, "white meat, no skin, piece of lettuce."

"The report says that the embassy showed the greatest possible willingness to cooperate in every way, but the ambassador urged an attitude of patience and understanding toward the problems of the current government and expressed his concern over the personal safety of the investigators."

"A threat," he said. "Intimidation. Those sons of bitches! So lesson number three is this: Here, if someone expresses concerns about your safety in a certain way, they are giving you a warning or something worse."

"I don't think this is meant that way."

"And what do you base that judgment upon, your considerable experience?"

Then after a pause he said, "I'm sorry, I didn't mean that. But patience? Understanding? How many times have we heard this?"

"It says they accompanied the Franciscan missionaries on a walking tour of the slums, and next the group met with leaders of the opposition parties, where the conversation turned toward electoral fraud. They also had a meeting with campesinos who brought to their attention twenty-one cases of human rights violations: murders committed by the National Guard and by ORDEN, including rape involving a girl of ten."

"They took a big risk," he said. "Those campesinos talked only because a trusted priest was with them and because they thought the congressman would do something to help. But this congressman, kind as he is, cannot protect them. And who knows what he's going to do with the information? Maybe something. Maybe it will just become part of some report in a file drawer."

"So you're saying that they shouldn't have talked to him?"

"I don't know. Maybe they shouldn't have. We'll see what happens now that the congressman has left."

"It says they next met with President Carlos Romero, and these discussions were frank, but no evident progress was made toward any solution to the problems of the political and religious exiles, nor that of the *desaparecidos*. They also met with Vice President Julio Ernesto Astacio, and in that meeting, it was suggested that a dialogue be opened between President Romero and Archbishop Oscar Romero. The vice president responded by urging the Church to become more conciliatory and make greater concessions, but as far as the government was concerned the vice president said, 'we are doing the best we can.'"

"I see."

"It says that late that night the group went to Aguilares for a meeting—"

"After dark?"

"It says."

"During a state of siege?"

"That's what it says."

"For the roads alone, I wouldn't have advised it."

"It says they met at an isolated farmhouse."

"Assholes."

"More than fifty campesinos spoke of the atrocities committed . . ."

"Fifty maybe soon-to-be-dead campesinos."

"And a priest said a Mass with them at 1:00 a.m. And in the morning, they met with labor leaders who testified that five hundred unionists have been imprisoned, and only two strikes have been allowed them since 1952. They quote one of the labor leaders as saying the United States must send out a signal that it believes in democracy in the whole world."

"And what signal would that be?"

I read on: "Quote: 'There was a final gathering at the ambassador's residence. The report notes that the Church is under significant pressure, its clergy and its people live in fear in a climate of severe repression, as do workers and peasants, and that through control of the press and the university and the stifling of every independent voice, the government has attempted to create a closed society in which all dissent ceases and the voice of the military government alone is heard.' End quote," I said, as the pages of the report flapped in the wind no matter how tightly I held them. Reading in vehicles always made me feel queasy.

"In the end, the report requests that exiled labor leaders and priests be allowed to return, that missing persons' whereabouts be disclosed, and the Public Order Law terminated. Such signs would indicate that General Romero's promise of reform was more than mere rhetoric. Until such indications occur El Salvador must, unfortunately, be declared to be in violation of human rights and its own constitutional guarantees."

I lowered the papers into my lap and put my head down between my legs as I had been taught to do as a child. I could never manage to read in moving vehicles without getting carsick.

Leonel's hand came to rest on my back. "Breathe. Take deep breaths."

He withdrew his hand to shift gears, and I breathed, but when I sat up again, he was whispering "Oh God, oh shit," and I saw what he was seeing: two bodies lying on the shoulder of the road, a turkey buzzard alighting on one, and as we coasted to a stop, the buzzard lifted and settled, lifted and flapped into the bushes.

"Stay here," he said. "Don't move."

He took the gun from the well near the gearshift and got out of the jeep, walking on the shoulder toward the bodies. I don't remember where this was precisely. I remember the light on the road ahead like a swarm of fish, as if the tarmac were water, and a buzzing in my ears, or a rush of air. Leonel had reached the bodies and was now on one knee. The buzzing rose and subsided, rose again, coming from the fields surrounding us.

When he returned to the jeep, he was pale and the back of his shirt was soaked. He started the jeep and drove slowly past them: two men, lying facedown, or rather a man and a boy, both with their hands tied behind them, both barefoot, and on the boy there was a large blotch of dark blood, almost black, where the vulture had been. Leonel didn't tell me to look away. He didn't say anything. When we reached the swarm of light, the fish had swum away, leaving blue-black road that no longer resembled water.

"They haven't been dead long. We have to get out of here."

"But what are we going to do? We can't just leave them."

There was a look on his face I hadn't seen before, and the gun was now in his lap.

"We have to leave them. I cannot lift them up, or at least, not by myself," he said, giving me a meaningful look. "Corpses are heavy, Papu. They don't help you when you lift them up."

Another swarm of light appeared, and there was a ticking sound against the undercarriage. Leonel turned the radio to white noise, then to an incomprehensible voice.

"There's a priest I know who works not far from here. We're going to find him. And as I said, they haven't been dead long, so whoever killed them cannot be far away, and I hope to God we don't encounter these killers, but if we do, listen to me, if we do, are you listening? Don't say anything, let me talk. And if we're fired upon, if a lot of lead starts flying around, I want you to get down and stay down and don't make any noise. Can you do that?"

I nodded, yes, but I had no experience to base this yes upon, and so the yes didn't mean anything.

We found the priest friend in a village not far away, just as he'd said we would. At our news, the priest covered his face with his hands, then sent the boy beside him on an errand, and shortly after that, women arrived, one sinking to the ground, rocking back and forth, the other hovering over her. I couldn't sit in the jeep anymore and do nothing, and why? Had it just become a habit of his to leave me behind? But when I reached his side, he didn't seem surprised. He patted my shoulder and introduced me as a poet from the United States.

"She's a friend," he said pointedly.

The priest nodded and said to the women, "We don't know yet, we must wait and trust in God."

Leonel drew with his forefinger in his palm to indicate where the bodies had been seen. An old white pickup truck pulled in beside us, driven by a wizened man in a straw hat. He seemed to know both Leonel and the priest. Two men stood on the bed of the truck holding on to the cab roof. Leonel said something to the driver, slapping the hood lightly as the truck drove away. One of the women held a cloth apron to her face. The priest was consoling her.

"Our business here is finished," Leonel said. "We have to get going. We have to get out of here—*now*."

———◆———

He rested his hand always lightly on the shift knob, watching cars parked against clay walls or nosing out of alleys, any truck with its hood raised, any van that appeared empty but might not be. He knew what to look for: panel trucks, with their sliding doors cracked open, and later, black, smoke-windowed Jeep Cherokees. I didn't understand what was happening, why we were driving all over the country, stopping here and there to talk to people, all kinds of people, many of them greeting him with open arms, while others held back and, on more than one occasion, with palpable hostility. Sometimes his visit seemed expected, and other times people appeared surprised to see him. I would be introduced as a poet from the United States, or else nothing would be said about who I was, to the point of awkwardness. Usually we were invited inside—into a house, a shop, a clinic, a rectory, even once a tobacco shed—and sometimes we were offered coffee and food. In the countryside, the offering was almost always beans with a dry tortilla, and on the outskirts of the cities, *pupusas* wrapped in paper, and among the affluent, we might be given almost anything. In restaurants, Leonel was partial to grilled shrimp.

In the beginning, I thought that these meetings and conversations with others were randomly undertaken, but as time went on, I noticed that after visiting a village with no running water or electricity, talking by the light of a cook fire, finding my way in the dark to the latrine and back among the braying animals and clucking hens, he would next bring me to an elegant house owned by a coffee grower or cotton farmer, or someone in the shrimping business, and we would be served by maids, and while the men talked, I would be led by the lady of the house onto terraces overlooking gardens and be told the names of the trees, and how pleased she was that her European species were now thriving among the date palms and bottlebrushes. We would talk about her children, away at school in Switzerland or the United States, and then we would run out of things to say.

There was nothing random about the meetings. Each seemed a puzzle piece to be locked into place so as to reveal a picture he imagined he was showing me.

"LET ME READ YOU SOMETHING, PAPU. THIS IS NOT WRITTEN BY SOME KUMBAYA. This is from Major Arthur Harris, U.S. military attaché to the War Department, December 22, 1931. You'll find it in your National Archives and I quote: 'About the first thing one observes when he goes to San Salvador is the number of expensive automobiles on the streets. . . . There are a few low-priced cars, but these are mostly taxis for hire. There appears to be nothing between these high-priced cars and the ox cart with its barefoot attendant. There is practically no middle class. . . . Thirty or forty families own nearly everything in the country. They live in almost regal style. . . . The rest of the population has practically nothing. These poor people work for a few cents a day and exist as best they can.' End quote.

"Nothing has changed, not a goddamn thing. This is how it was the year before the last uprising and this is how it still is, so is war coming? What do *you* think?"

"It's just breakfast," Leonel said, "but be careful. This man is the legal adviser to ORDEN, still the largest paramilitary group in the country."

"I don't want to meet him. I have no interest."

"Oh, but you do. You don't have much choice in the matter. His name is Ricardo. He's also a poet, by the way—which may interest you, and this meeting is being held at the colonel's request."

"Which colonel?"

"Never mind which colonel. You should know by now that there are things you can learn from these people, and there are also people to whom you cannot say no without arousing suspicion and making problems for yourself, not to mention for me. You should be saying, 'A sus órdenes, comandante!'"

"Is that supposed to be a joke? Are you making a pun? *Orden, órdenes?*"

"No, I was not. This is serious. You are now going to see how crazy these people are."

But the man we met for breakfast, Señor Suárez, was suave, elegantly dressed in a tailored suit, perfectly groomed, and charming. He held my chair for me, something Leonel never did, and, after seating himself, hiked his crisp white sleeve and with a gold pen sketched on the Sheraton place mat a diagram of his country's troubles, a map of the region with arrows drawn from Cuba, Nicaragua, and the ocean, all of them pointing at El Salvador.

"You see, they come from all sides, the Communists. Look at what they are doing to Somoza! But we are ready for them."

He pulled from his inside breast pocket a superhero, anti-Communist comic book that his organization had begun distributing to "the peasants." The cartoon Communists were depicted raping women, shooting children, and torching the packing-crate huts of the poor. Over a delicately folded omelet, Suárez told me with modest pride that he was a poet himself and, as proof, presented me with his book *Tarcos,* a leather-bound volume of poems dedicated to the fatherland, along with another titled *Meropis,* his prose meditation on the ancient history of Central America, indebted to "Generalissimo Franco."

"Thank you," I said. "I look forward to reading these."

"And there is one more. This one came to me in a dream," he said, setting a newer book titled *One State Under the Sun* near my water glass.

"It was a fantastic dream," he went on, "surely prophetic. The dream was not very clear, you understand, but the consequences were of utmost clarity. In the dream we ship El Salvador's campesinos permanently to the jungles of northern Brazil, and then a Great Lord emerges, born of the Salvadoran military to preside over the country, spreading his ideas like the nectar of hope. This leader, on the first day, would be seated at a big desk, with civilians, the military, and the diplomatic corps all surrounding him, all that corresponds to a real revolutionary government."

He sat back, blotted his lips with a white napkin, and went on: "In the dream the Great Lord would be called Anostos, which is also the name of a prehistoric volcano that erupted before the time of Christ. This eruption created Lake Ilopango, by the way." Then, leaning forward, he said in a low voice: "This is also the secret name for El Salvador itself."

"Mr. Suárez, do you believe in democracy?" I asked him.

Leonel made a face that only I could see, both surprised and amused.

"*Señorita, señorita,* of course I believe in democracy. We all believe in this. But unlike in the United States, we can only have a little democracy here. Just a little. We are a small country and most of our people are illiterate and live as the animals do. We have to take very small steps. If we had a lot of democracy here, you see, the peasants would win elections, and we cannot have that happening. The peasants vastly outnumber us. Surely you understand this?"

"Yes, I think I do understand."

"Anostos," he continued, picking up where he had left off, "is the name of the fatherland but is also its savior. The lost Mayans are like the Valkyries, celebrated by the great composer Wilhelm Richard Wagner. You have certainly heard his music? It was played loudly from the helicopters during a particularly brilliant sequence in the film *Apocalypse Now.* Surely you have seen this film?"

I couldn't look at Leonel, who was busy stabbing his breakfast with a fork.

"So it is my hope," Suárez said, "that you are going to write beautiful things about my country when you return to the U.S."

I told him that I, too, wished that this would be possible.

"We could pay you, of course. We have incredible resources. You could name your price. In fact, our resources are unlimited."

I tried to kick Leonel under the table but he was too far away. His egg slipped from his fork. Nodding to the waiter that yes, I would like more coffee, I assured Mr. Suárez that professional ethics precluded me from accepting his generous offer, but I would promise to write honestly about his country.

"The truth," he said, "you must write the truth."

He reached across to show me the ring he wore, a gold band crested with an eagle or a condor.

"This is a secret ring," he whispered, "which a Gypsy gave to me, a man with secret knowledge. I wear it because I am of the society of virtuous men. I founded our very own party here when I was still a student. We called it the Pyramid Party. We believe that the Great Pyramids of Egypt were not built by Egyptians at all but by people from Atlantis, which you will find on certain maps as the early name for the Americas. Well, but I am saying too much. Perhaps you aren't so interested in these esoteric matters?"

I told him I found it fascinating, and for the first time, Leonel's face seemed entirely readable.

"Let me autograph this for you," Suárez offered, stroking his illegible signature across the title page of *Tarcos*. Later, opening to the page, I saw that his book had been dedicated to the Salvadoran military, whose great capacity for combat, he had said, goes back to the Mayans and Olmecs.

———◆———

It wasn't long after we saw the dead man and boy that Leonel decided I would be staying from now on at another house, with his friend Margarita, her husband, and their three daughters. They lived in one of the better *colonias*. The husband seemed, these days, always to be away on business, he said, and Margarita had a guest room, and she had agreed to this arrangement.

"But she doesn't like North Americans much at the moment, so watch yourself."

It was a relief to know that I would be staying in one place, in a woman's house, and with a room. Up until now, he had been leaving me at places where his friends worked, sometimes for hours, sometimes days. I never knew when he would return. I didn't know anyone with whom I was left.

I have to go to see someone, he would say, or I have to go do something and it would be better if you didn't come. Let me, I'd plead, I'll be fine. I'll wait in the truck. *Mirá,* he'd answer, I don't know how long this is going to take. And it might be dangerous. And I cannot afford to have something happen.

Initially I believed him, as it was becoming obvious that the war he had been anticipating "in three to five years" might have already begun, as many wars do begin, he said, not with a major event reported in the news but with sufferings barely noticed: an unjust law, a murder, a peaceful protest march attacked by police. It begins, according to Leonel, with poverty endured by many and corruption benefiting the few, with crimes unpunished, a hardening of positions, the failure of peaceful means of appeal and redress. People were disappearing now every day, taken from the streets, from their vehicles and houses, at night and in the middle of the day. Yes, I thought, he's right, it's dangerous, but nevertheless I wanted not to be left behind, and I stopped believing that protecting me was his sole reason.

"I don't want to be left anymore," I said, "I'm not good at waiting."

He promised to bring me along more often, "when it's possible," he said, but there are some things, and there always will be, that he would have to do alone.

By then I had realized that most of these things seemed to happen at night. Where did he go? I wondered. And where does he live?

Margarita and I met for the first time not at her house but at a café that might have been near La UCA, the Catholic university, where she spent a lot of her time. She and Leonel kissed on the cheek, and a light scent wafted from her as she sat back down, nodding at me with a small, gracious, but perfunctory smile, and she began telling him something about a meeting she had just attended. They talked for a good while about the meeting, but Leonel was, finally, a bit dismissive of it, and this seemed to infuriate her, which was apparent by the way she tapped the ash from her cigarette. I thought she was beautiful, with her short-cropped hair and expressive green eyes that were perfectly made up, her lids powdered olive green, her eyelashes thick and black. She wore a close-fitting dress of the same green and she smoked elegantly, holding the cigarette aloft and slightly away from us.

"Tell Margarita what you have been doing since you got here."

"What do you mean?"

I felt self-conscious as my attention had wandered while they talked. Margarita looked at me, raising her eyebrows. I could tell that she would just as soon I wasn't here.

"Tell her where you've gone and who you've met. I think she'd be interested in your impressions."

Her expression belied this, but she leaned back and studied me.

"Forgive me, but this will have to be in English."

"Go ahead, I'll translate."

So, a few sentences at a time, I worked my way back to my arrival at Ilopango International Airport and the dinner at Benihana on a night that now seemed long ago, but was actually three weeks, my nights with Blanca and alone in the dictator's former house, the morning meeting with General Chele Medrano—

And before Leonel could translate this last, she blurted *"¿La llevaste allí?"*

"Yes, I took her there."

"Pero ¿por qué?"

"Just listen to what she's telling you, Margarita."

She gave him a meaningful look but what did it mean?

"Continue," Leonel said to me, and to her, *"tené cuidado."*

"—we asked about the whereabouts of Ronald Richardson, and then we went to the *campo."*

"¿Dónde en el campo?"

"Jesus Christ, Margarita, what difference does it make? I showed her a little of how people live, that's all. She's got to see for herself."

He was speaking in Spanish, but this is what I understood him to be saying. She turned her attention toward me again, and so I continued with something about Josita and the missing boy, the trip to Chalatenango, our daylong search for information about the boy, the arrival of the congressman and our disappointment—.

Leonel signaled me to stop so he could translate, but before he could do this she had a question of her own. *"¿Vos la presentaste a los jesuitas?"*

"No, Margarita, she met only one Jesuit. Briefly. The American. May I?"

"Por supuesto."

Why was he asking me to tell her these things? But Leonel continued to translate as I hurried through our trip to the farm, the metal backpacks, the bicycle and oil drum, and finally the bodies on the roadside and a little of what happened after that. Okay, I thought, I'm finished.

"¿Qué está haciendo aquí, Carolyn?" she asked. What are you doing here? *"Dígame."* Tell me. *"¿Está estudiando nuestro país? ¿Es ésta su laboratorio?"*

"No," I said, "no. I'm not studying your country. This isn't my laboratory." But I didn't know what else to say in that moment, and I must have looked to Leonel for help because she said to me sternly, *"No mire fijamente! Hable por sí misma,"* and then, in thickly accented English for the first time, and to avoid his translation: "Don't look at him. Speak for yourself."

"Well, to tell the truth, I don't know why I'm here. I'm here to learn, I hope."

"¡Bueno!" She dropped her pack of cigarettes into her purse and snapped it shut. "I have to go and pick up my girls from school. It was nice to meet you."

"Margarita," Leonel said, with more than a little irritation in his voice.

"Nos vemos más tarde, Leonel," she said, "I will see you later." And then I thought I heard her say in quick Spanish something like, "I'm not interested in this little project of yours."

At times, when alone, I thought that accepting Leonel's invitation might have been a mistake. I would think about that summer in Spain, and things that I didn't understand at the time began to reveal their meanings. I often waited for Maya in Mallorca, listening to flowering vines rattle against the wall, and wishing, somewhat to my surprise, that I hadn't come.

In Spain, I would wish this more often than I would have imagined: on the edge of the circle of exiled writers gathered at C'an Blau, Claribel's house, listening as well as I could to their variously accented Spanishes; as I walked mornings to the *panadería* for bread; sitting alone in the café drinking espresso with my buttered roll as the waiter Jordi swept up cigarette butts and paper napkins from the previous night, and his widowed grandmother sat in her corner peeling vegetables into a bowl on her lap. I wished at night, too, that I hadn't come, as I lay in *abuelita*'s bed, where Claribel's mother slept when she visited, in what had once been her room in C'an Blau, watching the moonrise over the sea between Mallorca and Gibraltar. I felt out of place here, despite how warmly I had been received, unable to share in the festive mood of Deià in the summer.

During my first waking hours, I began poems and abandoned them, erased what I had written the previous day, then held the pen to paper again, hoping it would begin to move on its own, as if the paper were a Ouija board and the pen a magical planchette. When the pen failed to move in this way, I would turn to one of Claribel's books and read in Spanish aloud to myself, hoping by such recitation the poem would yield its sense. On the days when I gave up on all of this, I wrote letters or worked on little messages for the postcards I would later buy and send to family and friends. In these letters and cards, Deià's ocher houses held fast to the hills and appeared shuttered against the light, and Maya and I were making "great progress" with the translations, and there were "too many interesting discussions to recount, so forgive the brevity," I would write, attempting a hurried nonchalance, and "I send you *besos y abrazos*," as I had learned to say. *"Mil besos."*

Some mornings I walked in the village, past the morning glories shivering on the wall alongside the *torrente*, the houses closed up and silent with only the *tienda* door open, a little grotto of a shop that sold eggs, lemons, goats' milk, and pastries. The only people I saw along the street were the widows, walking in pairs in their long black dresses, carrying baskets of lemons or eggs. If I greeted them, they nodded, and walked past in a cloud of quietness. Of those I met that summer on Mallorca, I most wanted to know who these women were and what had happened to them. In their dried faces and onyx eyes I saw my grandmother, back from the dead but no longer knowing me.

I walked alone among the twisted olives, or climbed the tamped goat paths up the Teix until the sea was visible, and the *calla*, as they called the stony inlet where the fishermen put in, and where we sometimes swam in the afternoons. Maya liked to sit on the wet rocks there while her other friends dived into the icy waters and emerged, shaking their long, wet pennants of hair and laughing at how cold it was. I felt myself invisible, perched beside Maya, watching the red-fleshed German bathers make their precarious way over the stones, and the willowy younger women remove their tops and walk with arms raised into the sea.

I might always have thought myself invisible, and I wasn't sure why, but it had by now become a comfortable state—not to be part of what was going on but to be outside, watching and listening. Once as I stood in an orchard, a sirocco arrived from the Libyan desert, shaking the almonds as wildly as if it were winter and the blossoms were snow, or a flock of snow geese had suddenly risen to fly north. I could barely breathe for the blossoms, and felt a surge of joy in my heart.

Sometimes I wrote on the terrace at C'an Blau, at the little table under the bougainvillea, the sun having risen on this side of the island, goat bells clanking in the heat, goats hidden beneath the olives below. The tiles were still wet from the daily mopping by the maid, and I watched the water shrink from them, with no words coming from my pen. I was blank then, as my mother's eyes had been on certain afternoons in summer. This was all right, I told myself, and then I would write: *the sirocco comes, a wind without beginning* and proverbs I'd read such as *the dead open the eyes of the living.* The lines of poetry seemed to come from elsewhere, from someone else.

Before I left, Maya stuffed an old, empty olive-oil bottle with special amulets for my protection: pebbles from the *calla,* a string of beads she was giving me, some pressed flowers. This bottle, she said, was a tradition on Mallorca. It would bring luck and blessings on my future life, which Maya much hoped would be an enchanting one, lived in some beautiful city, with poetry and music and most of all with a love who was a grand passion, this last in her perfect French. I couldn't fit the bottle into my already-overstuffed suitcase, so she offered to mail it to me, by slow mail, by boat, and it would arrive, she said, just as I was settling in again to the daily life of teaching, and it would remind me that much else was possible.

The bottle was lost in the mail. If it had arrived, perhaps things would have gone differently.

S hortly after my first meeting with Margarita, there was an auto-
mobile accident on a remote stretch of road outside the city. Leonel somehow received word of this, and he told me that Margarita's
aunt had been in the passenger seat. When we arrived at the accident site, there were no police. It was dark, but Leonel had brought a
flashlight with him, saying he wanted to investigate, and as the automo-
bile was still there, with its spiderwebbed windshield and accordion-
folded hood, this was the best time to do it, before any police arrived, and
when I asked why there was only one wrecked car here, he acknowledged
that this was a good question. The other vehicle must have left. The other
vehicle would also have been pretty badly damaged. But the other driver
would still be alive to drive away. Obviously.

Leonel bent down near the car, planting his boots in the crushed glass.

"Get me the keys," he said, "the keys from the ignition, could you reach
in and get them for me?"

The driver's door was crumpled but the passenger side was open. I
couldn't see, because Leonel had the flashlight, but he pointed it helpfully
toward the open door, and leaning on the wet seat, I took out the keys.

"I have them."

Leonel studied the tread marks in front of the wreck, not this vehicle's
marks but the other's. He knelt again and ran his flashlight across the

undercarriage, raised the hood, and shone the light on the engine, then tested the lug nuts on each wheel. We stayed quite a while, but by the time we left, the police still hadn't yet arrived.

"They must be busy with other things," Leonel said, "they don't have time for car accidents it seems, even fatal ones."

He had removed items from the car: a plastic tote bag, a small toy that had hung from the mirror. "Take these with you," he said, "but give me the keys." When I asked again what we were doing, he said we were trying to find out what happened.

"And did we? Find out what happened?"

"No. But we did learn that the police aren't interested in this. They are busy with other matters, or they aren't interested for another reason."

There was blood on my clothes but I didn't know this until Margarita saw me in the bluish light of the hospital entrance. Her dress was also splotched with blood, perhaps from pressing herself against the gurney used to roll her relative's corpse into the morgue. I held the tote bag out to her, containing the toy and some other things that I no longer remember, but she stepped back and held me at arm's length.

"You are—all right, Carolyn?" she asked in halting English, looking down at my bloodstained clothes.

Other people had arrived and were pulling Margarita toward them, embracing and surrounding her, while Leonel stayed off to the side, speaking quietly with one man after another until he came to my side and said it was time to go.

"I'm taking you to Margarita's. She'll be there later."

I had been watching the triage from the entrance, and it seemed that I had gone backward in time. Some of the nurses were Catholic sisters and wore traditional habits while the other nurses still wore starched white uniforms with white caps pinned to their hair. These caps had always reminded me of the sails of toy boats, and that would mean that the very air of the hospital corridor, of the nursing station, of emergency and triage, was a sea of something. Apprehension. Bodies under sheets. A sea of suffering.

"Papu, *what?* We have to go now."

"Does Margarita want me to stay with her? You're sure? I don't want to go unless . . ."

"It's okay. She was touched that you came tonight."

That night, he was driving an old pickup, finding his way through the darkened streets where people slept on flattened cardboard near rippled security gates. A few vendors were still selling their wares, and others were moving about as radio music came and went or a tarp wall fluttered. We drove in silence until he said that we had to pick up someone first, and then he would take me to Margarita's house.

"Margarita will be there by then. She will show you some things. I have to be away for a while."

"But where are you going?"

"Papu. Don't ask things like that. If I could tell you, I would."

After a time, he pulled to the curb under a sodium lamp that sprayed its cone of light to the walk, where a beautiful woman in a black dress stood. Leonel opened the driver's side door and climbed out. They stood close together, talking in the light, before she climbed into the truck from his side and sat between us, nodding to me, then turning toward Leonel, who was now at the wheel again. The truck filled with the light scent of jasmine, and the woman leaned close to him, her hand resting on his thigh.

"*Y mil besos!*" she whispered. Leonel laughed and said something I didn't understand, and they continued speaking in low voices, one and then the other, until we arrived in the *colonia* where Margarita lived.

"Carolyn, I will see you in a few days. Get some rest. Do some writing."

He called me by my given name in a voice slightly raised and business-like, with instructions about resting and writing, as if these amounted to the same thing and could be accomplished at the same time, and gave not so much as a name for this beautiful, fragrant woman in the whispering dress.

"Margarita's maid is just there," he said, nodding toward a woman at the gate with her hands in her apron. "She will let you inside. So. Take care. *Ciao.*"

"*Ciao*," I said, climbing from the truck in my bloodied, disheveled clothes, with the rucksack and bag slung one on each shoulder, trying to sound nonchalant. "A few days, then."

"Do you want some coffee?" Margarita asked, after showing me the room where I would stay, the bath I would use, the towels, and the way the louvers opened and closed.

"You don't need a key," she added, "the maids are always here to let you in or out."

"Coffee, thank you, if it isn't too much trouble," I answered, settling on the couch. Anything to keep her here, I thought, to learn something, anything, about her, about Leonel, and anything not to be left alone, and for what would probably be more than a few days.

Margarita told the younger of the two maids to bring us coffee and then, smoothing her skirt, sat on the chair near the couch and lifted a silver case from the glass table.

"Do you smoke?"

"Yes," I said, "a bit too much, in fact."

"You would like one?"

There was a lighter on the table, also silver, and she held it to me and then to herself.

"So, Carolyn, tell me. What are you doing here? Do you know where you are?"

"I'm not sure," I said. "What am I doing in El Salvador?"

"Look, Carolyn, I don't know what is your relationship with Leonel and I don't want to know, but our situation is dangerous, do you understand?"

"Relationship? I'm not in any relationship with Leonel. He's . . ."

"No? You are not? Then why do you look—so upset when you arrived here tonight?"

"Did I? I didn't mean to look upset."

Margarita exhaled her smoke and tapped her ash. The young maid brought a tray of coffee cups and saucers, a bowl of sugar cubes, little tongs for the sugar, a pitcher of cream, and set it down without rattling the cups. Margarita poured the coffee from the pot.

"Sugar?" she asked. "Cream? Or you prefer milk?"

"Margarita, I'm really grateful to stay with you. I hope we didn't get off to a bad start. And I'm so sorry about your aunt."

"Listen to me, Carolyn. I'm going to try to explain you."

That is how our Spanglish developed, with Margarita's artful and improvised English interwoven with my poor command of her language.

Explain me, I thought to myself, good luck.

"You have to be aware here, very aware, but more important, you have to be your own person. You have to think for yourself, do you understand? Leonel is very intelligent but he is working alone. He has his own—his own project. This is dangerous, Carolyn. Do you understand what I'm telling you?"

I nodded and drew on my cigarette. Margarita appeared surprised.

"You do? You are sure?" Then, leaning forward so she could speak in a low voice, "Listen. There are some things I must ask of you. Please don't tell anyone where I live, or that you are staying here with me. Don't tell anyone that you know me, and don't bring people here. And please, if you are going to do something with the project of Leonel, I should not know about it."

"Of course."

"And your clothes, give them to Alma. She will clean them. And in the morning, she will give you breakfast. I am going now upstairs to say good night to my girls. Maybe I see you tomorrow."

"Margarita? May I ask you something? There was a woman with Leonel—"

Margarita appeared irritated. "You want to know who she is? Is that what you want? I told you. Be your own person."

The maid, Alma, came to get the tray and Margarita whispered something to her while gesturing toward me. Alma nodded. She would appear a short while later at my door to take the bloodied clothes.

I lay in that room awake in the dark the first of many nights, with the guest bed pushed against the wall, beneath the louvered window opposite a half-empty closet with its doors open, books and papers stacked and jutting from the bookcase, painted figures on the top shelf: a peasant woman with a market basket on her head, a replica of the blue city bus painted with flowers, a cross on the wall with a bright, primary-colored village in the place of the crucified Christ. I should go home, I thought. No. There is no relationship. This has nothing to do with him. There was already a man in my life, even though I hadn't seen him for months. Or there was no one, and that was just as well. It was Leonel's secrecy that bothered me, I reasoned, not the fact that he may or may not be with someone.

From time to time I thought I heard a sound, just beyond my window. Headlights passed over the walls. The telephone rang in another room without being answered. When I woke, a door was slamming behind children's voices and shortly thereafter car doors, and then an engine started up.

"I am bringing the girls to school," she had written on a note left on the dining table set for breakfast: tortillas wrapped in a cloth, already-poured juice, a pot of coffee. As soon as I sat down, Alma brought the rest: white cheese, black beans, a papaya cut in half and filled with slices of lime. She poured the coffee for me.

"Thank you, yes, I have everything, *muchas gracias.*"

There was a clatter of dishware in the kitchen, and from the street occasional voices, dogs barking, motor scooters, and horns. I wondered what time it was, even what day. I scooped the beans and cheese with a bit of tortilla and ate.

By the time Margarita came back, I had wandered the house, studied the bookshelves, sat on the various chairs and sofas, taken off my shoes, and slipped through the sliding glass door into the garden, where birds of paradise spiked against the walls and coral bougainvillea climbed them. That is where I was when Margarita found me.

"*¿Qué tal,* Carolyn?" She touched my shoulder, leaning forward to kiss the air near my cheek.

"Fine," I said. "I'm fine, and you?"

"You had breakfast? You would like something else?"

She was different this morning in the way she held herself, relaxed and younger seeming, not much older than I was.

"I have to go to La UCA, the Catholic university. Would you like to come with me?"

"Yes I would! I mean—yes."

"Good, we'll go. But first I will show you something."

Her manner toward me had somehow changed during the night.

We wove through San Salvador in the exhaust of trucks, through barrios and past open markets, shut security gates, open shops and shacks, cook fires and roasting grates for corn, and in those days, *cántaros* that were still made of clay and seemed to float on the women's heads without tipping as if they were weightless. The women also carried baskets of live hens, and beside them their children, half clothed and barefoot, faces streaked, noses running, held or didn't hold on to their mothers or sisters, and there were skinny dogs hoping not to be noticed, spilled wash water on the street, blankets spread with vendors' wares, and all across the walls, acronyms written in black and red from spray cans: FPL, BPR, ERP, RN, FAPU, FECCAS-UTC.

There were whole words as well: *¡Cesen la represión! ¡La lucha continúa!*

Stop the repression. The struggle goes on. Then a bullhorn broke through the honking buses and traffic, shouts and radios, a voice bellowing something over and over.

"That is nothing, Carolina—an advertisement."

Like the knife sharpener's cry, I wrote in my notebook, or vendors calling out prices for vegetables in the market, a litany of prices. She had called me by the Spanish version of my name.

Margarita smoked even while driving and drove in the same manner as Leonel, always looking about and many times into the rearview mirror, but there was no weapon between us. We were on the outskirts approaching the Catholic university, La UCA, as she called it, when Margarita saw something and slowed the van: a group of fifty or so campesinos standing in line, waiting for something—men in straw hats carrying gourds and machetes, women with aprons over their trousers and skirts, holding baskets or *cántaros*, children surrounding them, waiting in line.

"Something has happened. Do you see them, Carolina? They rarely come into the city, so something has happened."

"Do you want to stop?"

"We cannot," she said emphatically. "I will explain. But we must tell someone that they are here."

She drove slowly past, then turned toward the campus still checking the mirror, expertly shifting and working the clutch.

"You must get a camera, Carolina. And you must write things."

"I have a camera," I said, taking the Olympus from my bag to show her, "and I have a notebook. But I'm no photographer. And I'm not a journalist either."

"This is not important."

She would often declare this, in response to things that I said. Most things were "not important."

SHE TOOK ME TO MEET TWO OF THE JESUIT PRIESTS AT THE CATHOLIC UNIVERSITY, Father Ignacio Ellacuría, and another whose name I didn't quite catch.

This might have been Father Segundo Montes. She also introduced me to her colleague Ricardo Stein, a scholar who was developing a center for documentation at the university and who invited me to come talk with him again.

Father Ellacuría, in a white guayabera instead of a cassock, motioned for us to sit in the chairs facing his desk. He had pushed his glasses onto his forehead as if he had eyes there. His gaze was fixed and intense and his language clipped and precise. Castillian Spanish. He began to speak in a manner reserved, I was later told, for visiting guests, as he did for students at La UCA, but when he learned that I was in El Salvador on a fellowship, he assumed that I knew much more than I did, and so his efforts fell on less fertile ground than he might have supposed.

That day he most wanted to talk about a recent law decreed by the government, the Law of Defense and Guaranty of Public Order, or what people seemed to refer to simply as "The Law." It prohibited rebellion, or the hosting of meetings to discuss rebellion, the encouraging of members of the armed forces to disobey orders, attempts by spoken or written word to oppose the established order, and everything having to do with opposition to the present military regime. There was also a provision having to do with the national University of El Salvador, which had been placed under a special body to assume temporary responsibility for governance, given the "present climate of unrest and violence" on the campus.

I took notes as best I could, and later Margarita would show me a copy of this law, with its eleven categories of offenses, its punishments, procedures, and articles, the whole of it placed at the disposal of the First Chamber of Criminal Matters and so on.

"This means," she said, "that they can arrest anyone at any time for any reason. They have legalized their repression. It is against the law to oppose them in any way. But, Carolina, only the lucky ones are arrested under this law. Only the lucky ones have a trial."

We were talking in the dark after the girls went to bed.

"What happens to the unlucky?"

"What happens? They are disappeared. They become *desaparecidos*. We don't know after that, unless the corpse is found, and even then we don't know because they are, how do you say it? Beyond recognition."

——◆——

All that day we went places together—to the empty gray cathedral without pews, flocks of doves flying in the clerestory; to the human rights office, with its red-and-gray-tiled floor, folding chairs and blue walls, where she showed me photograph albums, one with daisies on the cover, where the photos of the *desaparecidos* were mounted on sticky pages covered with plastic. Most of the photographs of the *desaparecidos* had been taken at school or on some occasion, such as completion of nurses' training, a *quinceañera* birthday party, a dinner in celebration of a betrothal. Therefore, most of the photographs were of young people, even if, at the time they disappeared, some were no longer so young.

"This sometimes makes it difficult," Margarita said, "to match the photographs of these *desaparecidos* to the dead that are found, but there are other factors making identification difficult as well. Some of them are found mutilated. Some of them have already been partly eaten by animals."

In the human rights office, these albums and some other folders were stacked high on a table. There was a telephone, and a fan turning side to side. People came and went, mostly older women. Some appeared desperate and anxious, clutching photos and scraps of paper, while others stared listlessly, waiting for some news. I turned the plastic pages, and it was like looking through a school yearbook of those most likely never to be seen again. I wrote as many names as I could in my notebook, not knowing yet what I would do with them. No one stopped me from copying these names down. A woman even crossed the room to bring me another album from the table, nodding as she pressed it into my hands.

Before we left, Margarita pointed to a particular photograph and asked me to remember the face. "I will tell you later when we're alone," she whispered.

We crossed town to the other university, the one taken over by a special governance body under the new law. Here the walls had been painted with murals, initials, and slogans, and there were flyers and posters, but much of this had been covered with paint so as to erase it. The walls were palimpsests of meetings and resolutions, marches and calls to action, layer upon layer of campus activism, as Margarita whispered to me. Otherwise everything appeared to be falling into disrepair: broken concrete steps, broken windows here and there, a filing cabinet with open drawers lying in a hallway. Desks left outside in the open. Empty desks. The students stood in small groups or walked arm in arm, moving between buildings and classes with their book bags. There were a few soldiers, with rifles slung over their shoulders, their olive helmets appearing wet in the light. The soldiers were as young as the students. Maybe younger.

"This campus is occupied," Margarita said in a low voice, reading my thoughts. "We should go. I'm going to take you to a special place—nothing to do with our situation."

"Might we stay a little longer?"

"No. I will explain later."

The fading graffiti appeared even on the walkways. We were walking on a quilt of flyers, some lifting in the wind, and through the cacophony of voices one would usually hear at change of class, there was a strange quiet; the mood of this campus was at once expectant and suffused with fear.

Back in the van, she lit her cigarette even before rolling down the window.

"You're shaking, Margarita."

"Everything is fine," she said. "But there was someone there and I think he saw me."

"Who did you see?"

"Someone."

As we drove and the city fell below us, here and there pastures grazed by cattle, and in the distance, a blue volcano rose into the clouds. We stopped at a scenic overlook. We were here because she wanted to show me something.

As we stood at the railing, she said: "I have come to this place for years, but I think it will not be possible much longer. Do you see that tree with the red flowers? They call it the marriage tree. Do you know why? It has beautiful blooms in the spring, but the flowers fall away and the tree becomes not so beautiful. Speaking of this, my husband is coming home tomorrow. You will see. We are not really together anymore. We do not have—relations."

"I'm sorry."

"Why? I prefer this. It would be impossible to share my life with him now."

She turned to look over the railing again. "He is not of the extreme right, Carolina. He has the politics of an ordinary businessman. Do you understand? We stay together because of our daughters, but I do not know how long this will be possible. I think there will be a war. I agree now with the people who believe this. We do not see—"

She caught the error before I registered what it was. This "we" didn't refer to herself and her husband.

"Are you organized, Margarita?" It was a term I had picked up, and she was surprised to hear it from me.

"You should not be asking me that. But no, I am not a militant. And if I was, I would not be telling you."

In the distance, volcanoes without smoke appeared. Sleeping volcanoes.

"The photograph of the woman I asked you to remember? That woman was my friend. The last time I saw her we were in a bank, standing in line at a teller's window. This was some time ago. She was dressed to go somewhere, or maybe she was on a break from work, I am not sure. But she seemed nervous—alert, like a *perico,* one of the small birds you see in flocks at dusk. She would barely look at me, and we were once close. She was looking all around, over my shoulder, out toward the bank entrance, and then she said in a quiet voice, I almost couldn't understand: *You must get away. You must pretend not to know me. Please.* And then she said, *I love you, and I will see you again someday.* I said I loved her too. The next week, I think it was, she disappeared somewhere near the market. I didn't sleep well after that, and I kept imagining where she might be, and what might they be doing to her. Then . . ."

Someone else had come beside us to look at the city or to meet there in that place above everything, two men who were joined by a third. They had come in two separate vehicles. Margarita stiffened in their presence. One of them had a pistol tucked into his belt and it's possible the others had them too. They were talking and laughing among themselves but not lightheartedly. One or the other glanced at us from time to time. Margarita turned toward me and looked into my eyes. She wasn't smiling. She opened her purse and withdrew a lipstick and a pocket mirror, holding the mirror at some distance from her face, then raised her voice to suggest that we do some shopping.

One of the men had been showing the others some black objects. At that moment, they all got into one of the cars and drove off, leaving one of their vehicles parked at the overlook.

"Two-way radios," Margarita said, then: "Well—I was telling you about my friend. Someone else, another woman, was put into one of the clandestine prisons but was released later, I'm not sure why, but this one who was released said she had seen Lil Ramirez, and said that "her hair had grown to the floor of her cell," that she was like a ghost. We should go now," and then she added, "before those men come back."

"You weren't afraid, Carolina?" Margarita asked as we descended toward the city.

"Should I have been?"

She looked over at me and then, downshifting with her hands white on the steering wheel, she answered, "Yes."

———◆———

That night, or the next, we stayed up late talking after the girls had gotten into their pajamas and kissed their mother good night, after the newly arrived husband had finished his scotch on the rocks, shaken my hand and nodded to his wife, and the two maids in their white uniforms had sailed through the doorway for the last time. As the moonlight splashed the rhododendron in the garden, we sat in the dark, the wall of glass doors open. It seemed we were both inside and outside the house. As with other houses, this one had walls surrounding it, with broken bottles embedded along them, and strings of razor wire that also caught the light. Margarita wanted to know how much I knew—how much Leonel had told me about what she called "this moment."

I went back to Leonel's history lessons: the conquistadores, Alvarado of the burning hair, the tortures inflicted on the Nahua, Pipil, and Lenca, the confiscation of their lands, all the way to the volcano Izalco's erupting on the eve of the uprising in 1932 and the ships in the harbor.

"*Pero, en este momento*—in this moment, Carolina."

"Well, he talks about corruption in the military quite a bit, and about the dead American Ronald Richardson—he's obsessed with that—and about Colonel Chacón, whom he thinks is responsible for Richardson's death. He talks about the labor union he is advising and complains that this union is being manipulated, as I understand it, by the Americans, but mostly he talks about poverty. He took me to one village to show me—I think mostly—the trench people use as a latrine. But now we've gone to many *caseríos* and villages, and talked to many people. Over and over he shows me the conditions in which people live, the majority of people. He says that if he could change the lives of campesinos even in the smallest way, he would be willing to dig ditches for the rest of his life. *I would dig them for two hundred years* is what he said."

"Does he ever talk about the *guerrilleros*?"

I remember wondering why she wanted to know these things about Leonel. She was his friend, wasn't she? And *as* his friend, wouldn't she know the answers herself? But my hesitancy at this time was overcome, I think, by the stronger desire for her friendship.

"He says the government exaggerates the size and strength of the guerrilla groups to get economic and military aid from the Americans. He says the guerrilla forces are small—militarily speaking, they are almost, he says, insignificant, but that this could change. He keeps saying that the country is going to blow up—that war is coming. But he's been saying that since I met him. The country is going to blow up. This doesn't make sense to me. If there are no guerrillas, how is it that war is coming?"

We sat quietly in the dark for a long while, the tips of our cigarettes making arcs in the air to our mouths. There was a bird singing in the garden despite that night had come.

L eonel returned the next morning, wet haired and beaming, having arranged my day for me, but first, of course, he wanted to sit down to breakfast, and joke with the girls and with Margarita and even exchange pleasantries with her husband, whom he later described as "a decent man."

I packed a few things to take with me just in case I wasn't coming back that night or the next. Margarita asked if I wanted to borrow a dress. She wore floral wrap dresses, closely fitted with low necklines such as I wasn't accustomed to wearing, but we were the same size, so she rolled and tucked one into my sack along with a pair of her dressy sandals that also fit me and a lipstick in a shade that would suit my coloring.

"Leonel would never think of things like this," she said, "and one never knows."

Then she put her hands on my shoulders and turned me toward her: "If you need me, call, and I will come and get you. Do you understand? And be careful and remember, be your own person. Call me if you need me."

She didn't walk us out. She let her maid open the gate. When I turned, I saw her standing in the doorway, watching us and covering her mouth with her hand. When she saw me, she waved.

I decided not to ask him where he had been. I wouldn't ask about the beautiful woman. We were here to work, as he said himself, so no more such questions. At this moment, I thought I was beginning to understand.

Margarita had insisted that I be my own person. Leonel was also adamant that I think for myself, that I let go of my preconceptions, although I hadn't, until then, been aware of having any. But all right, I thought. How to do that? Leonel had complained of my daydreaming, that I wasn't paying proper attention to things around me in my waking life, so from now on, I would pay attention, and try to see as much as I could, not the world as imagined in my continuous waking dream, but as it was, not only the obvious but the hidden, not only the water *cántaros* but their weight, not only their weight but why it was necessary to carry water such distances. I would try to learn from Leonel how to listen to what was said but also to what was *not* said, and I would also try to learn how to detect deception in others, which, he assured me, is a skill that can be acquired. I would learn to review my experiences for the missed details, and to keep in mind that while I was observing others, they were also observing me, and I would become less (how did he put it?) *readable,* and when necessary, I would attempt, in his words, to "manage the perceptions of others" so that, of the "five versions of the truth," in any given situation, mine might prevail.

"This place is a symphony of illusion," Leonel often said, "and an orchestra needs a conductor."

———◆———

The jeep bounced over the dry ruts of dirt roads, through the tin light of early morning. I steadied the bundle as Leonel drove from Margarita's *colonia* to the poorer barrios, and then to the outskirts, where cook smoke crawled the roofs. There was the white steam of morning piss above the ditches where each man stood, and where the women bunched their skirts to their waists and squatted, not far from their *champas,* whose windows were carved into packing crates with machetes, crates that had once contained appliances, so the walls read "Maytag," "White," or "Harvest Gold." The crates had been hacked apart and spliced together, bolstered with scrap lumber, straw, and mud; some of the roofs were nothing but drop cloths, others were of lámina. These were everywhere if one began to look for them, wedged between ditch and road, clinging to banana trees or slung between palms, their walls fluttering in the least wind. With the rains, they collapsed into the ravines and had to be built again. The ruins of earlier *champas* draped the palms like wet bedding.

We passed women walking along the highway with their children, one hand holding the hand of another child, especially as the heavy buses passed, trailing smoke, arms hanging from the bus windows and men riding on top, or when the open trucks passed with men standing shoulder to shoulder on the flatbed fenced to hold them as they were driven to the fields.

We were going that day to visit several more *caseríos*, Leonel said, settlements smaller than villages, clusters of houses inaccessible by road, so that I might continue to see for myself how people lived. We drove off the highway and onto a dirt road, and then bounced along a stony path for what seemed at least an hour. I pressed my palm to the roof to steady myself and took hold of a handle jutting out of the dash. Leonel kept both hands on the steering wheel, except when downshifting to avoid the largest rocks, as if he knew the location of each one.

"It's impossible to drive this road in the rainy season, so when it rains I have to walk," he said over the engine, "but the people who live here walk all the time."

On both sides there were *champas* hidden among the trees, and stands of corn, a dozen or so stalks. Fewer. Then ahead of us on my side a thin white cow, her bones jutting from her rump, loped behind a small barefoot boy who was leading the cow by a rope, her head rocking back and forth as she walked, the boy tapping the ground with a stick.

"He's taking that cow to graze. Do you want me to tell you a story about a cow? No, really, this is interesting. Several years ago, a small coffee farmer made arrangements for six campesinos from a nearby village to have a meeting with some businessmen in the capital. Well, okay, it was me. I was that coffee farmer. I thought it would be good for them to talk. On the morning we were supposed to go, the campesinos were late. I thought they had become nervous and had changed their minds. Finally, they arrived, all in clean shirts, their best clothes, but they were unusually quiet. One rode with me, the others in the back of my pickup. It happened that I knew their village needed a milk cow. On the way, I explained to the one riding with me that we would listen to what the businessmen had to say about their future plans for the economy and how these plans would affect campesinos. The businessmen were going to talk about farming cooperatives, new industries, and the improvement of roads, hospitals, and schools. I proposed that we listen to everything they said, and afterward the campesinos should ask the businessmen for a cow.

"We can do that?"

"Yes. Just ask them for a cow."

"Okay, so we go into this carpeted conference room where graphs and charts have been set up. The businessmen were more nervous than the peasants, but finally we got started. After the presentation, the campesinos asked some questions, but the businessmen directed their answers at me rather than at the campesinos. It was almost like they wanted me to translate for them. They said tell the men this and tell the men that. Then the campesino who had ridden with me thanked the businessmen on behalf of the others and said: 'What we really need at this time is a cow. We need milk for our village.' The businessmen looked at one another, then at me. 'A cow?' one of them said. 'We cannot give these people a cow.' I asked why not. 'You know why not,' he said to me. 'If we give them a cow—we can't be setting that kind of precedent.'

"So you see? Not even a goddamn cow."

"What did the campesinos think?"

"I didn't ask them what they thought. But I think they understood perfectly."

WE PULLED OFF THE ROAD AND STOPPED.

"We have to walk from here."

"Where are we?" He was already getting out of the jeep.

The sun bore down, but it was a beautiful day, dry and hot, and I remember listening to the hum of insects as I walked, and feeling the stones beneath my sandals, which were not right for this path. Leonel wore sturdy hiking boots, as he always did on terrain such as this. If I drew close enough behind him, I could hear the water sloshing in his canteen.

"How far?" I asked, catching up.

"Oh, I don't know. It depends on how you measure distance."

"Can I have some water?"

"Actually, I think we have to walk for just a few more kilometers, but we don't measure distance by kilometers here, we measure by time. A man will say it is a day's walk, or a day and night. But it's not far."

He stopped, unscrewed the cap, and handed me the canteen.

"We have to get you some better shoes."

I was winded and my sandals were cutting into my heels.

"Don't drink too much at once."

I thought about taking the sandals off and going barefoot, but maybe that would be worse. I wished he had told me we were going to hike, but he hadn't. For him this was a short way.

"You brought your other clothes with you? The ones Margarita gave you?"

I turned to show him my rucksack, which included the dress and shoes that I didn't want to leave in the jeep.

"Good. You might need them later."

A man was coming toward us on the road, wiry and wearing a straw hat, as all the men in the *campo* wore. He greeted Leonel by taking off the hat, and the two stood, talking, the man nodding, smiling a little, looking off into the distance and back at Leonel. I tried to hear but couldn't. The man looked over at me, then back. *Vale,* I thought I heard him say. *Pues. Bien.*

I didn't come closer. I thought I heard hens clucking but didn't see any hens. When I looked up the man was gone, and Leonel was motioning me to follow him through some trees. In the clearing there were four houses, and yes, there were hens pecking the ground. One of the houses had a veranda, or its main room was open to the air, where a woman sat on a stool with a metal tub at her feet. I couldn't tell what was in the tub. Leonel was talking with her, jokingly, but I couldn't understand what they were saying. He spoke differently with campesinos, a different Spanish, softer and lighter, with less swearing. The syllables were swallowed at the ends of the words.

"Okay," he said suddenly in English. "You're going to stay here tonight.

Fina is a good woman, an old friend. She's been through a lot. That was her husband we saw on the road. Manuel. They have, I don't know, about six kids. The grandmother lives here too and I don't know who else, maybe a donkey. I told them you are a Catholic."

"When are you coming back?"

"I don't know yet. Tomorrow. And don't wander off."

And then he patted me on the arm.

"You'll be okay. You can learn a lot from them, much more than you could from me. And if anything happens, just do what they do. Follow them. I'll find you later."

He handed me his canteen.

"Maybe it's better that you drink from this while you're here. I don't want you coming down with some rare tropical disease. Ask Fina to tell you about her life."

"*Buenas,*" she said, nodding to me, "*bienvenida.*"

Her eyes lit up her kind face. She motioned me to sit on the stool beside hers, and bent again over the tub, stirring the pale corn slurry with her hands. There were children darting among the palms, running off when I saw them, to reappear one behind the other, hiding from me near the wall. A dog with small teats hanging from her underside ran past, head down, not wanting to be seen. Where we were sitting began to seem like an outdoor room: There was a rough gray stone for grinding corn and a wooden box filled with corn ears. The two stools and a table had once been blue, but now the blue was worn mostly to bare wood. A few pans and bowls, of white enamel and of plastic, hung on the front outdoor wall. The earth had been swept smooth.

Did I want water?

"*No, gracias,*" I said, holding up Leonel's canteen.

Fina nodded, stood up, and carried the slurry to the table, then disappeared through the open doorway. She didn't come out for a good while. I smelled smoke then, the sweet smoke of a cook fire, and I wanted to go inside the hut too but dared not, so I sat in the hum of insects. This is what I did most of the afternoon as I was of no use here, and Fina had her work to do, and the children, too, had work it seemed, because I saw a small child carrying a bucket not far off, the water sloshing as he walked, and as I didn't know where I was to urinate, I went in among the trees and hurriedly squatted there, then returned as if I hadn't been gone. I sat with my notebook in my lap, pen in hand, the page blank, until I heard voices through the trees, and Fina emerged, wiping her hands on her apron, and the man we'd seen on the road appeared again.

It went like that, no talking, no wind, a cowbell, voices, Fina rubbing and rubbing a soft dough along the stone, then nightfall, lighting a stub of candle, and two thick tortillas were placed in front of me on an enameled metal plate, along with some black beans. I had been given the chair at the small table, and the others had taken the bench nearby, so I had the saucer of light from the candle, but in the half dark I watched them cross themselves before scooping a bit of beans to their mouths with a tortilla. I crossed myself too, as I hadn't since childhood, and ate as they ate while the candle flame flattened and rose.

Fina asked me if I wanted to sleep and motioned for me to follow her into the hut. I ducked under the lintel and followed her. It was now dark, but I could see that there was an open cook pit against one wall, its embers still rimmed with light and, against another, feed sacks of some kind piled, and beside them, a wooden pallet covered by a woven blanket, and it was to this that Fina led me, patting the pallet to show me that this was where I would sleep. Another woven blanket was folded at the end of the pallet. I sat there. Then she was spreading another blanket on the floor and the children, who were whispering even in their laughter, arranged themselves for the night.

As the embers died, the house grew pitch dark. I had no idea how I would see if I had to get up in the night. It seemed that Fina had anticipated this. In the dark, she took my hand and touched it to a metal can, making it somehow clear that I was to relieve myself in this if the need came. Then she left, and for a while I heard hushed voices outside, Fina's and the man's, and maybe another voice too, I couldn't tell. There was nothing to do but lie down and pull the other blanket over me.

With the darkness came the cold, and because of that I dreamed that my grandmother Anna was taking me with her through the blue snow as far as the boundary line of wintering poplars. She dragged a sack behind her and when she reached the rusted metal drum, she emptied the sack, stuffing its contents deeper into the drum with a stick. She lit several wooden matches until a fire began to waver and then roar through the debris, some of the paper escaping as ashen sheets framed in firelight. Sparks rose into the stars and hissed out. Anna's face was lit. She wasn't wearing her teeth. I was so cold that my hands went from rosy to white. *Never mind the cold,* she said.

IN ONLY A FEW HOURS, THE ROOSTERS BEGAN CROWING INTO THE LAST STARS and there were wild birds and braying donkeys or burros. The air was stiff and tinged with smoke. Men began calling out to one another beyond the cluster of huts. Only a few hours had passed since the candle had been blown out, and the moon still hung in a thin scythe over the palms, but the adults of the village were not only awake but already moving about, so I crawled from the pallet and went out to see that the women were headed toward a spigot and trough. There were no men with them. They stripped to the waist, shielding themselves with cotton cloths, soaping, splashing in the icy water from the spigot. I didn't have such cloth. It was too cold to strip, so without knowing what else to do I cupped water to my face. It seemed wrong to be here among them, and to see them this way, passing soap hand to hand. I was used to a hot shower, towels, toothpaste, and shampoo, but absent these things I was at a loss, and so I opened my blouse and pretended to be washing myself. When one of the women caught my eye, she smiled and nodded, then turned away. Later I would tell Leonel that I had been embarrassed at the spigot.

"Why?"

"Because I didn't know what to do."

"Just do as they do. Wash."

"But I didn't know how," I said.

"Well," he said, "think about that."

———◆———

Fina spent the morning grinding corn on the *metate* while I sat on the stool making notes, then I followed her around as she bathed children, fed hens, slapped clothing on wet rocks, scrubbed pots and plates, gathered dead branches, and swept the dirt floor. I was grateful when she gave me some small thing to do, and when she slowed her Spanish for me to point at objects and give me the word for them. She had no English, and didn't want any. Light poured into the hut through chinks in the lámina and wattle. In the midday, even the animals fell silent, but Fina didn't stop her work. That night it was the same: beans, tortillas, candlelight, only this night Fina said that someone was coming. We would not sleep yet.

The candle remained lit. Others arrived, quietly taking their places on benches near the table, the men taking off their straw hats as they sat, the women together, smoothing their aprons. I heard Fina say that I was a friend of Leonel's, that I was a poet. We waited in the dark, around a candle that cast light the size of a supper plate.

All stood when a young man in a moonlit shirt ducked under the porch roof. He greeted each individually. I thought I heard Fina whisper to him when asked about me, *Monja católica estadounidense*. American Catholic nun. At this, he nodded and opened the Bible he was carrying.

"*Hermanos y hermanas,*" he whispered, "you are children of God sent to transform the world. From the Book of Isaiah, chapter 61, verses 1 and 2. 'The spirit of the Lord God is upon me; because the Lord has anointed me to preach good tidings unto the meek; he has sent me to bind up the brokenhearted, to proclaim liberty to the captives, and the opening of the prison to them that are bound. To proclaim the acceptable year of the Lord, and the day of vengeance of our God; to comfort all who mourn.' What is the message of this verse?" he asked. "*Hermanos y hermanas,* what do you think? Who are the meek? Who are the captives? Who is bound? Who is in mourning?"

They answered in hushed voices: *la gente, los pobres, the people, the poor,* the flame rising, then guttering until another candle was lit from its stump, and in the light of this new candle, every face shone in the dark. The group held hands at the end.

"Sister?"

I had gone to a clearing to look at the stars and didn't hear him at first because I'm not a sister.

"Sister, may I speak with you?"

English.

"My name is Inocencio. Well, that is my name in this moment. You can say Chencho. I want to thank you for being here with us, in our community. Do you want to talk for a while? I would be grateful to practice English."

We sat on the bench talking and time passed until the last stars were visible. The roosters were awakening when he disappeared into a thick stand of jacaranda, and we had smoked almost a pack, and I had learned that he had been a seminarian but had decided not to become a priest. Instead, he'd become a catechist who traveled from village to village, bringing "The Word" to campesinos on nights such as this. The place I had been staying was a Christian base community, he'd said. A few of its members had already been killed and found dismembered near the farms where they worked. Others had come upon them and gathered their remains. After that happened, they were willing to die for one another, and for those who were already dead.

He told me that some of the men had begun sleeping in the mountains so as not to be captured in the night. It was enough, he said, to belong to a Bible-study group to be taken, and especially catechists and priests were in danger. *And also nuns,* he said.

I told him I wasn't a nun, and that I didn't understand why people thought this.

"Maybe it's because you smoke?" He smiled. "There are foreign nuns here, and some of them smoke, and they don't wear traditional religious habits like Salvadoran nuns do. You dress like them. And why else would a North American woman be here?" He paused for a moment, considering his own question.

"So if you don't mind me to ask, why *are* you here? Are you—working?"

Later I would learn that here "working" meant being part of the resistance to oppression, but at that time I thought he was asking if my job had brought me to El Salvador, and I said no, of course, as there was no job in that sense, and I must have mentioned the fellowship and the invitation because he began to appear bewildered, for which I couldn't blame him. For some reason, I didn't simply say that I was a poet, as I should have, because that answer would have made more sense to him than anything else. Salvadorans would expect to see poets anywhere.

"*¿Y por qué?* Invited why?"

"You know, I'm not sure. I was told it was because . . ."

He was listening more intently now. Was it all right to talk this way?

"Because war is coming."

"Who told you this?"

For some reason, I sensed that I shouldn't say Leonel.

"I would rather not say," I said.

"And what does this war that is coming have to do with you?"

"Nothing, but my friend asked me to come here to learn as much as I could about the country so that when the war began I could . . ."

"Could what?"

"Explain the reasons for the war to the North Americans, because my friend tells me that this will be important, that the real reasons be known, so that the people of the United States understand."

He seemed still to be listening, but a bit warily. I realized how it sounded, what I was saying, because it sounded that way to me too.

"This—this *amigo* of yours, why does he care so much what the *norteamericanos* think?"

"I don't know, but he does. He thinks the U.S. might enter the war on the side of the military. He thinks that this would be a mistake, so he's hoping to prevent it from happening."

This last seemed to interest him, but the questions stopped.

"Listen to me, *hermana,*" he said. "We are brothers and sisters in Christ, and Christ is moving through the world now, through us. He is acting through us in the struggle against injustice, poverty, and oppression. To be with God now is to choose the fate of the poor, to be with them, to see through their eyes and feel through their hearts, and if this means torture and death, we accept. We are already in the grave."

A song of insects rose in the underbrush, cicadas or crickets, a whirring through leaves that swelled as it rose in pitch. It must have been there before but only now did I hear it, as if I'd been away and had suddenly returned to be standing before this catechist who had grown visibly younger as he spoke. I handed him the crumpled pack with two remaining cigarettes and we shook hands.

"I hope I will see you again," I said. "Take care."

"You too," he said, *"y vaya con Dios."*

His white shirt tacked this way and that among the trees until he disappeared into the darkness or, rather, I could no longer see him. I went back to the pallet to sleep, but lay awake.

———◆———

After two days, Leonel came for me, and this time the back of the Hiace was filled with duffels and metal trunks. He was dressed in a clean white guayabera and pressed khakis. I nodded toward the duffel bags.

"Are we going far?"

"Maybe. I don't know yet. It depends on what happens. Do you have everything with you? In your rucksack," he added impatiently, "your nice clothes."

"Should I change?"

"No, not yet. Say good-bye and thank them. We have to go."

Most of the people were already in the fields, but I did say good-bye to Fina, who also wished me to *Vaya con Dios.*

The gun was wrapped in *Time* in the space between us, a sign that Leonel was worried, or that we would be traveling through areas where the coming blowup was expected, but after stopping along the road to make a phone call, Leonel, his spirits bright enough, pushed a cassette of flute music into the dashboard player and asked me how I was, how Fina had seemed to me, and when I described the young catechist, he nodded but, for the first time, didn't ask questions. We drove to the music of stuttering breath, the pitch of wind through bamboo, and beside us the green walls of cane gave way to the meadows of cattle.

"They thought I was an American nun."

"Really? Does that bother you?"

"A little. I'm not a nun."

"Well, it bothers me quite a bit. That isn't a good identity to have here."

On such drives as this, with the windows down, I would push the seat all the way back and brace my bare feet against the glove box. Sometimes we traveled in silence, but usually Leonel would take the opportunity to review the previous days, or recount a conversation we'd had with someone, or he would verbally assemble a puzzle he was trying to solve or a mystery that had as yet eluded him. Often, he retold the story of the dead American, beginning with Ronald Richardson's detention for failing to pay his hotel bill and ending with his being tossed from a helicopter into the sea.

"It's not as you imagine," he said. "When a body hits the water from that height, it is the same as falling into a block of stone."

The Richardson story was always the same, but more often lately the focus was upon Colonel José Francisco René Chacón, that *hijo de la gran puta* Chacón, who was believed to have ordered Richardson's death.

"He has his victims butchered and keeps their body parts frozen in plastic bags to feed to his dogs," Leonel reminded me, "most especially when he wants to impress a visitor."

He took his eyes from the road to be certain that I had again registered this information.

"His freezer is the kind that opens from the top, like a coffin or a treasure chest. His dogs are mongrels. I also told you, didn't I, that he anesthetizes his victims and . . ."

"You told me about that, yes."

"Who knows how many he has killed, Papu."

"I like this," I said, turning the volume up on the cassette player, but when the song came to an end, the cassette popped out of its slot, and I was about to push it back in when Leonel said, "Leave it, we need to talk for a while. We need to review."

"But you've told me this story so many times that I know it by heart."

"Do you? What do you mean by 'know'?"

"Is that another trick question?"

"It's not a trick, Papu. Chacón flays people alive. He kills a man's child in front of him and makes him dig the grave. I mean, goddamn it. You think you know this story from the few facts I have given you? What if I told you that Richardson might have been an intelligence agent?"

"You're kidding, right? That makes no sense."

"It doesn't? Why not? Look, the man arrives in Central America with no apparent reason to be here. The first thing he does, both in Guatemala and El Salvador, is to try to get work as a mercenary. From another perspective, he was trying to infiltrate the military. From another perspective, his target was Chacón, who happens to have his own small band of killers. But no one trusts Richardson until he starts talking about drugs. In this scenario, the flimflam man is an act. Richardson thinks he's getting close to Chacón. Apparently, no one brought the embassy into the loop, so they are busy trying to verify his driver's license and the addresses he has given, but none of it checks out. He isn't who he says he is. There is no Ronald Richardson."

"So what are you saying?"

"I'm saying that it is possible that the man who called himself Richardson was an agent."

"Which means?"

"Which means that the Salvadoran chief of immigration, one of the highest-ranking officers in the Salvadoran military, might have had a U.S. intelligence agent murdered. And despite the embassy's best efforts to find out what happened, there were no repercussions. The man who called himself Richardson is dead. End of story, except . . ."

He stopped, distracted by something: a cow, all hide and bones, loping along the road, the man following behind the cow, or something else he saw.

"Except what?"

"We can't let it be the end of the story."

Of course, he must know what I was thinking. Why did he care so much about this American? It had been months since his probable death, months in which dozens of campesinos had been murdered in the *campo*, had been thrown down wells, mutilated, left in the fields for vultures, and every day people were disappearing from the streets, abducted while walking to work or coming home from school, some to reappear in the morgue, but most never to be seen again, and if they were, by chance, alive somewhere, in secret detention, in a clandestine jail, they would no longer resemble the last photograph taken, the one that was meant to celebrate a watershed moment of their lives. Why was this one man, this Richardson, so important to Leonel? He more than others, and a North American? And if it is true that he was an agent, which seems a bit farfetched—well, the obsession with his death was even more puzzling.

He pounded his fist on the steering wheel.

"The man was a human being. That's reason enough. The question is: Why did the American government stonewall the investigation, and why was the new president so eager to accept the resignation of the ambassador to El Salvador before any other resignation in the world, and at a time when human rights had suddenly become so important? It was to be the centerpiece of the new president's foreign policy, or so they claimed. Believe me, I have thought long and hard about this question, Papu."

"Where are we going?"

"I told you, I was able to arrange something. We are going to Ahuachapán."

After the cattle ranches, we entered the sugarcane. The cane was ready for harvest. I watched from the Hiace as workers hacked the canes close to the ground with their machetes, hacked and stood and, with sun flashing from the blade, took the green leaves from the top and laid the stalk on the bundle, then disappeared again into the cane stands.

"What do you see?" Leonel asked, as he always asked.

"A cane harvest?"

"What else?"

"What else am I supposed to see?"

He nodded his head toward the cane fields and raised his eyebrows.

"Men are cutting cane with machetes," I said.

"Look at their hands. He slowed the car. Look carefully."

Their hands appeared black with soot.

"Do you know how sharp sugarcane leaves are? They are like razors. Do you know what happens to a man's hands when he cuts cane?"

There was movement among the cane stands, falling cane, a flash of machetes in the distance, and smoke.

"Why is the cane black?"

"It's been burned. That's how they get rid of the dead leaves. But the canes are filled with water, so they survive the fire. A good cane cutter can harvest a thousand pounds in an hour. If they don't work fast, they're sent away with nothing. Keep looking."

For some kilometers, I stared into the burned cane, doing as he asked. From time to time, a cutter staggered from the cane break with a bundle on his back many times his size and tossed the bundle to a waiting truck.

"Try to imagine, Papu, doing that every day, and for almost nothing."

I knew that he hadn't brought me to Ahuachapán principally to watch a cane harvest. After a time, he slowed the Hiace and pulled into some kind of compound, yanked on the emergency brake, and sat without speaking for a while.

"You want to know something about human rights? You keep asking me about human rights. The groups you are talking to—who are they? What are they going to do with our information? How far are they going to take it? What are they willing to risk?"

"I don't know what you mean."

"Well?" he said, and shrugged.

"No, really, I don't know what you mean. They are human rights groups, Amnesty International, and others. You know who they are."

"No, I don't. I have seen these groups, and you saw one too when you first got here. And look what happened."

"What do you mean 'what happened'? Nothing happened."

"Precisely."

"It's not their fault."

"Okay. Let's give this the benefit of the doubt. Suppose you were to give some good information to a human rights group, information about torture, about things going on even in a prison for common criminals. What would they do?"

I didn't like to answer these sorts of questions, but that was because, at the time, I didn't yet understand what he was trying to accomplish—in El Salvador or, for that matter, with me.

"I have no idea what they would do," I answered sarcastically, and then regretted this.

"Well," he said, "let's find out, shall we?"

He opened his door and gestured for me to follow him.

"Bring your sweater," he said, "it might be good for you to cover your arms."

It was a warm day, but I usually had a sweater with me for the cooler evenings.

"Leave everything else here. It will be all right."

As we walked a few feet from the Hiace, I saw the barbed wire for the first time, surrounding a one-story building, where soldiers had gathered near a gate.

"This is a prison," Leonel said in a low voice. "It's supposed to be for criminals, but there are quite a few political prisoners here too, and others who have become political prisoners during their incarceration. I went to school with one of the wardens. We're not friends, but let's say we know each other."

He stopped well short of the gate and looked at the clouds.

"Are you okay?" he asked.

"Of course I'm okay."

"Good. Now listen carefully."

He explained that I would be going inside to visit an old friend of his, who would now become instantly an old friend of mine too: "Miguel," or that's the name Leonel used for him then. Miguel had been in prison for several years for a petty offense committed when he was quite young, but his sentence was extended over the years as a result of his work as a prison organizer. Recently, he had led yet another hunger strike in an attempt to improve prison rations.

"He's a good man," Leonel said, "and he'll show you around."

"Me? You're not coming?"

"No, it's better if you go alone. But I'll be here."

"What am I supposed to do?"

"See as much as you can. Memorize everything. Especially the layout and the locations of anything you think human rights groups should see."

"Why are they letting me in?"

"I told you. I went to school with one of the wardens."

"But who does he think I am? And what does he think I'm doing here?"

There were two sharp cracks. Shots fired into the air. He nodded toward the building.

"Those are just warning shots. A visitor. Behave."

"Who should behave?"

"Everyone. Prisoners. Guards."

"What do they think I'm doing here?"

"I told them you were a friend of mine, and also of Miguel's family, and you just want to pay him a little visit while you are here."

"That doesn't sound credible."

"Well, can you think of something more credible?"

"What if anything goes wrong?"

"Things can always go wrong, but I really think you'll be okay. As I said, I'll be nearby. Just stay with Miguel, and when you see him, greet him like a friend and send good wishes from his family. Then stick close to him and pay attention."

"How long will I have?"

"I would guess about thirty minutes. As I said, stay close to Miguel and follow his lead."

At the entrance, there was a guard booth and a soda machine stocked with Fanta and Nehi, the grape and orange drinks of my childhood. There were several soldiers there, guards I supposed, but they looked like regular army to me, and they carried G3 automatic weapons, standard issue for the army. Leonel shook hands with the man I presumed was the warden, and they talked for a few minutes by themselves with their faces turned away from everyone else. When Leonel turned back again, a man was coming toward us, leaning on a crutch as he walked, his pants torn up the side to make room for a bruised and swollen leg. He dragged himself toward me by the crutch and smiled and held out his hand.

"It's so good to see you again, Carolina! How have you been?"

"Well. Very well. I'm fine," I said, or something like that, and then remembered to say, "Your family sends love. They miss you."

He was tender-eyed, unshaven, with crow's feet that belied his youth.

"*Gracias,* Carolina. Tell them the leg is a bit better. Would you like something?"

He was dragging himself toward the soda machine. Leonel was still talking to the warden. The soldiers were near.

"Oh, no, no, that's okay."

Miguel already had the coin from his pocket and he met my eyes and whispered, "Take it" as he handed me an opened bottle. "You'll need it."

I took a sip and Miguel smiled. He was younger than I thought he would be, perhaps thirty or so, not much older than me, and he was thin from the hunger strikes, but his eyes were bright and gentle.

"What happened to your leg?"

"Didn't *mi madre* tell you? I have thrombosis. But it's getting better. Shall we go?"

He nodded toward the prison entrance, where the gate was opening for us, and after passing through another set of gates, we were inside.

The stench came first, rotting coffee husks mixed with human waste, the hot smell of blood and sharpness of urine lifting from the pails that lined the hallway, an odor of unbathed humans together with smoke from the many tin-can fires, cans punched with holes holding burning coals, and over them, men were heating rations of beans and tortillas.

The prison had four wings and an open courtyard, the hallways on the four wings gave onto this yard, so the odors and cook smoke lifted toward the clouds, but the stench still hung, trapped in the air. I put the Fanta to my nose and Miguel smiled.

The men filled the courtyard lining all four wings, squatting on the tiles or sitting with their backs to the wall and their legs outstretched. When I walked through the hall, some of the men pulled their legs in to make way for me and some didn't. Some had tucked newspapers into the rims of their straw hats, and these hung down over their faces and all around their heads. They tented their heads with newspapers for privacy. They were wearing their own clothes, not prison uniforms but rags, filthy, torn garments pocked with holes. As Miguel walked on his crutch, the prisoners pulled their legs away to let him pass. I walked close to him.

"There is where we sleep," he whispered, pointing to a room that appeared to be lined with wooden shelves. "Those are the barracks. This place was built to hold about two hundred men but there are twice that number here now."

He stabbed the tile with his crutch and kept moving.

"Here are the latrines. Don't go in there."

The odd thing was that no one was looking at me. As I approached, they turned their faces away or looked down at the floor or at one another. Only Miguel looked. And it was quiet too. When we were outside in the beginning, I could hear a din of voices and shouts and even laughter coming from inside, but now nothing.

"Here are the workrooms."

These were long, narrow rooms with wooden benches, the walls made of peeling concrete painted aqua. I didn't see any tools or other evidence of work.

We turned a corner, where a group of prison guards had gathered in a circle, playing a game with dice, thoroughly occupied with the game, tossing dice and laughing or groaning. No one looked at us. We had made almost a full circle of this courtyard on all four wings. Miguel glanced around cautiously.

"*¿Listo?*" he whispered. "Are you ready?"

He locked eyes with me, then asked if I saw the dark open doorway nearby. I did. It was not quite ten feet away, a room with an entrance like the barracks, like the workrooms, but it was on the other side of the courtyard, the far side.

"No one is paying attention to you now. Just walk into that room and try to see what you can. Don't stay long, and control your face when you come out. I'll be right here. If anyone sees you and asks what you are doing, just make an absentminded North American lady face," and he imitated such a face, by looking at me blankly with his mouth slightly open. I had never seen anyone do that before and didn't realize that this is what we looked like to others.

"And just say that you got lost."

For a moment I froze, and then he smiled and nodded yes to me, tossing his head in the direction of the doorway.

"Go now, quickly."

I was inside the room. It was darker than any other room in the prison and it stank more. I tried to adjust my eyes to the darkness.

Try to see, Leonel had said. It was what he was always asking me to do. Try to see. Look at the world, he'd say, and not at the mirror.

What I saw were wooden boxes, about the size of washing machines, maybe even a little smaller. I counted the boxes. There were six, and they had small openings cut into the fronts, with chicken-wire mesh over the openings. They were padlocked. As I stood there, some of the boxes started to wobble a little, and I realized that there were men inside them. Fingers came through one of the mesh openings. Blood rushed to my ears, and I stood, trying to orient myself so that I could know not only where the room was but also which wall the boxes were against, and then I walked slowly toward the light of the open doorway and into the hall, where Miguel was standing against his crutch. As I came toward him he whispered, "Tie your sweater sleeves around your neck, *tiene urticaria.*"

I get hives, not as often as I once did, but in childhood frequently. Whenever I was afraid or nervous or sad they bloomed on my neck and face, so I did as he asked, and tied the sweater sleeves.

"That's *la oscura,* the darkness, solitary. Sometimes men are held in there for a year and can't move when they come out because of the atrophy of their muscles. Some of them never recover their minds. Tell them on the outside, tell them," and then, raising his voice he said, "Carolina, it has been nice to see you again. Give my love to Ana and Carlos."

He was walking, whispering again, *"Mil gracias.* It's time now for you to go. Go!" he said, motioning with his head toward the gate.

"But will you be all right?"

"¿Cómo no?" he said. "Go."

At the entrance, Leonel was waiting as promised, but beyond him, soldiers had surrounded his Hiace and were looking through the windows. He rested his hand on my shoulder and we began walking side by side.

"Why are they—?"

"I don't know. I guess we're going to find out."

We were between the building and the Hiace, which was parked close to the road. Leonel held the keys in his other hand.

"Don't turn around, just walk, and assume that everything is fine. We're just going to our vehicle, that's all we're doing."

Then he stopped. "Why don't you go up and say hello to them?"

"What?"

"I think it would be a good idea for you to say hello to them."

"Why don't you—?"

"It's better if you do it."

As I reached the Hiace, several of the soldiers turned toward me. They were smiling. I smiled back and put out my hand. *"Buenos días."*

"Buenos días."

They each shook my hand.

"This vehicle has four-wheel drive?" one of them asked.

"Yes, it has four-wheel drive."

"So it's like a jeep, then?"

"Yes, like a jeep."

"I will someday have a truck like this!" one of the soldiers said.

Leonel had reached us, and began talking with them, answering questions about the Hiace, then they walked off as a group, some waving goodbye. Leonel began driving slowly into the road. It was hot in the Hiace even with the windows rolled down. He was biting on his cold pipe, as he often did when he wanted to think, and ahead of us the road shimmered, and the stink of fire was still in the air and the whirr of blood in my ears and when I put my hands to my face, it felt wet, so that must have been why he kept looking from the road to me and back, but he wasn't saying anything, not even asking what I had seen, and then, in the next moment, I felt myself lurching forward, and vomited onto the dashboard. At the sight of this, I began to sob and, at the same time, tried to wipe the vomit up with my sweater. Finally, I threw the sweater on the floor and, still crying, turned away from him. Still, he said nothing. He stopped the Hiace and pulled hard on the emergency brake, I remember the sudden grind of it, almost as if he were angry but still nothing.

"Good," he said finally, "cry, go ahead." He didn't reach out to me or offer any comfort, didn't tell me that I had done well or that I was brave or that he was proud of me. I tried to stop.

"You know, Papu, I didn't think you would get this far. I didn't. I want you to pay attention now, and feel what you are feeling, really pay attention because you can learn from this. This is what oppression feels like. Now you have begun to learn something. When you get back to the States, what you do with this is up to you."

"I want to go back to the city. I need to take a shower."

"Papu, listen. You are always asking me why the people don't do something, why they put up with this brutality, why they don't rise up against it, this and that. Okay. You're exhausted, you're shocked, you're sick to your stomach, and you feel dirty. These things are what people feel every day here—and you expect them to get themselves organized? You expect them to fight back? Could you fight back at this moment?"

He seemed to be talking to himself now, and I didn't know any longer how I felt. Tired yes, still a little sick yes, but calmer, and I also felt angry with him for his lack of sympathy and for this lecture.

"Can we just go back to the city?"

"Yes, of course we can go. We'll go now. But we have a meeting tonight with those young poets, remember?"

"I can't go to any meeting. I want to go somewhere and rest. I need to think."

"Well, fine, but you promised. What am I going to tell them? We have to stop there and tell them you aren't coming, and I should be able to give a reason."

"Tell them the truth, then—that I feel sick, and that I'm tired."

WE DIDN'T SAY ANYTHING MORE TO EACH OTHER. THE CANE FIELDS WENT BY, followed by the cotton. It was dark when we reached San Salvador. The meeting with the young poets, arranged a few days earlier, was to take place in the barrio La Fosa.

"Wait here," he said, turning off the ignition and taking the keys. "I'll be back."

It was dark. There were small lights here and there, and voices of people passing by in the street, lights of cigarettes flaring, the sound of a glass bottle hitting a wall. I had the windows rolled almost all the way up and the doors were locked. I didn't really know where I was. I should have closed my eyes and rested until he returned but couldn't.

Even without the repression, Leonel had said, El Salvador is a violent country, with the highest murder rate in the world. I didn't know if that was true, but I was thinking of this as I sat in the dark waiting for him to come back. I heard radio music grow loud and then fade away. Leonel was often gone longer than he said he would be, but now at least an hour had gone by. I realized of course that I had no idea where he was, and no choice but to stay in the Hiace. As I pressed my head against the window glass, there was a tap, and when I turned, I saw a young man, motioning me to roll down the window.

"Carolina?"

He knew who I was.

"*¿Sí?*"

He told me his name and then said something about being sorry that I felt ill, and that of course all of them understood and everyone sent their greetings, but something had just happened in the *casita*. A poet's wife had just given birth. Would I like to come to see the newborn just for a moment?

I followed him through the darkness into a passage, then through the door lit by a candle and, by the light of it, saw people gathered and one of them, someone, took me by the hand and drew me into the circle surrounding a young woman who was lying on her side on a blanket on the floor, her head propped in her hand. There was a cardboard box beside her, and in the box, a newborn girl with her hair still wet, lying in a towel. Leonel was looking at me from across the room.

"She was born about a half hour ago," a young man beside me whispered. "She's early. We're going to name her Alma. *¡Bellísima!*"

We stood there I don't know how long, listening to the little sounds coming from Alma's mouth. The mother lifted the baby out of the box and held her to her breast, turning, shyly, toward the wall. The baby's father crouched beside them and the others moved toward the doorway.

"We're sorry about what happened to you," one of them said. "Leonel told us where you were today."

Happened to me? I thought. Nothing happened to me. But I nodded and smiled.

"We want to give you our *revista*," another said, handing me a booklet that smelled of fresh mimeograph ink.

"Not all of us have poems in this issue, but we can't find the previous one. We're sorry you got sick. We'd invite you to join us down the street, but we know you're tired. We've changed the meeting place because of this unexpected event."

Leonel was watching, a little quizzically. I heard myself say, "I'm not tired anymore. Of course, I'll come with you."

There was nothing in that *casita*, really nothing: a candle, a plastic basin, a ladle hanging against the wall, and, in the candlelight, the shadow of a wooden chair dancing on the wall. After touching the new mother's shoulder, I left with them, and in the next place, there was also very little. The poets, four young men, sat down at a wooden table and gave me a

Coke, and then the spokesman, the one who wasn't shy, told me the history of their group. I persuaded each of them to read a poem. Before I left, the spokesman cleared his throat, looked at the others, and said in a low voice, "Carolina, there is something we would like to say to you. First, we would like to thank you for coming here, not only to this meeting but also to our country. Second, we would like to ask you not to show this issue of our journal to anyone because you might accidentally show it to the wrong person, and that would be dangerous for us. Some of our poems are"—he hesitated—"militant?" and he asked Leonel if that was the word he wanted.

"Political," Leonel said.

"Yes. So. We were hoping that if you translate and publish them in the United States, you will be careful not to say who gave them to you. These aren't our real names, but there are other ways of finding out who we are, and we don't know all of those ways. It's just that we—we trust you, of course, but . . ."

"I'll keep your poems safe," I said.

That night I knew that something had changed for me, and that I wasn't going to get tired or need a shower or want to call something off so I could rest, and I hoped that if I forgot this I would somehow remember Alma in the cardboard box in the barrio, and the mimeographed poems.

I never saw the young poets again. I don't know what happened to them, if they survived or are among the dead. Shortly thereafter I wouldn't want to know who people really were or where they lived, where they were going, or who their friends were. After that night, I kept poetry mostly to myself, although the U.S. officials in the embassy knew that I was a poet, and the military officers I met also knew, or pretended to believe, that I was a poet.

"Yes of course," one officer said to me one night, "of course you are a poet. And I also write poetry."

The woman who went into the prison in Ahuachapán left herself behind in a barrio called La Fosa, the grave.

S ometime later, we went again to the region of Ahuachapán, this time as far as the sea, where there was an outdoor café that served the cockleshells that Leonel liked.

"There is something you should know," Leonel said. "I don't want this to worry you, but it seems that not everyone thinks you are a nun. Some people in the Salvadoran military think you might actually work for the CIA, or maybe the American embassy, they're not sure what."

The wind lifted the red-checkered tablecloth over the bowl of cockleshells, nearly tipping a bottle of Coke. The gray sea heaved upon the black sand beach below the café, one of the beaches where, he had told me, corpses sometimes washed up. We look for bodies regularly here, he'd said.

"I don't understand. Why would they think this? You told them the truth, didn't you?"

"They believe what they want to believe, and apparently, someone put two and two together in a certain way and came up with this."

"What two and two? You're scaring me."

"Well, you're a young American woman here on a foundation grant from the United States."

"For poetry."

"Yes, for poetry, but I don't think they believe this is the only reason you are here. They're paranoid these days and they no longer understand the Americans. For example, before the current ambassador arrived, your president nominated a woman about your age to be the next ambassador to El Salvador. My God, you should have seen the reaction. A woman!"

His pen wandered on the white paper protecting the red-checkered cloth, but the drawing was upside down: stick figures, corn plants, battleships.

"I don't see what this has to do with me."

"Well, at the same time, your president announced a new human rights policy. That really confused them. Years and years of keeping order by whatever means necessary, and in exchange, American military and economic aid, bank loans, investment, the works. And now? They have to be certified as respecting human rights in order to get this money. And unfortunately, they don't know what 'certified' means, much less how they are going to keep order while simultaneously respecting so-called human rights."

"About my mistaken identity. I need to know why they think this and what you're going to do about it, because . . ."

"I'm getting to that. Wait. Listen to what I'm saying, Papu. Put two and two together. For months after the former ambassador and political officer failed to get action on the Richardson case, and after their resignations were the first to be accepted by your new president, what happened? The embassy had no leadership for a good while. And during that time, the Americans nominated a girl."

"A woman, Leonel, they nominated a woman."

"Not according to the Salvadoran military, and right now we're trying to look at the situation from their point of view, remember? Think like a colonel."

Another bowl of cockles arrived with two more Cokes. We pulled the creatures with a small fork from their dark shells, and Leonel had a special way of doing this. He also liked to suck the briny liquid from the shells. He paused in his story to do this, so I lit a cigarette to calm my nerves.

"Where was I? Oh yes. After considering the possibility of a girl as ambassador, and trying to figure out if the gringos have lost their minds, you show up, at a time when, as far as they know, there is no new deputy chief of mission or whatever you call it. Maybe that person is you."

"Well, it's easy enough to check my fellowship, and that I'm a poet."

"They probably have checked. But to them, the foundation that gave you your fellowship used to be connected to mining interests in Latin America. And poetry? Many of them write poetry themselves. Ask them. It's quite bad, but they'd be happy to show it to you. And Yale. Your poetry book was published by Yale, which has educated a fair number of intelligence officers and agents."

"So what are you saying?"

"I'm saying that they think you might be the new something-or-other at the embassy, the new *jefa,* or at the very least, you work for intelligence. So this is why they want to talk to you."

"Who does?"

"More officers have asked me if you would meet with them."

"And what did you say? You said no, right?"

"What could I say? We're talking about the Salvadoran military now, remember, in a country that has been under dictatorship for more than fifty years. Say no to them? I don't think so."

He finished the cockles and licked his thumbs, then wiped his smudged glasses on a paper napkin.

"Don't worry. I think this development might even be useful."

"What does that mean?"

"Well, for a little while at least, you will be watched closely and your opinions will matter. They will be reading you for signs of what the Americans think. Maybe we can even convince them that this human rights policy is serious."

"Isn't it serious?"

"I don't know, but I have seldom seen the Americans serious about human rights unless it is politically convenient for them. So if this time they are truly interested, it's something new—to me, at least."

"I'm just going to tell them the truth—that I'm a poet and that's it."

"Precisely. And at that moment, they will know that what they suspected is true. There is a saying we have here that might even have originated in your own State Department. 'Never believe anything until it is officially denied.' If I were you, I would let them think whatever they wish to think."

"Did you have anything to do with this, Leonel? Tell me. Did you lead them to suppose I'm someone I'm not?"

"No, of course not. This fell into my lap, as your people like to say. But I could not have planned it any better. Let's go now," he said. "I have time to take you to El Imposible. Would you like that?"

The Impossible, yes, I thought. Whatever that means. Why not?

"Actually, it is no longer quite El Imposible. You will see."

We drove toward Cara Sucia through a green silence hung with fog, through a nowhere of highland coffee guarded by a blue volcano.

"Izalco," he said. "Remember? The volcano that erupted on the night of the uprising in '32? That volcano is sleeping now, but the fire in the earth is close to the surface here, Papu, all through this area there are geysers, fumaroles, and small volcanoes, some with lakes in their craters, some sleeping, some pretending to sleep. Over there is Apaneca, a classic volcano, such as children might draw, with a little puff of smoke coming out of the top. They used to bring the coffee harvest through this forest by mule train to the port of Acajutla, and they had to pass through the Hacienda El Imposible, and then across a gorge. They built rickety, makeshift bridges across this gorge that sometimes didn't hold. Mules, sacks of coffee, men and boys, all dropped into the gorge to their deaths when these bridges gave way. That is how the gorge came to be called El Imposible. The people would then build another bridge and the same thing would happen. Some of them held for a time, of course, which made matters worse because this made people think there was a chance."

I tried to imagine a wooden bridge letting go of a gorge wall and tipping the mule carts: mules running in the air, wild eyed, straw hats falling just above the men's heads, coffee sacks breaking open, and beans ticking into the sharp rocks at the bottom and forming hills of coffee.

"The government built a solid bridge in 1968 and announced that El Imposible was now 'possible.' I don't know about that. It's getting dark."

By then no one wanted to be out on the roads at night. Leonel opened a trunk in the back and retrieved a .357 Magnum and its clip. He leaned into the jeep, slid the clip into the weapon, and laid it beside a 9mm Smith and Wesson. Night fell to the volcanic peaks, and spilled into the valleys like ink.

"I've never seen anything like this," I whispered. "Even in the desert, even in Deià."

I was closer here to the equator than I had ever been, on a night gauzed with starlight.

"Leonel? Can we just stay here for a little while? I've just never seen . . ."

"I know, but the answer is no. Maybe I can show you the stars another time, in a place just as dark but safer than this. Let's go."

We drove slowly and without headlights as the moon rose so as not, he said, to draw attention. We were going to Santa Ana, or near there, to stay the night, in the town where Leonel was born and where Claribel Alegría had spent her childhood. What I knew about Santa Ana, I knew from her poems, a city whose poor children grew carnations in the crater of Ilamatepec, carrying bright sheaves of them down the mountain during harvest. This procession, seen from a distance, resembled lava flowing into the mountain's folds. I knew things like this, and that a man called Don Raimundo had magical powers to turn the electric lights throughout the town on and off, and that faces in the photo albums smelled of camphor. The Santa Ana of her poems was a city of neglected gardens, a closed-down pharmacy, abandoned houses, and dead birds.

"You wanted to know where I live. This is one place."

We had pulled in front of a wall. He turned the engine off and checked the side mirrors and the rearview.

It wasn't late, but it was dark, not as dark as the road from El Imposible, because here a few windows glowed among the palms. This was not an elegant *colonia*, nor quite a barrio. There were no armed guards near the gates on the one hand, and no *champas* hanging on to the ravines on the other—neither rich nor poor. I hadn't seen many such neighborhoods.

"Don't move. I'll be right back."

He left the weapons in the vehicle with me and disappeared down a narrow walkway. I picked up the smaller of the two guns, just to see how it felt in the hand, but when I saw him returning I quickly put it back. He opened the door and told me to gather my things and follow him, pushing the guns into his waistband. We went down a walk lined with banana palms. He unlocked the front door with a key he took as if by sleight of hand from a trellis of bougainvillea. Before holding the door open, he turned and said, "Be careful. And don't touch anything."

"What are these?"

There were objects wrapped in newsprint secured with tape standing upright on the floor in rows.

"Especially don't touch these. Come this way and step carefully."

He led me into the kitchen and began opening and closing cupboards.

"I'm trying to find some coffee for you for the morning. I'm sure we have some. Here, here it is, and here is the pot, and what else? Drink the water from this bottle but not from that spigot. We'll go out for breakfast."

He opened the refrigerator door to reveal empty, lit shelves.

"Yes, well, that makes sense," he said.

"What does?"

"Come this way."

He held back a curtain, clicked on another lamp beside a bed neatly made up with plumped pillows. There was a stack of extra blankets folded at the foot, and a poster of Che Guevara mounted over the headboard. Leonel pulled the bedcover back on one side, revealing beneath it an AK-47, which he placed high on top of the armoire, out of reach.

"Someone else also lives here," he said.

It would not have been the moment to ask him about this.

When I asked him about the Che Guevara poster, he said: "Yes, well, I have posters of Mussolini too, if the need arises. You can sleep here." He patted the bed. "I'll be back in the morning to pick you up. The bathroom is down that hall."

"Where are you going?"

"I have to meet with some people. I'll probably sleep at my brother's house."

He saw that I was looking at the top of the armoire.

"You won't need that," he said, adding, "don't put too many lights on, just try to sleep. This isn't my first choice for you, but we had to get off the road. Don't poke around, Papu."

"Why the telescope?"

A telescope was mounted on a tripod in front of a window.

"Yes, well, with that I can watch a fly crawling on the neighbor's roof tiles."

As soon as it was light I climbed from the bed. I went to the kitchen and filled the kettle. Someone had been taking good care of this place, I thought: Dishes and bowls had been piled up and nested by size on the open shelves, and there were watered plants and a basket of unripe mangoes. Books were everywhere, stacked and shelved, mostly in Spanish: *Cien años de soledad,* the poetry of Rubén Darío, and *A Short Account of the Destruction of the Indies.* The magazines were organized by volume and number, and covered Leonel's subjects: weaponry, motorcycles, and Formula One racing cars. Books on warfare and military strategy were also here: his Sun Tzu, his Carl von Clausewitz, and the diary of Ho Chi Minh. As expected, I also found a Machiavelli, held together with a rubber band. Leonel had written in the frontispiece: *There is no avoiding war; it can only be postponed to the advantage of others.*

The kettle startled me with a high whistle. I took the Clausewitz to the kitchen, where I poured the boiling water over coffee grounds and sat down to leaf through this book that Leonel had recommended back in San Diego.

This passage was underlined: "Many intelligence reports in war are contradictory; even more are false, and most are uncertain." Also this: "All action takes place, so to speak, in a kind of twilight, which, like a fog or moonlight, often tends to make things seem grotesque and larger than they really are." I would ask if I could borrow this from him.

For an hour or so, I wandered barefoot on the cold clay tiles, carrying the coffee from one place to another. The armoire held women's clothes and several pairs of shoes. There was a perfume bottle and one earring on the chest of drawers. The wooden soap dish in the bathroom smelled of jasmine. On a shelf of photographs beneath the bookcase I found framed pictures of Leonel with his daughters, of his daughters alone, of Leonel with a group of campesinos standing in front of a pickup truck, and the portrait of a beautiful young woman, not the one who had joined us the night of the accident, I didn't think, but a different one, and last, a black-and-white photograph that seemed fairly recent but also oddly historic: a slightly younger Leonel sitting beside an Asian man with a receding hairline. There were flags behind them and an electric fan off to the side. Leonel and this man were shaking hands while looking at the camera rather than at each other. I resolved to ask him about this man rather than about the woman, and then I heard footsteps.

"I see you didn't follow orders!" he boomed in his joking voice.

I quickly replaced the photograph and spun around.

"I was just—"

"You were poking around, Papu. But it's okay. Is there more coffee?"

"I can make more."

As I turned to the sink, he pulled out one of two chairs.

"Where is your—roommate?" I asked, as lightly as I could. I was still turned away from him.

"Papu, you know not to ask about people," but then he added: "She's been away."

He tipped three heaping spoons of sugar into his cup.

"We have something important to do today."

"Should I change?" I asked, hoping he'd say yes. I had, after all, slept in clothes that had already been to the sea and to El Imposible, and I felt stale in them, and disheveled.

"No, not yet. Wait until we get where we are going."

He took a sip and said something that didn't seem all that significant at the time, something about how the Salvadoran military had passed on the baton of power more or less peacefully for fifty years, that there hadn't been the bloody coups d'état that occurred in other countries, that the system here was set up in such a way that the military always closed ranks and protected its own. He also said that even if there were reformists among the officers, and even if they were inclined to support social change, unless there was an *apertura* in their ranks—

I must have looked at him strangely.

"An opening, like you have in a camera. Or you could think of it as a space, or a crack. Something that, how shall I say it, weakens the structure."

He turned to unlock a trunk on the floor. When he opened it slightly and closed it again, there was a whiff of petroleum in the air.

"What's that? I smell gas."

"That's Cosmoline. It's an anticorrosive for storing metal." Then he added, for no apparent reason: "Everything's fine."

Before we left the house, which he would now begin calling his, he took the AK-47 from atop the armoire and set it down again on the bed beneath the coverlet, smoothing it briskly and plumping the pillows. He then washed the coffee pot, dried the cups, and pushed the chairs back beneath the table, leaving everything just as it was.

"What are these?"

I was following him between the rows of objects wrapped in newspapers, on our way to the door.

"Be careful not to knock anything over."

Some of the objects were larger, leaning against the wall. By their shape, I guessed they were rifles.

"Sports trophies," he said, "some of them anyway."

"What sorts of sports trophies?"

"Don't ask so many questions."

"I thought I was supposed to pay attention to things."

"Just not my things, okay? Okay. Some are trophies for marksmanship. Others are weapons."

As we drove toward San Salvador, he expressed his disdain for the new American ambassador, predicted that war was coming, and condemned the oligarchs for their inhumanity. He also marveled that there were still ocelots roaming wild in El Imposible. Then, out of nowhere, he surprised me by mentioning the leadership of the guerrilla groups.

"Some are well meaning but lack knowledge of military strategy," he said quietly. "There are others I respect. A few might turn out no better than Pol Pot. Still, it is one thing to be—"

"I thought you said there were no guerrillas to speak of."

"I didn't say that. I said the Salvadoran military was exaggerating their number and strength to get more money from the U.S. government."

He downshifted behind a bright blue bus with a load tied to its roof that included a cage of hens. Two men stood on the narrow bumper in the back and held on as the bus swayed in its black smoke. Leonel looked over at me, seeming to have decided that it was safer not to pass.

"We have no Sierra Madre here," he said, in the voice of a father about to tell a story to a child. "We have no jungle. There is no place to hide. If the people take up arms, those arms must come from somewhere, and the ammunition from somewhere, and the fighters must be fed, and have continual access to potable water. Equipment and supplies must be moved from place to place without interruption and without detection. Fighters who are killed must be replaced. They must also be transported back to their homes or buried. Wounded fighters must receive medical attention. Doctors and nurses are needed, as well as surgical and medical supplies, and all of this must also be transported, again, continually, again without detection. Do you see how challenging this is, Papu?"

He kept taking his eyes from the road to see if I was paying attention.

"Revolutions do not go according to plan," he went on. "There must be thinkers among the commanders who understand the tactics of the battlefield, who can think strategically, and whose plans can be executed successfully so that they may command loyalty and respect. There must develop a strong bond among the fighters so that they will risk their lives for one another, not once but every day. And these fighters, who will nevertheless be hungry and thirsty, wounded and in pain, must respect the lives of the people, must not steal from them or harm them. And when the enemy is captured, he must also be respected and not harmed. Those captured must be housed and fed and clothed and treated for their wounds. None of this is easy," he said. "Armed uprising is one way to attempt to lessen repression and begin building a just society, Papu, but it is not the only way, and it is, without question, the most difficult, and when it is over, and let's say you have triumphed, you must guard with great vigilance against becoming an oppressor yourself. This is the greatest danger. If you are defeated," he went on, "that's another story. Waging a guerrilla war takes something more than waving red flags with hammers and sickles at the bull."

He wasn't exactly talking to himself, but he certainly seemed to have said all of this before, and possibly many times, but to whom?

"As Sun Tzu teaches us, 'the supreme art of war is to subdue the enemy without fighting.'"

"Leonel, are you a Marxist?" I wanted to know this because it seemed to matter so much here.

"Marx was a great social philosopher."

"But are you a Marxist?"

"I have told you, I'm not a religious man."

The bus had pulled to the shoulder to disgorge passengers. The women bent down to hoist the water *cántaros* back onto their heads, and the men swung large sacks over their backs.

Perhaps to dissociate myself from those he considered ideologues, I might have said something critical about the Soviet Union at that moment. It hadn't yet been a decade since the Warsaw Pact invasion of Czechoslovakia, and that is the lens through which I viewed the Soviets: from the kitchen table where Anna sat, listening to the radio with a handkerchief over her eyes. The Soviets had crushed the Prague Spring. They had sent their writers to the gulag.

"Remember that the USSR lost twenty million people during the Second World War. Twenty million. Leningrad was under siege for nearly nine hundred days. They were pulling wallpaper from the walls to eat the wheat paste. And, remember, they won that war in Europe for you. Without the Soviets, Hitler would have been victorious. What? You look surprised."

"No, not surprised. Well, maybe a little."

"Don't get caught up in the rhetoric. If the Salvadoran campesinos fight, and I think they will, they must win. If they do not win, they will suffer for another two hundred years. But to win, they must defeat the Salvadoran military, and if, in this engagement, they are perceived as so-called Communists, the Salvadoran military will have the backing of the largest military force in the world. So. If you are going to wave a red flag around, you had better know where is the bull."

W e were someplace I had never been. It was near the city, or perhaps it was a *colonia* within it, but the houses were set farther back from the street, behind gates and walls posted with guards, and through the gates, gardens and fountains flickered as we passed. He drove slowly, perhaps searching for a place he had never been. Finally, he seemed to reach his destination. He rolled down his window to show identification to a guard, then spoke to a second guard, and the gates slid open.

"What is this? Where are we?"

Water swirled from the mouth of a marble fish leaping into the air, about to be netted. The water veiled the air and rained into a fountain. More guards opened the doors for us. Leonel had put his weapons away somewhere but he asked these guards if I could bring my handbag and rucksack with me. They opened both, but without looking carefully inside nodded yes, I could bring them.

Leonel whispered, "Keep your purse with you at all times no matter what."

I had no idea what this meant, but I kept it.

"Where are we?" I asked again.

"This is the house of a high-ranking government official, *very* high. We have been invited to have lunch. Remember what I told you about your mistaken identity? I think that has something to do with this. Just listen, pay attention, and be calm, and oh yes, when you get inside, ask the wife if you might freshen up and change your clothes."

A maid admitted us, but the lady of the house arrived quickly, dressed in a cream bouclé suit, high-heeled pumps, and tasteful gold jewelry. She smiled, held out her hand, but did take notice of my clothes. Her husband was greeting Leonel.

"Forgive me. May I freshen up and change? We've had a long trip and I wasn't quite expecting—"

"Of course, the maid will show you. Help yourself to anything you need." She never stopped smiling.

That is how I found myself in the spacious bathroom, with its teak bench, Egyptian towels, a basket of milled soaps, and the shower with its many jets that sprayed water from all directions. Standing in the spray, soaping and rinsing, I realized what a comfort it was to have hot running water, and such was the pleasure that I lost track of time, or thought I had. When I rejoined the group, even Leonel looked surprised.

Fine, I thought. Let him see me in another light. Margarita's dress fit perfectly, as did her shoes. For the first time since arriving in El Salvador, I had put on makeup and had dabbed a bit of cologne on my wrist, the scent of the lady of the house.

Both men stood up, and Leonel introduced us with the man's official title. I shook his hand, keeping my purse in the crook of my other arm.

Lunch was served around a long table covered in linen and set with crystal stemware, china, and silver. The centerpiece was a sprig of white blossoms that smelled of oranges. Lunch was chicken. Two young maids served, rushing to and from the table. Leonel seemed relaxed and happy, and the conversation was light. Only an hour ago, he had been holding forth about guerrilla warfare. I tried to catch his eye but couldn't. When the small, light clouds of caramel flan served for dessert had been eaten, the gentleman of the house rose from his chair and set his napkin on the seat cushion. Leonel also stood, so I reached for my purse, which I had tucked under my chair.

"Shall we?"

We were led into a living room, where a large Persian rug, the pale blue of the volcanoes in the distance, covered the tile floor. Leonel was offered the large, comfortable chair and I was asked to sit beside the high-ranking official on a long white sofa, from where I could see the foyer, walled with mirrors and lit by a chandelier. Two guards in military uniform and white gloves stood on either side of the entrance door, their reflections multiplied in the mirrors.

When, during the past few weeks, Leonel had taken me to meet other high-ranking members of the government, we usually talked in cramped army offices, where a colonel presided in his dark olive uniform with epaulets, his hands folded upon a dossier he'd been reading, his brow glowing in the close air. In these conversations, I listened to a briefing about the worsening situation, heard praise heaped upon my country and its historically close relationship with the officer corps, along with muted expressions of disappointment at the recent deterioration of that relation. These usually included the conditions under which American aid might again be restored and, one hoped, increased so as to "meet current needs." I would try to be attentive, but usually said very little, and at the end, the officer in question often expressed confidence that we "understood each other."

This was something different. This high-ranking official was an elegant civilian in a well-cut suit and silk tie, gold watch, and cuff links, whose wife, now in another room, was fashionably thin, well coiffed, and gracious. The house was at once airy and opulent. Through a wall of sparkling window glass, the volcanoes rested on the distant horizon.

One of the maids brought a tray of cups and a silver pot with its handle wrapped in a linen cloth. Leonel, who seemed almost at ease for a change, asked after the man's extended family, who seemed also to be involved in the cultivation of coffee, if I understood him correctly, and Leonel apparently knew several family members. All was well with all of them. Soon, however, the man changed the subject to matters that concerned the current government: a pending international bank loan and the recent strain in relations with the United States.

"Tell me, Leonel, what is it that they want?" the man asked. This question seemed not to be rhetorical. "What can we do to improve the situation?"

Now he was looking directly at me, but Leonel said, "I can help you with that." And he began to talk about Richardson, and rather than wave the subject away as several of the military officers had done, this man listened intently. Leonel didn't start at the beginning to tell the story, as he had in the past, so he must have known that the man was well aware of the details. Rather, he began with the futile efforts to solve Richardson's disappearance, emphasizing how hard the previous ambassador and his political officer had worked, suggesting that Washington remained seriously concerned about the case, and perhaps this accounted for the cooling of relations, and it might be why Washington was sending strange signals to the Salvadoran government, such as nominating a young woman to be ambassador and instituting a policy demanding respect for human rights, whatever that might mean.

The man leaned forward, resting his arms on his thighs, and clasped his hands together in the empty space between them.

"This shouldn't be so difficult," he said. "We should be able to take care of this."

"The problem is Colonel Chacón," Leonel pressed, as if he were diagnosing a minor repair, "because it seems that Richardson might not have been the petty thief he was pretending to be, and if this is so, and I'm not saying that it is, there is only one course of action. You have to deal with Chacón. You have to send a signal to the Americans that you are serious."

The man leaned back and turned toward me.

"Is this the case? Do you agree?"

I don't know what I was thinking in that moment, for it was only that, a moment. The name Chacón had come to mean butcher, with images of thawed human limbs in the mouths of dogs. I nodded, rather than saying yes. I nodded yes and transferred my purse to my lap to signal that the conversation had come to an end.

"You are very young to be doing what you are doing," he said, and smiled.

Somehow, I knew not to smile back.

"Please wait here, I have something I would like to give to you—a gift, as a token of our friendship."

As he disappeared down the hall, Leonel walked over to the wall of glass, as if he wanted to take in the view. The official's wife slid in beside him, laughing and touching his arm while pointing to something in the distance. When he turned to rejoin me with his back to her, he was no longer smiling and his eyes were grave.

The man returned, holding a small wooden plaque with El Salvador's coat of arms: a triangle and, within it, five volcanoes, a sun falling upon them, a rainbow, and a cobalt sea, the whole of it surrounded by flags raised on warrior spears and hung with feathers, encircled by a laurel wreath.

He said something about my purse, almost jokingly, that I "certainly kept it close."

We all shook hands. The wife returned to walk me through the mirrors to the front entrance. Our Hiace had been pulled into the circular drive for us, and the guards were opening the doors. Our host stood with his hands behind his back and his feet slightly apart, as a uniformed officer would stand, rather than a man in a finely tailored suit.

Leonel started the engine and when his back was to the house, he turned to me and put his finger to his lips. We drove in silence for several kilometers. Leonel checked the rearview mirror frequently. He turned the volume high for the pop song whose lyrics bounced in the air on a refrain having to do with taking chances. *Take a chance on me,* the group sang over and over. We stopped at a machinist's shop with its security gate open to the street, and he got out to talk to a man bending over an engine, and then we went to a small house I hadn't seen before, and he emerged with a satchel. We drove again.

When Leonel was lost in thought, he often pinched his mustache between thumb and forefinger, or else he dug under his nails with a tiny screwdriver used for repairing eyeglasses. If we were alone in a room and he was truly deep in thought, he would take his weapons apart and put them back together. But it was unlike him not to talk for such a long stretch of time.

"Leonel, what is it?"

"We just did something."

"What? What did we do?"

"You were there. Now, either he believed us or he didn't. Or he was pretending to believe us. We are either going to see some results or we'll be lucky to be alive at this time tomorrow. You can't stay at Margarita's tonight, and I can't go where I was going. We have to do something else."

"What? What else?"

"We have to stay someplace where we'll be safe, at least for a little while. By the way, you did very well back there. I couldn't have asked for better."

"Did what well?"

He looked at me. "Come on, you *know* what you did. That took guts. Now let's get out of here."

W̲e reached the edge of the city, or what felt to be the edge, and he pulled in beneath a sign that read EL EMPERADOR. Behind the building, there was a row of garages with some of their doors wide open. We pulled into one of them and the door closed behind us.

"We're staying here tonight," he said. "Welcome to El Emperador, flophouse of the colonels. There is another one across the street just like it, El Conquistador, but I prefer this one."

He opened the door as if he were at home, to a clean room with a large bed and two pillows propped against the headboard. There was a night table, but little else. A window near the ceiling on one side framed a walled garden of palm fronds darkening in the twilight. Leonel picked up the phone on the night table and asked for two more pillows, a blanket, and two Cokes with ice.

"Do you want anything else?" he asked, cupping the phone's receiver.

As I wasn't sure what sort of things I could want, I said no.

After a few minutes, there was a knock, and Leonel opened a small cupboard door in the wall. Behind the door, a young woman's arm passed pillows through to him, along with a folded blanket. After another knock, two opened Coke bottles and two glasses of ice swiveled into view. Leonel took them, left a stack of bills in their place, and closed the door. As soon as he did this, music filled the room. I remember the song playing over and over that night: "Feelings" by Morris Albert, set to the tune of *"Pour toi,"* an older French melody by Louis Gasté. This version had Spanish lyrics.

Díme. Solamente díme. Tell me. Just tell me. Over and over.

"Now you understand why we have extra pillows—so you can put one over your head to drown this out."

"Can't we just ask for it to be turned off?"

"No, my dear, we cannot, because we aren't actually supposed to sleep here. This is not a hotel for sleeping, and for that very reason, it suits our purposes perfectly."

Leonel sat on the edge of the bed and loaded the .357 Magnum, and then spilled the rounds of the 9mm onto the night table.

"I call this place the Chicken House," he said, reloading those same rounds. "If you've ever been in the sort of building where hens roost."

"I have, yes, when I was young my mother would take us to visit a woman we called the egg lady. They're called coops in English, not houses."

"Well, then you know that if someone makes a loud noise in a chicken house, there's quite a racket, with feathers flying and hens scattering in every direction. And, for example, if someone was to fire a weapon in a place like this, every colonel and lieutenant colonel in here would be running to the parking lot, pulling up their boxer shorts, with their mistresses right behind them."

He poured Coke into the glasses.

"This place has a certain, shall we say, specialized clientele. No one knows who might be sleeping in the next room, if we can use the word 'sleeping' loosely. Therefore, no one is going to fire a weapon in this place and be responsible for having a military officer caught with his pants down, so to speak. It's all very discreet. Once the garage doors are closed, the cars are hidden from view. Not even the girl who took our money knows who we are. We're safe. I think. However."

"However, what?"

"If something should happen I want you to put your back against that wall over there and keep as flat against the wall as you possibly can. Don't make a sound. I'll take care of the rest. Or you could slide under the bed if there's room."

I reached over the side of the bed and felt the distance between the frame and the floor.

"There isn't."

"I didn't think so."

He handed me one of the Cokes and touched it to his own. *"Salud.* Remember your Machiavelli, Papu. *Never was anything great achieved without danger."*

We lay side by side on the stiff bed in the dark.

"Leonel? Before you put the pillow over your head . . ."

"What?"

A moon had slipped among the palms in the window.

"What happens when they realize that the Americans don't actually care about this?"

"Well, do you think they don't?"

"If they did, I'm sure I wouldn't be the one making this clear to the Salvadorans."

"You're right. That's an excellent observation. But don't worry. No one is going to admit having listened to a poet. That's your protection. Now try to get some sleep."

He put both pillows behind his head, closed his eyes, and folded his hands over his stomach. The moonlight slid onto the grip of the 9mm and silvered the ice in the empty Coke glass. I couldn't find a way to position the pillows so as to block the music. The *"Díme"* version of "Feelings" played again, followed by "Tonight's the Night" by Rod Stewart in English. I must have fallen asleep because the next thing I knew, Leonel was bolt upright with a gun cupped in both hands, pointed at the ceiling.

"What is it?" I whispered.

He touched two fingers to his mouth twice.

The music had stopped. I thought it would go on all night, but there was no music now. A palm leaf ticked against the window in the wind. Leonel motioned for me to go to the wall on the side that would position me behind the door to the garage. I pressed my back against the wall as if it might be possible to disappear into the cinder blocks. There seemed to be a bird trapped in my throat. A hummingbird. There was nothing I would not have done to have been somewhere else in that moment. Leonel turned his head so that one ear was trained on the garage. I thought of my mother and father, at home in Michigan in their bed. They didn't know where I was. No one did.

Leonel turned, planted his feet on the tiles, and rose without a sound, all the while holding the muzzle toward the ceiling. He met my eyes and once again raised his finger to his lips. He turned the knob and pushed the door to the garage open, keeping himself against the wall on the other side. I flattened myself to the wall behind the door, but I could see Leonel through the hinges. He reached into the garage with his left arm and flicked the light.

"It's nothing, Papu. You can go back to bed."

"What happened?"

"I thought I heard something. Never mind."

We lay side by side again, door closed, light off. The wind slapped the palm broadly against the glass.

"It might have been wind. Whatever it was, it woke me up. You were very calm, by the way. That surprises me. Other times you have seemed easily rattled."

"Yes, well, the worse things get, the calmer I am. I must have thought they were pretty bad."

"Actually, they might well have been. We're lucky."

"Well, try not to scare me, okay?" We were whispering for some reason.

"Let's be clear. I was not trying to scare you."

"Well, you did. Scare me."

"I'm supposed to say I'm sorry at this moment but I'm not going to say it. You know what the good Christian base communities call the 'preferential option for the poor'?" His hands were again folded on his stomach and he was drifting off. As if reading my thoughts, he added that if we are to share the fate of the poor, we must be willing to share their justifiable fear of dying.

In the morning, we went to a shuttered ice cream parlor for coffee, and I said I wanted to call Margarita, so Leonel asked the proprietor if I could use the phone.

Margarita would not yet have left with the girls for school. It rang several times.

"*¡Hola!*"

"*¿Diga?*"

"*Habla Carolina—*"

"*Un momento.*"

After a while, I heard footsteps, and then the sound of a receiver's being fumbled or dropped and retrieved.

"*¿De parte de quién?*"

"Margarita, it's me."

"Where are you? Do you want me to come and get you?"

"No, no. I'm fine. I just called to say . . ."

"Carolyn?"

"I'm here. I just—"

"*Un momento, Carolina.*"

She had muffled the mouthpiece and was talking to someone in the background, and then I heard the receiver come back to her. I was trying not to cry, but I wasn't sure why, and I didn't want Leonel to see this, but Margarita heard it.

"Carolyn, what is wrong? Can you talk?"

"No. I mean, not right at this moment."

"Are you coming?"

I didn't know if I should answer this over the phone. I had begun to wonder what I should say and not say, to whom and when.

"Margarita—"

"It is all right, Carolyn. I understand. You can't talk. See you soon. *Ciao!*"

The line went dead. I blotted my face with my sleeve and went back to the table. In the Hiace, I saw myself in the side mirror and knew that he would have noticed but had not remarked on my swollen eyes.

"Let's go to the coffee finca," he said. "I need to gather my thoughts."

———◆———

The harvest was coming to an end, so everyone was off in the coffee. The bicycle-powered water drum idled in the shade, with the metal backpacks arranged in a row beside it. There was a whining sound in the metal swing-set frame that held the drum as the wind passed through it.

"I have some things to take care of here, so why don't you write for a while," he said almost gently, "write some poetry."

Write some poetry, I whispered to myself when he had left. Just like that, I thought, pick up the pen and open the notebook to a blank page.

Draw, Antonio, draw, said Michelangelo to one of his apprentices. *Draw and do not waste time.* In my mind, I changed this to: *Write. Write, and do not waste time.* Leonel would have liked this. In the back of this particular notebook I had copied something from Paul Valéry: *Provided the pen touches the paper and is full of ink, and I am bored and abstracted . . . I create!*

But at this moment the pen touched paper and bled as I was neither bored nor abstracted. A poet had once cautioned me not to live a life that was more vibrant and intense than my inner life, that inner and outer must at least be kept in balance, but if one was to gather strength over the other, let it be the life within. Beneath that, I had copied this from the French Resistance poet René Char: *the poem rising from its well of mud and stars, will bear witness, almost silently, that it contained nothing which did not truly exist elsewhere, in this rebellious and solitary world of contradictions.*

Later I would find something written in pencil in my notebook:

walking in a field in the *campo:* the light, the day, sky, wind, a man drinking from a dried and hollowed gourd, another leaning on a hoe, a woman with an aproned skirt over her trousers, the light, the rattle of sorghum and its flower, a spray of seeds resembling barley, and then we come upon something that begins with flies, the soft drone of a squadron of flies, as if the field were humming to itself.

In the same notebook, I found this, also written in pencil:

People from the countryside are coming into the cities some live between road and the fence with no place to relieve themselves houses made from shipping crates stamped This Side Up stamped Maytag Harvest Gold roofs weighted with rubber tires walls lighted by coals set on fire in lard cans punched with holes the light dances on walls and coals give off sparks like the salt of stars in the fields cane smoke blackens the air coffee ripens on the high slopes red coffee cherries in white mist it is the time of bloody stool in the ditch of maggots in wounds of flies in the clinic bodies found by the roadside are covered with lime no one wants to eat the fish from Lake Ilopango anymore the fish have been eating the dead.

And that is where it ends, words strung together into notes that are not a poem. I don't remember when I began writing this way in pencil, or why, other than pencil lead is faint on the paper, so the words evanesce, waiting to be erased—however, rather than using the eraser, I usually cross out unwanted words and phrases. Whole sentences crossed out. In the notebooks from El Salvador, entire pages are struck through or left blank, not only at the end of the book but within, as if I couldn't continue without turning to a new page. I wrote down in pencil what I saw, what I heard, and was careful not to use people's real names. There are no addresses or telephone numbers, and my birth name is nowhere to be found inside, so any lost notebooks remain lost. The others are here with me. I have heard it said that to write is to dream on paper. In these notebooks from the time of El Salvador there are no dreams.

W RITTEN IN PENCIL:

Sometimes in the countryside he said you will come upon a tree that has been decorated with strips of paper rags and garbage this is because the tree failed to bear fruit in its good year the people tie things to the tree to make it feel ashamed to embarrass it in front of other trees so that the next year fruit will come one day in the *campo* in an area where there had been some killings there was a tree with human skin and hair hanging from its branches it looked like rags and garbage the soldiers who had done this were from the *campo* they knew what it meant to hang things on a tree.

On Sunday, Leonel came for me early, saying that there was something important, and yes, everything was important, but this was more so, and I should wear something "appropriate," but appropriate for what? Church. The man he was taking me to see was the most important person in the country, and more than that: Without this man, standing where he stands, saying what he does, without him there would be no voice for the people whatsoever. There is no one, no one more courageous than this man, he assured me, and you will not ever again in your life encounter anyone like him.

"Are you coming too?"

"No. I never enter churches."

"Why not?" He was already climbing into the Hiace.

"I told you, I'm not a religious man."

The streets surrounding the cathedral were thronged, as were the steps leading to its doors. The Mass was to be celebrated today by the archbishop, Monseñor Oscar Romero.

"It will be crowded inside. Try to get close to him. I'll be here when you come out. Stand on the steps and I will find you. *Ciao.*"

This is how I first saw Monseñor Oscar Romero: from a distance, over the heads of the congregation in an unfinished cathedral, in his white vestments before a spray of microphones, giving a homily ending with a litany of the names of those disappeared or found dead that week, some of whom were in coffins lined up at the altar, with windows cut into the lids to reveal their faces, except the mutilated. In shafts of sunlit dust sent from the louvers of the two bell towers we stood, shoulder to shoulder: women in scarves or mantillas, men holding their straw hats, children sitting along the altar rail as the homily was broadcast to thousands of radios throughout the country, to machine shops, bodegas, to pickup trucks, and the battery-operated radios in the villages. When his homily giving guidance and counsel came to an end, Monseñor walked toward the coffins with an aspergillum, sprinkling holy water on the dead, and then he walked through the congregation, and we parted to make a path for him, the water sprinkling down on our bowed heads, as it had on the coffins. Later I would understand that here the dead and the living were together, and those who stood alive before him, he was blessing in advance.

W e need to rest," Leonel said, when he found me at the bottom of the cathedral steps. "We're going to Guatemala for a few days. There's someone I want you to meet, and there are certain things that it might be time to show you."

"You don't take rests."

"Relatively speaking, then. You'll see. I think you will be pleasantly surprised."

He assured me that he had let Margarita know where I was going.

The Hiace was packed inside almost to the roof, to which I had contributed only a rucksack and a small duffel bag. I didn't ask What is all this? I knew not to ask and, moreover, no longer wanted to know such things. It was a beautiful day. That was good enough. Only one strange thing happened. We were driving along, listening to music, and Leonel suddenly braked, backed up, and turned around to drive in the direction we had come, saying he'd seen a green tree branch lying in the road, and branches with green leaves were a sign of something, often a warning sign. When I asked what the sign meant there was the usual silence, and then he finally said: "There is some kind of roadblock again, maybe military. Or something else."

"How do you know this?" I asked, to which, of course, he said nothing.

He pushed in another cassette, this time of Silvio Rodríguez playing the song "¿A Dónde Van?"—a tender song about the transience of all things that asks where everything and everyone is going.

"We're going to a beautiful place where you can forget about things for a while. Besides, it's a good time for us to be out of El Salvador."

The next song was *Madre*, a love song for mothers, or at least that's what I had thought as I'd listened, before Spanish became clearer to me. Taking my bare feet from the glove box I sat up to press REWIND. The song ended with *Madre, en tu día,/Tus muchachos barren minas de Haiphong*, and then he repeated the line, as he repeated all the others.

"Haiphong," I shouted above the wind. "It's about the mining of the waters of Haiphong."

"So you know about that?" Leonel called back, sounding impressed. "The song is not about Mother's Day. What do you know about Haiphong?"

We were close to the border now, in Ahuachapán, with here and there a *champa* with a wisp of cook smoke, but I was elsewhere, one moment standing on the sidewalk in Michigan, for the first time watching rather than marching, wearing the army jacket that my former husband had given me, with the name FORCHE sewn above the breast pocket. It was May but still cold, and one moment the crowd was chanting to stop the mining of the waters of Haiphong, and the next I felt a sharp blow to my head, and then I was in a white tent set up by medical students, and there was blood spatter on the army jacket. When I put my hands to my face, they came away covered with sticky blood.

Leonel glanced sideways from the road to me. He asked what was wrong and I shook my head *Nothing*.

Could I tell him now that I wasn't quite the person I seemed to be? I was alone in my life for a reason, and it was for this same reason that I preferred long-distance relationships or none at all. It was perhaps the reason why I had agreed to accept his invitation to come here, and to see another Vietnam "from the beginning," although I no longer believed that what he was showing me was, as he had suggested, "the beginning of another Vietnam."

IT IS 1969, SUMMER. I'M NINETEEN YEARS OLD AND HAVE TAKEN A WEEKEND away from my summer job as a nursing assistant in a convalescent home to visit one of my friends at the college I attended, an hour north of where I grew up. My friend lived in a group house in the Grove Street neighborhood, where antiwar students lived, along with deserters, draft dodgers, and young, would-be revolutionaries. Pot laced the air. Everything was new to me as I had lived only at home before that, and for one year in a college dormitory far across campus, where some of the football players and the students bound for fraternities and sororities were housed.

Now I was in the midst of people near my age and even somewhat older, living on their own together in large stucco and wood-framed houses and bungalows. My friend Linda had a lover who was visiting her from Harvard then, so she didn't have much time for me. I understood this. She also knew that I was still a virgin, and therefore a little young to be with her in her present surroundings. With twelve years of Catholic-school indoctrination behind me, I was on the verge of adulthood. Linda felt protective, I think, but she also wanted to find something for me to do while I was there, someone to "be with," and she knew just the person.

One afternoon, I'm holding a box of kitchen matches. One by one they don't strike. I'm trying to light a gas burner on the stove in Linda's communal kitchen. The gas is hissing out below a black cast-iron grate. Behind me, a man is walking into the kitchen to be introduced to me.

The box of kitchen matches explodes in my left hand, the matches catching all at once in a burst of fire over the stove. The man entering grabs a kitchen towel and tosses it over this fire, then leaps to turn the gas knob off. He spins me around and thrusts my palm under cold running water in the sink, then makes me hold ice cubes wrapped in a napkin. His long blond hair falls to the shoulders of his army shirt. It is olive colored but faded, and over the breast pocket is the name FORCHE. Later I would ask him why there is no accent over the *e* on his pocket.

"The army doesn't do that," he'd said. "The army doesn't do a lot of things."

I was still in high school when this man, whom I would soon marry, crossed the South China Sea to CủChi, and made his way along the trails of the Filhol rubber plantation and the Ho Bo Woods; when he killed his first man, whose body was thrown into a small trailer hooked to the back of a jeep and taken to base camp, where people put lit cigarettes in the dead man's hand and placed a beer can in the huge hole in his skull and then laughed and took pictures. A man in his company cut off ears and kept an ear garden with little crosses, and the man I would marry climbed down into tunnels with a flashlight, a bayonet, and a pistol, and was never so afraid in his life. There is more, of course, but I wanted to stop thinking.

My own moment had nothing to do with CủChi or Pleiku, where he later helped build a base camp for the 4th Infantry, or with other events that were important to my fellow university students, such as the Christmas bombing of Hanoi and the carpet bombing of Cambodia. Those were important, but for me the moment came after everything else had happened and I was no longer living with him in the firebase he had constructed in our attic apartment by stringing blue Christmas lights along the walls and taping playing cards to the blades of a rotating fan to mimic the sound of a chopper muffled by clouds.

My moment was the mining of Haiphong Harbor in May 1972, when I was neither marching toward the police phalanx nor chanting anything at all, but merely standing on the sidewalk upwind from the tear gas, a month from my college graduation, watching what might seem to be a holiday parade if viewed from a distance.

"I can't talk," I said, waving my hand near my ear. "It's too loud."

By the time he might ask me again about Haiphong, I will have thought of something to say.

———◆———

We crossed at Las Chinamas on the Salvador-Guatemala border, which involved going into an office and showing identification, then waiting while several uniformed border guards considered whether to give us entry visas, or whatever the documents were that we were given, including permission for the Hiace to enter Guatemala. Leonel had obviously been through this process many times, not with these guards, but with others, who were all, he said, more or less the same. *A zebra is a zebra,* he would say. *Zebras have stripes. A guard is a guard. You just have to know how to talk to them.*

Once across, he asked me to notice how the campesinos walking along the roads were dressed, which I thought odd, until I saw that from the border onward, there were no more campesinos. The people walking the roadside, mostly women, bearing *cántaros* filled with water, were Mayans dressed in many-colored *huipiles* and head wraps, the men in purple-and-white-striped trousers and bright woven shirts.

"But they aren't campesinos," I said, "they're Mayans."

"K'ichi' Maya, but yes, and the campesinos on the Salvadoran side are Indians too, Nahuat and Pipil—Lenca in the east. Some few still wear their native dress and speak their native languages, but most do not—1932 changed many things, Papu. In the aftermath of the massacre, the people burned or buried their native clothes and adopted Western dress. They stopped speaking their native languages and began to use Spanish. And why? Because to be Nahuat or Pipil or Lenca was to be Communist, complete with Carlos Marx and orders from Moscow. It is difficult to imagine now, but 1932 drew the border between Guatemala and El Salvador as indelibly as it is drawn on most maps. We're talking about cultural death. Forced assimilation. Now you will see something of what El Salvador once was, at least in that respect. There are other views of this history, of course, but this is mine."

Leonel had chosen a small, old hotel in Antigua, an hour away, with a fireplace in every room. He would be right next door, he assured me, and if I needed anything, I could pick up the old-fashioned heavy black phone and ask. Logs and kindling had been stacked, and because night had already come, the bed was turned down and the curtains were closed. Sleep, he'd said. I changed into a nightgown, splashed water on my face, and was given a start when I saw myself in the mirror, tired and drawn. I had become an older woman.

With the lights off, the room was utterly dark. I felt for my cigarettes and lit a match, the flare illuminating the blackened, hand-hewn rafters along the ceiling. I wouldn't sleep much, as it turned out. I would strike another match to the fireplace and sit on the floor, close to the fire, hunched over, tending the flames with the metal poker and opening the flood of thoughts released by the name of a port city in Vietnam. I had not allowed myself to think about this in a long time.

"It would have been beautiful," my former husband said, "that trip through the jungle in the highlands to Pleiku—were it not for people continually shooting at us, and hitting mines that threw tracks off the tanks, and getting mortared while attempting to change the track parts. It would have been beautiful. Water buffaloes standing in silver rice paddies.

"When we arrived at Pleiku, it was different. There were Montagnards to help fill sand bags, but our base was continually fired upon," he said. "That is where the pictures of me in the torn uniform were taken. Claymore mines were always going off on the perimeters. We carted off the dead and then the night filled with light flares and fire missions. It was always wet. I was always scared. One night we had both tracks blown off the tank and I was left to call in artillery strikes, even though I had flunked out of officer candidate school, and howitzers were pounding us within thirty meters.

"I was sent to Taipei for a week of R&R, and after a week of drinking, I had to go back to the war, excuse me, 'the conflict.' We were some of the first soldiers sent to Vietnam, and we were young, and we kept killing and counting. Our commanding officers loved nothing more than body counts."

At one point, I remembered him telling me that his armored personnel carrier had been hit and he was trapped inside, the only soldier not dead in that can of death, and after that he was assigned as door gunner on a Huey helicopter charged with picking up the wounded. He remembered a tarp blowing from the corpses of two men who no longer had faces. None of this was unusual, he said, nothing that happened to him was different from what happened to anyone else.

I WOKE UNCOVERED ON THE BED. THE FIRE WAS OUT, AND LEONEL WAS KNOCK-ing on the door, asking through it if I might rouse myself and meet him outside.

After standing in the shower for a while, I dressed and went out wet headed to the Hiace where he was reading a topographical map.

"How did you sleep?" he asked cheerily.

"All right."

"Get in, then."

It was cold, and the sun had not yet cleared the ridge of mountains, but the east was scudded with fuchsia and cantaloupe cloud pack, and a few faint stars were still visible.

"We have to get to Chichi early," he said. "It's market day."

"I need coffee first," I said.

"Did you sleep at all?"

"Yes, I slept. I just need coffee."

"Don't tell me you can't wait for just a while. If you can't, you're addicted."

"Yes, well, you grow the stuff. You should know."

"It's meant to be enjoyed in moderation, my dear." He was holding his pipe away from his mouth to say this.

"Why don't you just smoke that thing? I'm certainly going to smoke if you don't mind."

"I see we did not sleep well. Never mind. You'll get coffee in Chichi. It's about two hours from here."

"So, not far then," I said, blowing smoke out the window.

"No. Considering the terrain we will cover, it isn't far at all."

He looked over at me but I looked straight ahead.

"All right, then, I'll get you some coffee," and after a few kilometers, he pulled into a fast-food breakfast place on the edge of Guatemala City and returned with a cup of instant.

"Okay now?"

I would have said no to instant under any other circumstances, but instead held the hot paper cup against my cheek and felt soothed.

"Yes, okay."

It was still early when we reached Chichicastenango, but the cobbled streets were crowded with people, mostly Mayans, their wares spread before them on blankets: baskets of ground herbs and tied bundles of dried herbs, clayware, burlap sacks of beans, mottled, pink and black, woven tote bags, kitchen utensils, sandals with soles made from tire treads, pyramids of mango and papaya, weavings both hanging and folded, painted masks and woven belts, bananas and pots of food stewing on grates, corn turned above coals and rubbed with limes, painted ceramics, and over the whole of it hung a gray haze of smoke from copal burning in braziers on the stone steps of the Iglesia de Santo Tomás, bright white in the sun and built, according to Leonel, on the foundation of a pre-Columbian temple. We climbed its eighteen steps, one for each month of the Mayan calendar, toward what once was a Mayan temple and was now a Roman Catholic church, as it had been since 1545, but don't kid yourself, he'd said, without elaborating as to what this kidding of myself might mean.

We climbed and he pushed open one of the two great wooden doors and we were inside, standing in the coolness before several pallets covered with rose petals and burning tapers affixed to the pallets by their own melted wax. The people were removing burned stubs and lighting new ones, sprinkling the petals with a liquid and strewing more petals from a basket, all the while whispering in their language.

"This is not something Catholic," Leonel said quietly. "This is the *costumbre*. There are Catholic elements, but on a deeper level, this is much older."

The people who were tending the candles and roses seemed not to mind our presence, but there was no sense that we would be welcomed to light candles ourselves. In and out they went, stopping for visits to the pallets, where, according to Leonel, they placed their problems and sorrows.

From the high steps, the market stalls were a flotilla roofed by market tents like sails, white and hard to the wind, luffing at the edges, bright and taut, and beneath them people moved like schools of fish in the swells of commerce.

He took me to a place called Cofradía de Pascual Abaj, where ceremonies were performed by a K'ichi' Mayan *cofradía,* which he translated as "brother in a religious sense," who builds a fire to a Mayan deity, growing the blaze by spewing *aguardiente* on the fire from his mouth.

"Alcohol," Leonel whispered, "very strong. It is said that writings carved here record the actions of the god Tohil, who presided at the time of the Spanish conquest, and whose name might be translated as 'obsidian' or 'rain' or 'tribute' but is also understood as 'fate.' He was among the first of the gods the Spaniards attempted to eradicate, but, as you can see," Leonel said, "without success. But the god of fate, Papu, can you imagine! They wanted to eradicate even the god of what the Mayans were destined to become."

We walked back into the market, where he seemed to know some of the vendors, who showed us many different weavings, some brought from behind the counters, where they were kept because of their finer quality. There were woven bags, *huipiles,* and other pieces. The textiles are texts, he whispered, where stories are written concerning wildcats, horses, and birds, both colorfully plumed and plain, and also dogs, flowering trees, and corn plants, snakes, antlered deer, and geometric designs that might refer to lightning or maps, tilled fields or stars. Every figure speaks, if one knows how to read the weave.

The shops and all fabrics within them smelled faintly of woodsmoke. Leonel asked if I would like something, and when I said no, thank you, he chose a black-and-white woven bag for me, such as the one he carried that first day in San Diego, but this one had a jaguar standing on its hind legs.

"This is for you. No, I insist. This is your bag, because it has the jaguar. Someday I will tell you why. Mine, if you remember, also has the jaguar."

He took me deeper into the market, past the street of tomatoes, to an alley of flat iron griddles where women were patting tortillas between their palms.

We ate there, in the fog of griddle smoke, and in the next alley, bright and open to the air, he bought pink clouds of cotton candy. I didn't want mine, so he ate both, followed by roasted corncobs with salt and lime and then he said it was time to go because we had to meet with someone.

We drove again on dirt roads up into the hills, under a moon like the light at the bottom of a well, the dark air laced with woodsmoke.

"I have an adviser here. You might think of him as a teacher. I've been with him for a while. We first met some years ago after an earthquake, when I came here to help set up a camp for refugees. He's quite old now. He doesn't speak much Spanish—a little, but not much. I had to learn some K'ichi' in order to talk to him, so I will translate for you."

"I'm going to meet him?"

"He's been expecting you in a certain way, so yes. But we might have to wait for him to wake up. He's often asleep when I arrive. I almost think he does that on purpose, but never mind."

Leonel held a small flashlight, spraying a wedge of light on the ground leading to the house. A woman held the door open, but didn't smile. We crossed through the candlelit dark and when my eyes adjusted, I saw that the house consisted of one large room, with weavings folded and stacked almost to the ceiling along one wall. At the far end, there was a fire pit with a grate, a basin, and metal pans hanging from nails. An old man was seated against the wall near a hammock that rocked by itself, as if someone had just left it.

"That's his daughter," Leonel said in English, nodding toward the woman, who now stood grimly with her arms crossed over her chest. She waved us toward a wooden chair and a stool that had been positioned near the old man. Leonel was too large to sit on the stool so I took it. The old man hadn't yet said anything. His hair was straight and white, he had no teeth, and his skin was dry and grooved, but deep in their sockets his eyes shone as if he carried a lamp in his skull. He leaned toward Leonel and whispered.

"He welcomes you," Leonel said. I nodded, but no one was smiling here, so I didn't smile.

There was silence. The daughter stood her ground, arms folded, jaw set. Leonel spoke in halting K'ichi'. The old man leaned forward. Still nothing. More K'ichi'.

"He's seeing who you are," Leonel said. "That's what he does."

"Is his daughter angry we're here?"

"No. If she was, she wouldn't have let us in, believe me. But don't expect her to make jokes with you. Now stop speaking English. They can't understand and we don't want to show disrespect."

The old man seemed surprised at something Leonel said then and even I could tell he was asking for clarification.

"It's about your horse," Leonel said in Spanish.

"¿Mi caballo? Qué caballo?"

"El caballo rojo," he said with exasperation, and the old man nodded firmly. Red horse, I thought. I had no idea what they were talking about.

"It seems he hadn't realized that I would think the horse was real," Leonel said in Spanish. "Your horse, Papu, is a statue. I think he's amused at this mistake."

"I'm lost," I said, forgetting not to use English, and failing at the time to connect this conversation to the red papier-mâché calliope horse in the corner of my living room at home.

"He says you are even younger than he thought you would be."

"*No entiendo.*"

The old man understood this and nodded.

"No," Leonel said, "it's just that he was expecting someone older, and I think he wasn't expecting a woman, although he doesn't say this."

Leonel repeated what he said in K'ichi' and the old man nodded and said something back.

"Yes. He thought you would be a young man, but he knew that the horse was a statue, and he thought that I had understood this." Leonel laughed for some reason. I decided not to try to make sense of this conversation, but instead would sit here in the intense quiet, as the room seemed to amplify the man's labored breathing into a gourd-rattle sound.

The woman brought us two cups of a sweet drink and withdrew again. In K'ichi' mixed with Spanish, they spoke for a little while more. The old man then turned to me and said something like *Oo-mi-al.*

"He's calling you 'daughter,'" Leonel said gently. "*Su hija.*"

"Thank him, Leonel."

"You don't thank him for that. Just accept it. He wants to give you something."

The man had left his chair and gone to a trunk on the floor beside the weavings. He returned with what looked like a sash or belt, of tannish-pink cloth with darker pink designs. It appeared to be old.

"He wants you to give this to your grandfather as a gift from him."

"My grandfather? Both of my grandfathers are dead."

"No, he means Grandfather Goodmorning."

"How does he know about him?"

"Well, in this case it's nothing strange. I told him. And now I'm going to tell him that you accept his gift on behalf of your grandfather."

The man waited, looked at me again, and said, "*Quilib la nan,*" then louder, "*Quilib la nan.*"

"It's time to go now," Leonel said.

"What is *Quilib la nan?*"

"He is telling you to be careful."

"*Xpe ri jab.*"

"It will soon rain. Or something like that," Leonel added. "I'm not sure what it means."

———◆———

During the next days, we drove through the western highlands, climbing the slopes into the clouds from Chichi to Santa Cruz del Quiché, then north near Nebaj, where we spent a cold night in an adobe house offered by another man Leonel knew, who also gave us ears of roasted corn and tortillas wrapped in cloth, which we ate by candlelight. When the flame died out, he told me to get some sleep. I lay down on a pile of rugs with his field jacket over me and heard him cross the floor and then the door close behind him. He was not going to the hammock slung on the other side of the darkness. He was leaving me alone.

It was as I imagined the grave would be, with the coffin closed and the earth shoveled onto its lid, an absolute dark with no escapes, shovel after shovel until there is no sound, the ear cupped so as to hear nothing, the lid inches from the face, a darkness like boiling tar or an unfinished tunnel.

The Mayans don't distinguish between past, present, and future, he'd said. They have one word to describe all instances of time, meaning something like "It comes to pass." If you know the past, you know the cyclic forces that created the present, and by knowing the cyclic influences exerting themselves on the present, you can foresee the future, and this, he said, is why the present interests him so much. If you can learn to read the present, without preconceptions, you will better know which of all possible futures will come to pass. There is nothing magical about this. It is a skill that can be acquired by anyone with the inclination and discipline.

In the morning, I found him loading several bundles of what appeared to be Mayan weavings into the remaining space at the back of the Hiace, because something was going to happen here soon, he said, and the women wanted for us to take these things to safety and bring them back someday when and if the time comes.

"When what time comes? What is going to happen?"

"I don't know. They say they will be forced to leave and they won't be able to carry anything with them, and it could be even worse than that."

"What do they think?"

"I'm not sure. This place has been tense for a long time, but this is something new. I'm just reporting to you what they tell me. I don't know what it means."

As we drove away from Nebaj, a group of women and girls watched us from the middle of the road, clustered together but not waving to us as they grew distant in the mirror.

"What's in the bundles?"

"Head scarves, slings for tying children to their backs, belts such as you were given, and something that surprised me." We had gone around a curve in the road and the women had disappeared. "Something that told me how serious the moment is. We may not be able to come back for a long time."

In Santa Cruz del Quiché, I asked him again: "What else is in the bundles?"

"Their wedding *huipiles*. It takes months to weave one. A weaver might have a thousand patterns committed to memory, and each of these *huipiles* is one among a thousand. Those women want us to keep the *huipiles* safe, and you are going to do this, Papu, because soon nothing will be safe with me."

———◆———

That night we stayed in a small hotel near the shore of Lake Atitlán. My room had an adobe fireplace, like the *fogón* at Grandpa Goodmorning's, where wood had been stacked for a fire. The bedstead was high from the clay floor, but there was a wooden stepstool provided for reaching the bed. I had never before slept in such a bed, in a room such as this, with its low, dark-beamed ceiling and windowsills wide enough for a basket of papayas. The hotel had once been a house, built before electricity, so the wiring was sent up the walls in tubes bolted to the clay. My lamp opened a small yellow hole in the dark, not enough to do more than light a glass of water at the bedside. The darkness panted like an animal beyond this light. I was drifting off when Leonel knocked and asked if I would like to take a walk, in the dark, to the lake.

His flashlight fanned out across the ground ahead of us until we reached the water lapping against the stones and he flicked it off. For a moment, it seemed that I was upside down, that the black sky clouded with starlight was below me, but there was only the lake below, mirroring the stars above us. We were standing in a globe of stars, with bats singing in the air. There was no wind, and neither of us spoke. This was the all-at-once of sacred time, as Leonel's mentor had told him, the same man who had also said that rain was coming. On the way back through the dark, I decided to ask him to explain about the red horse.

———◆———

We had one more stop to make, in the town of Panajachel on the northeast side of the lake, where, he said, some Americans and hippies lived, and we were going to pay a visit to one of these hippies.

"But why?"

"Because before he was a hippie, this man was an engineer."

"How do you know that?"

"He's an acquaintance of a friend of mine."

"Well, that narrows it down."

"Papu, this will take only an hour, and it's important."

"Everything is important. Even the hippies, it seems."

"You'll see. Bear with me."

The man who opened the door of a small pink house was no older than I was, with long blond hair and a deep tan, more surfer than hippie. He wore khaki shorts, a T-shirt, and no shoes, and had tied a red string of amulets around his neck, something that resembled an animal tooth and a pierced pebble.

"Hey," he said, moving aside to let us into the house. "I just made some chai. Would you like some?"

I didn't know what chai was, but said yes, and it turned out to be a spicy tea.

The man's name was Greg, and he spoke no Spanish at all, which I found odd for a person living in a Guatemalan town. Leonel set his tea on the table and said what he usually said: "I don't have much time. But," he continued, "I heard that you are interested in helping."

"That'd be great, yes," Greg said. "I've always wanted to do something real, you know? I would go to Nicaragua but, well, I've heard it's hard to make contacts there, so yeah, I'm glad I'm finally getting a chance to talk to you. I don't know anything about guns, but I'm willing to learn."

"Guns? This isn't about guns."

"Well, I mean there is going to be a revolution, right?"

"I don't know yet what's going to happen," Leonel said, "but I'm here to talk to you about a way that you, especially you, could help us."

"Me? Well, anything. Just tell me what you want me to do."

"I want you to design a portable bridge that could bear the weight of a light truck. We don't have trucks yet but if the bridge could support a truck, it could support anything and would be fine for our use. It needs to be somehow portable, so you would probably have to design something that folds up or comes in sections."

"A bridge? What does a bridge have to do with revolution? I don't do bridges."

"But I was told that you are an engineer."

"Yeah, well, I studied engineering but it was boring. I don't, you know, want to get involved with that stuff anymore. I came here to get away from all that. Truth is, I hated it."

"So, you won't help us with the bridge. Do you know someone who can?"

"No, man, I don't. I'm sorry. Not too many engineers around here."

Leonel rose to his feet and thanked the man for his chai and his time. He said something about perhaps being in touch, and we left.

"What was that about?" I asked when we were back in the Hiace.

"Okay. It was a bit of a waste of time, but only an hour. Let's go."

"Why did you think he could design a bridge?"

"I don't know. Someone told me this Greg was an engineer, so I just thought I'd give it a try. In the rainy season, many of our roads are impassable, and there are also many small rivers. So, say you wanted to set up a cooperative farm in a remote place, but you wouldn't be able to get access to the land, or take supplies there, or carry out your crops, so I had this idea for a portable bridge. Something you could set up, and after the vehicles had crossed, you could take the bridge apart and carry it with you somewhere else. This Greg, he thinks he's Che Guevara. But he won't draw plans for a simple bridge. This is something you should learn, Papu. Lesson number four: If someone promises to do great things, ask them first for something small, like a bridge or a cow."

W e returned to San Salvador the next day, crossing again at Las Chinamas. When we reached San Salvador, Leonel took me to the convent of the Sisters of Divine Providence, the Carmelite nuns who ran a small hospital for terminally ill cancer patients. He often joined the nuns for meals and seemed close to one older nun in particular, Madre Luz, who listened to the story, or half the story, of what I had seen since coming to the country. (Leonel left out the meeting with the high-ranking official concerning what was to be done about the "Richardson case.") When he complained that I hadn't been allowed to join the delegation to Aguilares, Madre Luz suggested that I accompany her sisters when they made their bimonthly visit to the village to provide, among other things, dental care.

"I didn't know you were taking care of teeth these days."

The nun kept her smile and threw her head back a little at this joke and told him that they bring along a dentist. Then she looked me in the eyes, nodded, and put her hand on my arm.

"You could wear the habit of our order," she said. "That might be the safest way."

I pictured myself in the habit of the Carmelite sisters, brown dress and veil, white headband, white robe and veil in the warm months.

But Leonel didn't think this was a good idea. If we were stopped while coming or going, it might be discovered that I was not a nun, that I wasn't even Salvadoran, and if that happened, it would also bring the sisters under further suspicion. Things were already bad enough, according to Leonel. Monseñor Romero, who lived in a small room here on the hospital grounds, was the only person speaking out regularly against repression and the right hated him for it, and by extension hated the nuns. Yet no matter how endangered the archbishop was, he refused to have bodyguards, and he insisted on driving himself around the city in his own car. The nuns also refused. Their protection, they said, was God.

"They get death threats every day," Leonel said. "Madre Luz takes the calls."

As the elder nun listened to this, she reached across the table and patted my hand again. Lunch was set before us, a blessing asked, and then she said she would pray about it, and at that moment, everyone was rising to their feet and pushing back their chairs as Monseñor Romero himself came to the table, gesturing for all to sit down, apologizing for coming late, saying that there were so many meetings this morning, so many problems to address, that he had lost track of the time. He sat at the head of the table in his white cassock, smiling at a joke someone had apparently told, while a plate was hurriedly put before him, and after crossing himself, he held his fork aloft and exchanged news with Leonel and Madre Luz.

I had heard so much about Monseñor, especially from Margarita, but had seen him only from a distance in the cathedral, and now he was here, at this kitchen table, chatting over chicken. I heard my name, then something inaudible, and Monseñor nodded his head yes, glancing at me. Then he said yes again. To what had he said yes?

Monseñor took off his eyeglasses and rubbed them with a white handkerchief he had retrieved from his cassock, then put them back on, and as he rose from the table, all rose and crossed themselves for his blessing. As quickly as he had come to the table, he was gone, and we were back on the road.

"What did he say, Leonel? What did you tell him?"

"Nothing. Why?"

"You were saying something about me. What did you say?"

"I told him that you were a poet visiting from the U.S."

"That's all?"

"What do you mean 'that's all'? Maybe I said something else, I don't remember. And what else would you have me say? *Mirá,* Papu, about Aguilares—the nuns must be protected at all cost. They must be above reproach. You cannot be running around in their clothes, and this means you will not be going with them. If you want to go to Aguilares, we will find another way. But I don't advise that you go. Why would you? To meet with people who would soon after be killed maybe because they were seen talking to you?"

"Leonel."

"I know what you're going to tell me. You're going to tell me that I'm not being fair. It's something you Americans say when you are told the truth."

"And that isn't fair, either. Where are we going?"

"It's not safe for us to stay in San Salvador at the moment. Not until we see what comes of that meeting we had the other day. If anything comes of it."

"Which meeting, Leonel? I'm losing track of all the meetings."

"The meeting we had the day we had to sleep in the chicken house. That meeting. *A la gran puta,* Papu, what meeting did you think?"

"I'd forgotten."

"Yes, well, lesson number five. It is best not to forget things like that."

WE SPENT THE NIGHT IN ANOTHER HOUSE BELONGING TO YET ANOTHER FRIEND in Santa Tecla, and the next morning drove to meet with campesinos on a cooperative farm some distance from the city, so by afternoon, we were both sweaty and covered with dust. Nevertheless, Leonel insisted that we had to go, right then, to the Estado Mayor, the headquarters of the Salvadoran military.

"We have to meet with one of the younger colonels," he said, "actually a lieutenant colonel, to be more precise."

"Why? I don't really want to go. I have had enough of the colonels."

"Well, that's up to you, of course, but I advise that you come with me.

He's expecting both of us. You don't have to say too much. Just listen. You may learn something. Have you ever seen the headquarters of a military dictatorship? No? Well, here is your chance."

"Like this?" I asked, sweeping my palms over my dusty clothes.

"Yes. Especially like this."

THE UNIFORMED GATEKEEPER STUDIED LEONEL'S IDENTIFICATION, MADE A telephone call, and waved us into the compound. Leonel walked slowly, almost casually, talking about other things while in a lower voice he told me to look around, to take things in, but not to make notes until later. Don't say too much, he said. Walk slowly. Act like you are comfortable.

At every encounter with a soldier, we were stopped, questioned briefly, and waved past until we reached the row of folding chairs against a wall where we would wait for a quarter of an hour. What I remember is how much light shone on the waxed tile halls, on officers' portraits, on the buffed shoes of the soldiers patrolling the halls and the rifles they carried, light pouring through the open door, catching on their helmets, and sounds? I didn't hear shouts or screaming in distant rooms as others would later report. I heard only the opening and closing of doors.

The lieutenant colonel's office was smaller than I expected. There was a little Salvadoran flag on the large wooden desk beside an inbox and an outbox, both full, and a brown felt blotter where the young lieutenant colonel placed his folded hands after shaking ours and gesturing for us to sit on the chairs opposite the desk. A fan, yes, there was a fan, turning back and forth near the open window, but not so much as a paper stirred. The voices of the two men blended with the hum in a blur of small talk that grew louder as the minutes passed, until they were talking about the many murders and disappearances that had been taking place in the capital and around the country.

"People are starting to blame the army," Leonel told the lieutenant colonel, who bristled visibly at this. "The army has to prove its professionalism. It has to clean itself up," Leonel said.

The lieutenant colonel responded with something I didn't understand, but it seemed that he was defending his fellow younger officers and attempting to refute Leonel's suggestion that they might be involved in the disappearances.

"The reality doesn't matter," Leonel said. "What matters is perception. And right now, the army isn't looking very good."

Given what was happening in the country, I was surprised that he would speak this way to a member of the armed forces, but I sat stone-faced beside him, hoping for the meeting to come to an end.

"By the way," Leonel said, "you have a shower here, don't you, Colonel? Do you mind if I take a quick shower before we leave?"

The lieutenant colonel looked as surprised as I felt.

"Why not? As you wish."

He ordered a younger aide to show Leonel to the facilities, and then he left the room.

"Wait here," Leonel said. "I'll be back shortly. Make yourself at home."

Some minutes passed, according to the clock on the wall, and there were sounds of distant, echoing voices, boot soles on tile, and the fan grew louder, something was wrong with it, like the sound of the fan my former husband had rigged in our attic apartment, *pocketa pocketa*—the sound of a chopper in fog flying over a firebase.

The lieutenant colonel kept his desk clean, but in the ashtray there were several twisted paper clips. I noticed that one of the drawers in the file cabinet wasn't quite closed, and it crossed my mind to go leafing through the manila folders that I could see plainly from my chair. The second hand clicked audibly. There was no wife, there were no children; the only photograph in the room was the portrait of the president of the republic wearing a dark business suit and a blue-and-white sash such as beauty contestants wear. Somehow this reminded me of Leonel's story of the Miss Universe pageant held here just two years earlier. "So much poverty," Leonel had said, "and this is what the government spends money on, this is what they're interested in, a goddamn beauty contest. Well, the people protested as of course they would. They even occupied the cathedral for a week, and when the protest march was fired upon by security forces, as marches here always are, thirty-seven people lost their lives.

[217]

They say fifteen, but they are wrong. It was thirty-seven. Most of the dead were students. The president of the republic called them Communists, of course, and charged them with plotting to overthrow the government. All because of Miss Universe."

The mild-seeming man wearing the sash and smiling from the wall was the minister of defense and public security at the time, so he either ordered or approved the attack on the marchers.

Later, as we drove out of the compound, I confessed to Leonel that I had wanted to search through the lieutenant colonel's files but had been afraid.

"You wouldn't have found anything."

Leonel's hair was still wet, as was the neckline of the fresh guayabera he wore.

"Leonel, why the shower? Couldn't you have waited? And how do you know I wouldn't have found anything?"

"Think it through. We were seen, the two of us, going into the Estado Mayor, one of the most important military facilities in the country. And an hour later, we were also seen walking out, and I'm all cleaned up, looking like a goddamn nightclub singer. Whoever is watching us has to imagine that I'm on quite friendly terms with someone in the military, and I have the sort of access civilians don't usually get."

"What do you mean 'watching us'?"

"Watching. Believe me, someone is always watching."

The radio was between stations, two voices interweaving, one selling something, the other singing to a past love, and the rest pure noise.

"*Mirá*, Papu, who is Leonel Gómez? It's a serious question. Gómez is seen talking to campesinos in Cabañas, but also in Santa Tecla and San Miguel, although his coffee farm is in Santa Ana. He frequently visits retired military officers but also nuns and priests. He comes and goes from the U.S. embassy, from certain military garrisons, even a goddamn ice cream parlor. He talks to this one. He talks to that one. Gómez pays many visits to Divine Providence but he doesn't believe in God. So who is Gómez? Nobody knows."

"Last summer Claribel's husband told me that some think you work for the CIA."

"Bud told you this? That's a good piece of information. Thank you."

Leonel had tuned the radio more precisely now, so we seemed to be listening to a single voice: an announcer for a sporting event, *fútbol* maybe, and as I knew this didn't interest him, the radio was on for another reason.

"What do you mean 'information'? *Do* you work for the CIA?"

He laughed. "Some people say so. Those visits to your embassy have paid off."

"What are you talking about, Leonel? Stop playing games. What 'good piece of information'? If it's true, tell me. If it isn't, why do you want Claribel and Bud to think so?"

"I don't know what they think, but this confirms something for me. I know who started this rumor and now I know who is spreading it."

"That doesn't answer my question."

"Do I work for those sons of bitches? What do you think?"

"I don't know."

"Well, that's what I want: for people not to know but to have all sorts of suspicions. This is my only protection—this, and my trophies for marksmanship. Without these things, I would have been dead a long time ago. Do you think Chacón is alone with his band of killers? There are quite a few others—in the army, in the treasury police, in the national guard, and some civilians too, who are on the payroll of certain oligarchs. There is even a dentist among them they call Dr. Death. At least I think he's a dentist. They use machetes, knives, ice picks, blowtorches, and primitive electrical equipment. Many of them have had sophisticated training in the so-called School of the Americas, where they learn more refined techniques. But, Papu, this is a poor country, as all of these rich sons of bitches will tell you, and they don't have special equipment and facilities, so they make do with lit cigarettes and rope, plastic bags and toilets full of shit. I'll let you use your imagination."

We had entered a narrow street clogged with traffic, and people were weaving among the vehicles. One by one the drivers honked their horns and shouted from their windows the equivalent of "What's the problem?" The radio lost its way between stations, so there were several voices speaking at once.

"Roll your window up. We're going to use the air conditioner. Something is burning. Can't you smell it?"

"Yes, now I do."

"This is usually a shortcut."

"Where are we going?"

"Well, now we are going to wherever this fire is."

"Why do you think I wouldn't have found anything in the colonel's office?"

"And why would you have looked? That was a stupid idea, Papu. Goddamn Mata Hari. What if you were caught? What do you think would have happened then? And what did you think you would find, a list of who is next?"

"I told you. I thought the better of it."

"You *thought the better*. Let me tell you something. These people don't keep records. They don't give written orders. Orders are simply understood. They aren't even given verbally. There is no need. A nod and a phrase or two is all that is required. 'Take care of this,' for example, is such a phrase. What you are going to find in that colonel's basket is an order for a hundred kilos of cornmeal for a barracks kitchen."

"Then what does 'take care of this' mean exactly?"

"It means to kill the person. Or that's what it means in this context."

SOMEHOW THE TRAFFIC HAD THINNED, OR VEHICLES HAD PULLED ONTO SIDE streets to avoid driving into smoke. Now there were mostly people on foot: thin, small, poorly dressed, their hands and faces smeared with soot. They were surrounding the Hiace, pressing their hands against the glass, cupping their palms in a gesture to receive coins, touching their hands to their mouths to ask for food, then falling back to be replaced by others, many of them young children whose hands left sooty prints on the windows. We were coasting slowly, and the windows muted the street noise.

No. There was no noise. No sound. The people were moving in slow motion now, mouthing words I couldn't hear or understand, holding up their gray hands.

"What's wrong, Forché?" I heard Leonel asking. "Are you okay?" He had broken the strange silence, and there was also a rushing of air.

"Drink some water," he said, reaching into the back for his canteen. "You look like you've seen a ghost."

The crowd was still moving alongside us. We had reached the still-smoking wreckage, where several buildings appeared to have burned and then collapsed.

"Maybe the smoke got to you."

"No," I said, and then heard myself saying, "I have seen this before," as if in the voice of someone else.

People were crawling over wood and debris, rummaging in the ruins.

"They're looking for something," Leonel said, "something, anything they can use: a bottle, a comb with a few teeth, maybe a spoon. You'd be amazed what you can find after a fire like this, and as it is, they have nothing."

He was right. An old woman was dropping things into her apron and looked up as we passed, her eyes bright in a face now the color of smoke.

"Tell me what happened back there. I thought you were going to pass out or some goddamn thing. I'm glad to see you are okay. Did you inhale too much?"

"I don't know."

This wasn't the truth. I would try to tell him the truth, but not right this moment. I had to first think about it for myself. Instead I asked him to tell me what he thought had happened here.

"Simple. This is a barrio where the poorest people in the city live, and someone wants this property, so they want these people out. They pay some guy to torch the place, usually during the day when most people are at work, not because they care how many die but because too many deaths would draw more attention. In fact, no one is going to investigate arson even when committed in broad daylight. So the buildings burn and the insurance company pays the owner, who turns around and sells the land to the buyer waiting in the wings. Nothing happens for a while, and then, one day, construction begins, but not to replace housing for the poor, you can be sure."

"What do they build?"

"Often, these days, they build a fast-food restaurant. It used to be banks."

"What about the insurance companies?"

"What about them?"

"Well, they seem to be the ones who pay."

"No, they are not. Insurance companies are also insured against loss, and there are ways of making these arrangements so that everyone wins, you see, everyone except the people who have been displaced. They are the ones who pay."

"How do you know that this fire wasn't accidental?"

"Do you see any fire trucks?"

Our windows were covered with handprints, but the sound of hands slapping the windows had stopped. There were no trucks, there was no water running down the street, no hoses stretched out or rewound on their reels.

———◆———

I have to go back now to childhood for a moment in order to make some sense of this. My mother is standing at the stove in the kitchen stirring pudding in a double boiler. She is busy. The baby, one of the babies, is on the speckled linoleum floor crawling around at my mother's feet, and my mother wants me to pick up this baby and take it away from the stove, but I'm carrying an issue of a magazine, large for me, held open in my hands to photographs taken by American soldiers from the Second World War who came upon the bodies of concentration camp prisoners. I am six or seven years old. Do I pick up the baby? Probably, but I don't remember picking her up. I ask my mother to tell me about the photographs in the magazine and she says something like *Not now, I'm making dinner,* and probably something else, either about folding the cloth diapers that are always mounded on the sofa or pairing and rolling the socks, also in a mound.

"What is this?" I ask, holding the magazine pages open for her to see.

"Give me that. You're not supposed to have it."

"But what is it? What are they doing?"

She is still stirring the pudding. The baby isn't there any longer. A door slams so hard that the flies fastened to its screen rise off in a buzzing cloud—someone coming in or going out—a little chaos in the kitchen, too much for my mother. Already three younger siblings born and three more to come, and she can't really pay attention, but I need to know who they are because the people in the photographs have also appeared in my dreams.

She takes the magazine away from me. Through the steam from the stove she said she would tell me when I was grown.

ALL THROUGH MY CHILDHOOD THE NIGHTMARES CAME, AND THEN SOMEHOW the faces disappear, the terror and the black wings, the lunging of that world, like a roller coaster in pitch-black space, and having always to sleep with blankets over my head. Then another dream replaces these flights of darkness, and in this dream people appear whose faces seem to be smudged with coal dust, or so I thought. Their palms are blackened, and pressed open against something that comes between us. No sound comes from them, but they want something, and I don't know what.

WHAT HAD COME BETWEEN US WAS A WINDOW, WHERE NOW THE SAME SOOTY hands were pressed against the glass. Later I might tell Leonel how I might have seen this place more than twenty years earlier: this place, this fire, these people with soot on their hands. Would I tell him that I had seen them during recurrent night terrors as a child? Could I possibly tell him this?

This all happened almost a decade after the Second World War. My parents were young and exhausted, but they would lift me from the bed and walk me down the hall and back until I stopped screaming *"The people"* and woke and realized where I was. Always in the dream it was the same: men, women, and children standing before me, holding up their blackened palms and asking for help, but seemingly unable to come closer. I knew that there was some barrier keeping me on one side and them on the other, as sleep is kept apart from waking, but I hadn't known the barrier was glass.

"It's time for you to get some protection too," Leonel said, once we were back on the highway.

"I don't want a weapon. I don't know the first thing about them."

"Do you need coffee? You seem like you need coffee. You're right, however, you'd probably wind up shooting me in the balls. But I wasn't talking about that. It's time for you to pay a little visit to the U.S. embassy and introduce yourself to the new ambassador."

"You have to be kidding me. I can't meet the ambassador."

"Why not? You're a U.S. citizen, aren't you? He's your ambassador, isn't he?"

"But I'm no one. Why should he meet with me?"

"He will meet with you because you are visiting at a time when there are almost no gringos here, no press, no nothing—a few Peace Corps, but aside from that and other than embassy staff, no one. He will meet with you because he doesn't know who you are and he will make it his business to find out because his contacts in the military might have already said something. To get an appointment, all you have to do is pick up the phone. Here is the number for the main desk."

"But I don't need to talk to the ambassador. I have no reason. I have nothing to say to him."

"Oh, but you do. The symphony of illusion, remember? You need to be seen entering and leaving the embassy, and if possible, you need to get yourself invited to an embassy function, a cocktail reception or, better, dinner at the residence. You can bring me as your guest. The food is excellent at those dinners, and the views of the city . . ."

"Leonel. I'm not interested and I'm not going."

"You're a goddamn Pekingese, Papu."

"What's that supposed to mean?"

"Otherwise known as 'the lion,' or Peking Palasthund. The breed originated in China. Barks a lot. Mop of hair in the eyes. Courageous. Not easy to train. I'm going to start calling you 'The Pekingese.' Or maybe 'Great-Granddaughter of Genghis Khan.'"

Where were we? I didn't know. Often, I didn't know. We were on the road I called the road of the blond billboards—advertisements for expensive scotch and liquor made from sugarcane, frosted drinks, pearls, blond women with glossed lips.

"You are going to talk to the ambassador so as to remind him of his duty to protect American citizens and to investigate incidents having to do with American citizens abroad. Ask him how things are going with the Richardson case. I'll be curious to know how he will answer you. Remember, Richardson is still classified as having disappeared while in the custody of the Salvadoran government. And oh yes, mention something about the San Lorenzo hydroelectric dam project. They don't need to build it. We are a net exporter of electricity. If the U.S. approves the loan to build it, you will only be pouring American money into the pockets of military officers."

"And what should I call you? What's going to be your nickname?"

"Mein General. As in *Jawohl, mein general*. Or maybe just always say *Jawohl*. Or maybe something Greek. Have you seen the film Z? Costa-Gavras? We can name me after that guy."

"The one killed at the beginning?"

"No, the one who investigates—Christos. Don't forget to mention San Lorenzo."

———◆———

As we were waved into the building by the white-gloved marine guards, the air changed, and I realized that I had not been in an air-conditioned building in a while. There were potted palms near the planted flags on either side of the reception desk. The leaves were glossy as if each had been polished by hand. We clipped the visitors' badges to our shirts and the elevator doors closed behind us.

"Welcome to the United States, my dear." Leonel was laughing, looking around the elevator, up to the mirrored ceiling where we saw ourselves, then to the steel doors, and the numbers of the floors lighting up as the elevator rose.

"You're not coming in with me, are you?"

"No. The son of a bitch can kiss my ass. I'll wait for you outside his office. There's a nice lady who works there, and I enjoy talking to her. She works for every ambassador, son of a bitch or not. But most of them are sons of bitches."

The elevator doors opened.

"You realize," he whispered, "that you are in the United States now. This building is their territory. It smells different in here, doesn't it?"

"If you aren't coming to this meeting with me, then why did you come here at all?"

"I enjoy visiting the United States. Besides, as I think I have told you, it is good for me to be seen coming and going from certain places. It helps with the symphony of illusion."

The receptionist, the "nice lady," had seated us in a waiting area and left to get the coffee Leonel had requested. He put his finger to his lips and pointed to the ceiling, the wall, the desk, and then to his ear.

"Be careful," he whispered. "Here's what I know about this man. He's a graduate of the War College. A Catholic. Before this, he was posted to Colombia, Uruguay, Chile, Portugal, the Dominican Republic, and Venezuela. He's a seasoned career foreign service officer, as they say, which means that he has read not only his briefings, but also the back files. He knows how hard the former ambassador worked on the Richardson case. Ambassador Lozano worked his ass off and put his job on the line. And he also knows how involved I was in the case, but he hasn't asked to meet with me, and so far he has said nothing at all about Richardson. The thing to keep in mind is that this man is afraid. The right wanted him dead even before he got here, and they wanted to blame his death on the left. Now they are saying that some on the left would like, possibly, to kidnap him for ransom money, even though it is common knowledge that the U.S. government never negotiates in abduction cases."

The receptionist returned, cheerily setting a tray before us in the center of a low table scattered with American magazines—issues of *Time, National Geographic,* and for some reason, a few issues of *Popular Mechanics*—then she motioned me to follow her to the ambassador's office door, and opened it to let me enter.

He was already coming around the desk to shake my hand as if I were an important person, inviting me to sit in the chair across from him. He was clean-shaven and wore a well-cut suit, a crisp white shirt, and cuff links. "White collar," my father would have said.

"So—what brings you to El Salvador?"

Leonel was pacing near the elevators when I rejoined him, as he didn't want to be in the reception area, in case the new ambassador walked me out to the door. He had not wanted to shake the man's hand, he said. Not yet. He gave me a look that I understood to mean we were to keep quiet until we were well away from what he called the jurisdiction of the United States, so we were back in the hot vehicle by the time he said, "Well?"—by which he meant: *Tell me everything the man said, word for word.*

I began with the ambassador's "deep background" briefing, the speech he gave to all journalists, and to all "NGO types," as Leonel called them, and all congressional delegations, the speech that described conditions in the country as he had found them upon his arrival, and as he expected me to find them as well, and the situation as it currently was, in the estimation of embassy personnel. This was followed by a summary statement of the U.S. policy line, and warnings against staying "too long" here, or going out "into rural areas," as it was extremely dangerous for American citizens now, as he was hoping I well understood, and when I took my chance to ask about Ronald Richardson, he shook his head and explained that this particular disappearance didn't happen "on his watch," but that of his predecessor, and he regarded the case as unsolvable and hence closed. While he was talking about Richardson, I remembered, the ambassador kept clicking his pen. At other points in the conversation, the pen remained on the desk.

I watched him as he talked, trying to keep my face, as Leonel would say, unreadable. I asked about the upcoming review of the Salvadoran government's human rights record, and about certain names of the *desaparecidos*, about which he had nothing to say, and then, as instructed, I inquired about the building of the San Lorenzo hydroelectric plant, and about the money that had disappeared well before the project was even begun. He asked how I knew these things about the San Lorenzo. I didn't answer. He wanted to know how many Third World countries I had visited in my life. When the answer was "none before now," his manner became, for a brief time, almost fatherly, and he warned me against having much to do with Leonel Gómez because, as he said, "we don't know who he is." And then he advised me to go home.

"That's it?" Leonel asked.

"I think so, yes. Oh, there's one more thing—there is an aquarium in his office filled with freshwater tropical fish. I used to have one too, so we talked a little about that. His tank hadn't been cleaned in a while I noticed, but the ambassador said he found the aquarium soothing."

A few days later, Leonel heard back from someone in the embassy regarding my meeting, and it was "good news." Apparently, I must have upset the ambassador quite a bit.

"Congratulations, my dear," Leonel said, "the ambassador said he was appalled by you."

———◆———

I had to remind Leonel that I would soon have to return again to California, if only for a while, as I hadn't yet taken a leave of absence. I would be back at the semester break, and then for the summer, but for now, my time was up.

"Yes, yes, of course."

He was squatting down in a dark machine shop, where his motorcycle had been disassembled for repair, the parts spread neatly on an oily tarpaulin, the chrome gleaming under a work light held by the mechanic who, for some reason, did not seem to know quite how to put the bike back together again. The only other light came from a broken window resembling a block of ice.

"You're not listening."

He fished through the parts, picking them up, setting them down, as if something were lost, and something might have been, because next he asked the mechanic if he was absolutely certain this was everything.

"*Sí, estoy seguro, señor.*"

"*¡Vale!*" Leonel said, getting himself to his feet. "Okay, then. We'll see you in a few days."

Apparently, the mechanic had assured him that he just needed a few more days.

Leonel seemed distracted, but he was always distracted around this motorcycle, and in matters concerning this disassembled bike, the mechanic always needed only a few more days.

The sunlight blinded me, and there was a whiff of what might have been a plugged sewer. He stopped at a market stall and bought two bottles of warm *refrescos* and, handing one to me, said: "But you have to get back here soon, because it seems that some other military officers would like to meet with you."

Other military officers. I kept walking. This probably meant nothing. He was trying to intrigue me in some way, perhaps so that I wouldn't leave yet, but I had to leave just a few days later and, for a time, fulfill my responsibilities teaching, grading papers, writing letters and notes toward poems. In those months, it was as if I were asleep, dreaming of finches singing from curtain rods and ceiling fixtures, a field on fire with carnations, rabbits gnawing on cabbage heads, the blank, salted air of that town on the coast. The call came about a week later, around midnight, so that it seemed at first that the ringing, too, wasn't real.

"Papu?"

"Leonel! How are you? Is everything—?"

"Listen to me carefully. Chacón is dead. He was killed this morning, ambushed by his own military at the house of his mistress. I don't think he had time to pull his pants up. They shot him like an animal."

There was silence on both ends of the phone.

"I thought you'd want to know," he said, and hung up.

A week or so passed, and he called again and asked me if I could possibly fly to Texas. There was someone he wanted me to meet. "I'm already here," he said, "in San Antonio."

"Texas?"

"Just for a few days. It's important."

"Can it wait until the weekend?"

"Yes. But look—"

"I know, I know. It's important."

"Yes, my dear, it is. Here is the number, call when you know your flight."

Just like that, I thought, hanging up the wall phone in the kitchen after I heard the click on his end. He thinks I can drop everything to fly to Texas. Texas, for God's sake.

"Who was that?" Barbara asked, probably from the stove, where she would have been making herbal tea, as she often did to soothe her migraines.

"Nothing. I have to go to Texas."

She would have turned toward me, blowing on the tea to cool it a little, studying me over the rim of the cup, and asked if this had something to do with that man, Leonel, about whom I couldn't seem to stop talking since I had gotten back, and when I said yes, concern flared in her eyes, but she wouldn't have said anything. Almost all of my friends seemed to feel the same way about my new interest in this strange person and his distant country, although I had known enough not to tell them everything. *We're worried about you,* they all said. But this concerned Texas now, not El Salvador, and so she agreed to drive me to the airport on Friday, if I came back by Sunday night, in time to resume my normal life.

———◆———

As it turned out, he had driven the Hiace to Texas right after he learned of Chacón's death. He needed time to think, he said, to lie low to assess the situation, and that is why we were going to a motel bathed in pink neon on the outskirts of San Antonio, near an American military base where one of El Salvador's junior officers was in training.

There was no moon, so other than the bright wedge of our headlights on the road, and the red blinking lights of communication towers in the distance, there was only arid darkness.

"If they really listen to all the phone calls, why did you tell me about Chacón over the phone?"

"*Because* they were listening. I wanted them to hear me report this to you."

I rolled the window down for the night air. "I'm not following you. And by the way, where are we going?"

"It's not far now. *Mirá,* Papu, they shot one of their own, and for the first time. They have never, *ever* before moved against one of their own. If you think of the institution of the military as an impenetrable wall, well, now there's a crack in that wall."

"Are we really almost there? I have to use a toilet."

"And there's a group of younger officers who are not at all pleased with this *tanda* now in power, but they have been afraid to make a move."

"Move as in make a coup?"

"Move in any way. It isn't so much that Chacón has been *ultimado,* but by whom. I'll pull over. You can go in the bushes."

"No, Leonel. No bushes."

"So tonight we're going to meet with one of these young officers, and tomorrow we'll pay a visit to the base, and then, if you insist on getting back by Monday morning, we'll hit the road, as you people say."

"We're driving back?"

"Yes. It will take us about eighteen hours. I already studied the map: El Paso, then Tucson, then Horseshoe Bend, but you have to promise not to drive us over a cliff when it's your turn."

"You're coming to San Diego?"

"No, I'm coming to your house for a few days."

Barbara will appreciate that, I thought.

"I need to study," he said. "I need to know everything about the war in Vietnam. Do you think you could bring me books from the university library?"

"If you tell me what you want. Or we could go there together and . . ."

"Military strategy. Logistics: strategic, operational, and tactical. And bring me everything the library has that is on, by, or about General Võ Nguyên Giáp, who, by the way, happens to be one of the greatest military strategists of the twentieth century."

"I don't know who that is."

"No, you probably wouldn't. He defeated the United States in Vietnam. We're here."

"We're meeting at a motel? Why? Isn't your friend meeting us on the base?"

"Because here he will talk more freely. He didn't want to have this meeting on the base."

"But we're going there tomorrow, you told me."

"Yes, we're going there, but not to talk, to shop. I need some things."

It must have rained sometime during the past few hours. The pink VACANCY sign flickered upside down in a puddle.

Just before he knocked on the door that gave onto the parking lot, Leonel warned me that this man might seem a little bit nervous, a little bit scared. "Don't say much," he said. "Play it the way you did in El Salvador."

"Play—?"

"He doesn't know who you are, and that is a good thing. He does know, however, with whom you have been talking."

He put his hand on my shoulder. "Be yourself," he said.

The young officer's uniform was sharply creased, his dark, wavy hair neatly combed. It was clear that he had come to this highway motel strictly for this meeting, and other than the full ashtray, there was nothing that suggested he had been here long. The ashtray told me that he was nervous before we arrived, or else he was a heavy smoker, but he didn't smoke in our presence, so—. Propping himself against the headboard of one of the twin beds, he stretched out with his polished shoes set neatly on the floor. We were on the other bed, Leonel the closest to the officer whose name I don't want to recall. Some of their conversation went past me, and this wasn't only because the Spanish was colloquial and rapid but because, as Leonel later told me, I wasn't familiar with the "actors"—with "who was who"—and why this was "the moment," and how dangerous things would be going forward, so important was this moment and vital to the integrity and professionalism of the army and so on. The *ultimado* of Chacón, he added, had surprised the younger officers, but also heartened them.

"There is hope," he said.

The next morning, this particular young officer met us at the entrance to the base, then rode with us to a parking lot and, before leaving the car, handed a small package to Leonel across the well of the gearshift. Leonel thanked him, tucked the package under the driver's seat and, when we were outside, carefully locked the Hiace.

"We're going to the PX," Leonel announced gaily. "It's like a department store, but for military personnel and their families. They have everything: groceries, clothing, electronics. If you want anything, put it in the basket, and our friend here will buy it for you as if it were for himself and you can pay him later."

Then he added: "We don't have military ID cards, so we're not allowed to shop here, technically speaking. But it's all at reduced prices, and there is no tax."

The young officer calmly pushed the cart but bought only cigarettes for himself. Leonel, on the other hand, added a small tool kit, khaki trousers, pipe tobacco, a camping stove, and some other things to the cart, walking at a slow pace through all the aisles, examining many items, all the while talking in a low voice to the officer, who sometimes nodded yes and sometimes no. I decided not to purchase anything.

We shook hands and left the officer there, standing where we had been parked, one hand shielding his eyes, and he watched us drive off. Leonel waved through the window. The young officer raised his hand slightly but didn't really wave back.

"Excellent," he said loudly over the blast of wind on the open road.

I had him stop at a Circle K convenience store so that I could telephone Barbara to warn her that we were coming, and so that Leonel could buy an ice cream bar and a soda, but otherwise we drove for the next eighteen hours under the pulsing desert sun, and through the night as the air cooled, taking turns behind the wheel and stopping only for gas. He would talk most of the time, except when he took his short naps, usually in the back of the Hiace. During one of these, I remember having the feeling, vividly, that he was no longer in the van.

Barbara had left a note on the kitchen counter: *Have gone to stay with B and M. He can use my room. Let me know when he leaves.*

She must have left only a short time before because the bowls in the finch cage were brimming with millet and the paths she had vacuumed into the carpet were still visible. Leonel set his things neatly against the wall in the living room, eventually including the stacks of books I would borrow for him, which did not, apparently, include as much as he'd hoped they would. He was not interested, he said, in the history of U.S. involvement in Vietnam, nor in analysis of the American prosecution of the war or our domestic debates concerning it. He wanted to know about how the war was *fought* on the *other* side, during the "Second Indochina War," "The Resistance War Against America," sometimes shortened to "The American War in Vietnam." He wanted to know about the tactics and strategy of the North Vietnamese Army and the National Liberation Front, about their tunnels and movements, their booby traps, and how they used the element of surprise.

He was happy that I had found two books by Giáp himself, translated into English: *The Military Art of People's War* and *How We Won the War,* and he stayed up several nights reading these.

Never in the history of warfare, he would say over and over, *never in the history of the world. I mean—God.* This was his mantra, *Never in the history,* whether we were walking through the fog on the beach or he was pacing the living-room floor: air power, firepower, weapons, chemicals, thousands of pounds of explosives, B-52 bombers, F-4 Phantoms, UH-1 helicopters, armored personnel carriers, howitzers, Mk 2 grenades, napalm—armaments such as no people prior to the Vietnamese had ever had inflicted upon them in this kind of war.

"I mean, Jesus Christ, Papu, the U.S. sprayed nineteen million gallons of herbicides over four and a half million acres of Vietnam, the most destructive defoliation the world has ever seen. And you know what?"

He would pause at this moment of the speech, as if waiting for an answer, and then he would ask again. "You know what? The Americans lost, that's what. They lost. I think I know why, but I'm trying now to answer the more interesting question: Precisely how did the Vietnamese win? And by the way, we have to go to a hardware store."

"What do you need?"

"Foam rubber. Chicken wire. I have to build something for the trip back. For this," he said, setting the small package on the table given to him by the junior officer in Texas. It was wrapped in aluminum foil in a brown paper lunch sack: a small brick of something, a little larger than a box of kitchen matches. He unwrapped the aluminum foil, revealing a substance that resembled modeling clay or marzipan, the almond paste my mother used to sculpt realistic-looking fruit candies. This was also almond colored.

"It's made of plasticizer, synthetic rubber, some mineral oil—and RDX."

I was now lifting it to my nose to smell it. It weighed just over a pound.

"That's short for research department explosive."

I put it down.

"Careful," he said. "Treat it gently. Even though, as far as I know, it won't explode without extreme heat and a shock wave from a detonator of some kind. I could probably shoot it and it wouldn't explode. But just in case, I'm going to make a special package to contain it during my drive back. I do go through the desert, after all."

The smell was now becoming apparent. Motor oil?

"*Mirá,* if you just light it with a match, it will burn slowly like a wet log. Soldiers used this in Vietnam for various purposes," he said, "in small amounts for heating rations, even though the fumes are somewhat toxic, and they would sometimes eat just a little bit to get high, or a little more to get sick enough to go on leave. It didn't usually work. Papu, as I said, even if I shot it with a rifle, it wouldn't—and look, you can work it like modeling clay. You can shape it any way you want. It pushes easily into holes and cracks in walls, and it will stick to anything . . ."

"Leonel, can I ask what you are doing with this? And can you please take it back outside?"

"Of course. I'll keep it in the van, and I'll build the cage outside, don't worry. I just brought it in to show you. I thought you'd be interested."

Why would I be? I thought to myself. He still hadn't answered my question. What did he want with something like this?

"I may have need of it," he said, reading my mind. "One never knows. I may have to blow up the front of my fucking house if they come after me. Or I'll have to blow up the front of the priest's house if they come after the priest. Excuse my language."

We found the things he needed for the packaging of the little cage at a fabric house and a feed store. Foam rubber, chicken wire, wire cutters, and duct tape.

"Is it legal for you to have this?" I asked him later over cold pizza.

"I have no idea. That isn't actually a big concern of mine at the moment."

"But how did you get it?"

"My dear, if you have the money and know the right people, you can buy anything you want on a U.S. military base."

The little cage didn't take much time, and he was careful to clean up the random bits of chicken wire and foam rubber. He even took a razor blade to the piece of duct tape left on the porch rail, where it had baked in the sun, and carted the whole of it away in a white plastic trash-bin liner, fitted neatly among the black storage lockers he seemed always to have in the Hiace, and once again it was *Ciao,* a peck on both cheeks, and a pat on the shoulder.

"March, no later," he said. "You have to get back in March."

After Leonel left, the dry Santa Ana winds began, the so-called devil winds flowing down to the sea from the hills, whipping up wildfires, and carrying spores of valley fever. People in Southern California believe this wind affects their moods, much as the sirocco from Libya was said to have driven people mad in Spain. It was not quite time for the Santa Anas, but here they were, bending the palms toward the ground and stirring dry earth into dust devils.

During a lull, Barbara and I pitched a makeshift pup tent for the rabbits as they'd outgrown their hutch, but we kept having to go outside and stake it down. After telling Barbara and the rest of my friends as much as I could about what I had seen in El Salvador, and somewhat less about what I had done, we moved on to other things, mostly writing and work, but when the subject of Leonel or El Salvador came up, I caught the meaningful glances exchanged as one, then another tried to change the subject.

This was hardly the Spanish Civil War, they said, a subject that interested North American poets at the time, nor could it possibly be Vietnam as there was nothing about it in the newspapers, which seemed odd, given the butchery I described, nothing even in *The New York Times*, which was, at that time, at last covering the "dirty wars" in Argentina and Chile. My friends attempted gently to discourage me from returning in March. I think I listened, but nothing anyone said seemed to have any effect on me.

At the discount store Gemco, I bought some of the items on the list of things Dr. Vicky had mentioned needing: sanitary pads to use as field dressings, iodine, isopropyl alcohol, adhesive tape, elastic bandages, finger splints, cold packs, sterile gloves, burn ointment, antibiotic ointment, aspirin, tweezers, petroleum jelly, thermometers, and penicillin in any form, expired or otherwise. To this I added baby bottles, nipples, an aspirator for sucking phlegm, and a bottle of multivitamins for Dr. Vicky herself. All of this I packed into a rip-stop duffel bag, set on the carpet near the mattress where I slept and beside piles of books: versions of *Teach Yourself Colloquial Spanish,* vocabulary flash cards, Leonel's rubber-banded Machiavelli, the poems of Roque Dalton in Spanish, and a copy of *Donde no hay doctor,* the village health-care handbook by David Werner et al., bought so I could learn enough to be of better help to Dr. Vicky in the months to come. The doctors' offices that I called couldn't help me with the penicillin, or any other prescription medicines for that matter. One suggested that I look in the Dumpsters behind health facilities as things were always being thrown away. The Dumpster was my best bet, they thought.

"What you need," one of my few sympathetic friends said, "is a convoy of trucks and millions of dollars, not only for this year but also for next year and the year after that. Do you really think that one duffel bag stuffed with first aid supplies is going to do anything at all?"

Then it occurred to me: Imodium, the new diarrhea drug. I needed to buy as many boxes of Imodium as I could afford. I had to turn around, drive back to Gemco, and buy Imodium. The chief cause of death in children is amoebic dysentery. We had to turn around.

"I think," this friend said, "that you should take a step back." She was still talking as she followed me indulgently into the store. I must have been listening as I usually try not to ignore people when they're talking to me.

"The card," I said. "I can put it on the card."

The pharmacy employee who had led me to the aisle of the antidiarrheal medicines showed me the different brands. There was also Kaopectate and Pepto-Bismol. I began loading up the cart, and I realized, of course, that I would need more duffel bags. Of course, I realized that.

I t was Leonel himself who came for me this time. He was standing beside a jeep just outside the terminal, where the taxis waited. The sun was blazing but he was wearing a jacket. When he reached me, he did something he had never before done. He held me close to him. I felt something then, just under his armpit: a gun in a shoulder holster.

"I'm happy you are here. We have a lot to do." Now I was at arm's length, his hands on my shoulders as he seemed to study how much I had changed in the intervening two months.

"You're armed."

"Everything is fine."

"But you don't usually—"

"Wear a weapon? Papu, don't worry too much. When things get dangerous enough to worry, you'll know."

"And Margarita?"

"She's waiting for you. Get in."

He hoisted one bag, then another into the back of the jeep, duffel after duffel, and despite having so much with me this time, I was waved through customs without so much as a glance.

"Jesus Christ, Papu, what have you got in here?"

"Supplies."

"Don't I feed you enough?"

"They're for Vicky. Only the blue one is mine."

"How much time do you have?"

"Two weeks."

Now we were shouting over the engine, the traffic, the wind flap of canvas, and I was back, as if I hadn't been away, and as before we were driving somewhere known only to him. Things have changed since you were here, he told me over the engine noise. Many more people have disappeared, and many more have turned up dead, and if you want to find a corpse, people say to watch for vultures or schoolchildren as both are drawn to corpses, and it's time not to be seen in certain places with certain people, and to remember always and everywhere that they are listening, they are watching with many eyes and ears, and at night, especially at night when people think they are safe in their beds, well, that is no time to relax anymore because any moment they might come and break your door down and drag you out and shove you into a Jeep Cherokee with black windows or a panel truck and that would be it and you don't want me to tell you how the end will come.

I n those days, the people I knew in the city moved around, house to house, never staying long in one place or traveling by the same means or route. No one was known by his or her given name, and several had taken more than one pseudonym: a woman I knew as Ana someone else knew as Carmen; Roberto became Mario and then Balthazar; and I knew even less about Leonel's whereabouts, or what names he was known by, but as I was later to learn, he was called El Gordo by one faction of the guerrillas because they regarded him as fat. He knew *my* precise whereabouts most of the time.

"You will always have a person," he'd said, "a contact, a compañera, and you're to stay close with this person. You might spend the morning with the nuns, the afternoon with Margarita, then Rene, Alfredo, but as often as I can, I will be there, and if something ever happens, I will find you. If by some chance you are taken, talk. Right away. Say anything. Say everything. It's a myth that people don't talk under torture. We know what you know, and we can take care of ourselves. Unless this happens, you will be all right. If you get scared, go to the hotel Camino Real where the journalists stay, but always, always let someone know where you are, at all times, so I will know. *¿Vos entendés?*"

Did I understand these instructions? Yes. But the full nature of our situation, its precariousness, the invisible guillotine blade that hung above us, no. When I worried that his life was in danger, he would say yes, yours too, everyone's, but what matters is to work, to bring the sin to the eye, to make many acts of denunciation, large and small, to get word to the world and to arouse conscience, this is what matters, and fate will decide which of us survives, fate or God if there is a God, but not us. We don't get to decide. And by the way, in my opinion, he said, there is no God, but we could help our chances a little by following some basic principles, and these he spelled out, drilling them into me whenever there was a free moment between his monologues of endless analysis.

On three occasions things would go wrong, but, as he would remind me years later, all three times I hadn't followed the rules.

When I awake, there is a chink of raw sun coming through a break in the lámina, and the yellowed newspapers that serve to cover the window openings aren't flapping as they did during the night. It is too still for that. The animals' brays, grunts, and barks that woke me earlier are now quiet. The hammock tied to posts across the room is no longer spread like an open wing, holding the sleeping mound of someone already asleep when we arrived. I was not given a hammock for myself, but rather a more comfortable bed, a pallet raised from the ground and covered with flat-woven rugs. Pallets are the hardest beds I have slept upon, but I did sleep without waking until the rooster crowed and scratched the ground, tilted his head, and with his quizzical, black bead of an eye seemed to ask what I was doing here. A village pig also came to the hammock. I heard and smelled the pig before I saw it.

I went deep under the rugs, which smelled of smoke. That morning I had asked Leonel again what he was doing, why he had brought me here, and I thought he would give his usual answer having to do with educating a poet, or he would say that his reason had evolved over time, but this time he had another answer.

"I'm learning to imagine being a North American," he said. "In order to think in a certain way one must learn how to enter the mind of another, as a guest to be sure, but to feel another's reality from within. I'm not

[247]

studying you," he said, "I'm learning you, and you could use your time here to learn what it is to be Salvadoran, to become that young woman over there who bore her first child at thirteen and who spends all of her days sorting tobacco leaves according to their size. Now that would be an education."

L eonel thought it might be a good idea for me to pay more visits to the U.S. embassy, or at least to be seen coming and going from there, so he arranged for me to meet with the health programs officer. I believe that was her title. He wanted me to ask her about U.S. aid to El Salvador in the area of human health. I was again on U.S. territory, and even the air felt carpeted.

"We do have some excellent programs," she began, smiling, "the most important being a promotional program designed to encourage campesinos to use their local facilities."

"Hospitals and clinics?"

"Well, yes."

I remembered that, according to Dr. Vicky, the people passing by her hospital could hear screams coming from the operating room. They were afraid to come here, she'd said. I wondered what sort of promotional program would remedy that.

"Have you visited the local health facilities?"

The health programs officer patted her stiff hair and stared at me.

"The clinics," I prodded as gently as I could. "Have you visited them?"

"Well, there are only so many hours in a day, and as you can see, I have plenty of work to do right here at my desk."

It was true. Her desk was stacked with papers, bound and loose, some in manila folders, the topmost marked CLASSIFIED. There were no personal photographs to link her to any other life. Her nameplate was such that it could be slid from its holder and replaced by the name of someone else.

"We also have programs for population control and latrinization," she said.

Perhaps the look on my face prompted her to elaborate, so she added: "To provide condoms to men and also latrines to the rural areas to help prevent contamination of groundwater."

She handed me leaflets for these programs, with cartoon instructions for how to put on a condom and how to set up and use a latrine. There were no words to accompany the cartoons.

The U.S. embassy was located in the city then. When Leonel took me there, he preferred to wait outside in his jeep or the Hiace, parked on a side street. He would read while he waited, usually a magazine, especially the ones he asked me to bring him from the States, having to do with marksmanship and racing cars. It must have been May when I met with the health programs officer, because the Formula One Grand Prix at Monaco was one of his consuming interests at the time, and most especially he hoped that this race would be televised in El Salvador.

He had advised me always to walk slowly out of the embassy, to stop just outside the fence and look around, as if making sure of something.

"Pretend that you are taking precautions against being followed or watched."

"Am I?"

"Of course not, my dear! Remember the symphony of illusion. One of the reasons I bring you here is so that you can be seen going and coming. The other is that I want you to learn something about your own country.

"Welcome back to El Salvador," he sang out as I climbed into the passenger seat this time. "How did it go?"

"It was odd. She doesn't go out. Never leaves the embassy except to go home. She stays in the compound all day and that's it. I think I have seen more of this country than she has. And it's her job!"

"What's her job?"

"She's in charge of the U.S. aid for health programs here. Presumably—"

"Don't presume, Papu. Never presume. She arrives each morning at eight forty-five a.m. wearing her badge. She leaves precisely at five in the afternoon. She moves pieces of paper from one basket to another. That's all. Her job, my dear, is to move papers."

We passed the front entrance, not heavily guarded in those days. Two U.S. Marines in their dress blues stood on either side of the glass doors like nutcrackers beside the two flags. Through the iron fence and the rattling palms, the building was blinding white.

The Americans did something about twenty years ago," he said over the wind. "There was malaria, and they sent crop dusters to spray for mosquitoes. The malaria disappeared for a long time. After that, they wanted to clean up the country because there was so much dysentery. This is because the poor have no place but the fields to relieve themselves, as you have seen. They sent several thousand latrines they called portable toilets. Johnny on the Spot. They were blue plastic, with doors and ventilation, and it was explained to the campesinos how to use the chemicals to get rid of the waste. The campesinos live in houses made of mud and cardboard. One man said to me, 'How can we live in a cardboard box and shit in a plastic house?' So what do you think? They took apart the latrines and used the materials to make better houses. Even now, today, walking in the countryside, you will find the blue toilet seats scattered around."

All of this was shouted as we drove with a jeep's canvas roof rolled back.

"Latrinization!"

"What?"

"That's what she called the program. 'Latrinization.'"

"Yes, well. You see how well that worked. And the condoms? You find those too. The kids thought they were balloons. As for using the rural hospitals, a supply of anesthesia would be helpful."

"What about the incubators Vicky showed me? They looked new."

"The Swedes. Actual supplies seem always to come from the Swedes. And some crazy Pekingese poet, a descendant of Genghis Khan, who shops in San Diego."

He winked and patted my leg. "Let's go find a television so I can watch the race at Monaco."

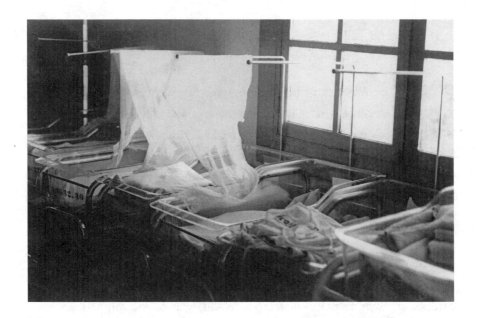

With most people, especially rural laborers, I never said anything about writing poetry, not because I was hiding something but because it didn't seem important. There was one night when I did confess that this is what I did in my other life, my life in *los Estados Unidos,* a place still remote in the imaginations of most Salvadorans, not yet a destination for survival, economic or otherwise. I was in a *casita* on a cooperative farm with a group of labor organizers, and one of them, José Rodolfo Viera, a friend who would be killed within a year, was, on this night, in a house full of guns—not military weapons, but small arms carried for protection—and he was talking quietly with the others about the possibility that paramilitary death squads would attack that night, or soon. They were discussing how to preserve the cooperative in the aftermath of their deaths. It was a calm, matter-of-fact conversation concerning what was to be done. My friend turned to me several times and asked if I was afraid, as if he were asking if I was cold, if I needed a jacket. When I said yes, of course, there was supportive laughter all around, and when it died down, there was more serious talk.

Finally, one man asked me something I didn't quite understand, which happened a lot in those days.

"He is asking what your work is," Viera translated.

"My work?"

"Yes, not here but at home. What do you do at home?"

That is when I confessed that I wrote poetry. It seemed an odd thing, and I was a little embarrassed about it at the time.

Poeta, poeta went around the room. A man, fingering a straw hat shaped like a fedora, asked me if I would please say a poem for them.

"Recite?"

Yes! came from all around the room. "Can you say one of your poems?"

"I'm sorry, from memory? One of my own? No, I don't know them by heart."

This seemed to surprise them. "Do you know of the poet Roque Dalton?"

I was relieved to answer yes, I know his poetry.

"He was one of us. The poet Roque Dalton."

"Our *compañero*," added another, holding his fist against his heart. "And he was killed also by one of us."

"I don't understand. One of you killed him?" This couldn't be true, I thought. There is something I'm not understanding here. I would ask Leonel later about it.

"We are honored that you are a poet and are here with us," Viera said on behalf of the others, and then there was a bit of commotion, suddenly it seemed it was time to go. Trucks and jeeps had pulled into the compound. We had to move somewhere else.

"*¡Apúrate! ¡Apúrate!*" someone was shouting.

"Come with me, this way," Viera said, taking hold of my arm and steering me toward his truck as one by one the other vehicles skidded off in clouds of dust. Once I saw him behind the wheel, I realized how small he was, thin, more so than the others, and he was without a weapon, which, in any case, he didn't need because, according to Leonel, Viera said that he wasn't even able to kill a chicken, let alone could he take the life of a man, and so to reassure me that he could well outrun anyone who might have been coming for us, he took his eyes from the road to smile so broadly that some source of light from the truck cab caught on his gold front tooth that matched the gold crucified Christ around his neck.

The death squads left their marks and warnings, publishing lists of their targets in newspapers, making calls in the night and hanging up. The dead click was enough to send the message. In San Salvador, the warnings of Mano Blanca appeared: fingers and palms dipped in white paint and slapped against doors and walls at night to dry by morning, handprints that resembled the paintings of schoolchildren if they weren't also a sign of being marked for death. I asked Leonel why he never entered churches, on whose doors many handprints appeared.

"I believe with my life," he said, "with how I live."

Wwe were somewhere near the unfinished cathedral and the plaza where for a few hours in the afternoons and also at night vendors sold holy cards, ice cream, and open sodas from stalls that closed with rippled security gates. I was with Monseñor Ricardo Urioste, a quiet, studious priest whom I knew as a friend of Monseñor Romero's. He was walking calmly but with long steps, and I walked beside him, but it was hard to keep up. The weather was white with the coming rains.

We had been talking about the views of the religious community toward the armed struggle when suddenly he fell silent, holding his hand out before him, palm down. He had stopped walking and had fixed his gaze on the street ahead of us. I tried to see what he was seeing but saw only the traffic, bumper to bumper, brightly painted buses with their black exhaust and sacks tied to their roofs, cars nosing behind them with windows down and radios blaring. The voice in the commercial was calling out *"Domingo Domingo Domingo,"* then the horns, voices, and motor scooters died down. The cars had stopped too, many of the drivers now seeing what Monseñor Urioste saw.

A panel truck had stopped just ahead of us in the street, and men were leaping from the back. Two of them grabbed a teenager wearing a student's rucksack and wrestled him into the vehicle. Everyone stopped, or moved away from where they had been, some ducking behind the buses, and right beside me a security gate was suddenly slammed onto the side-walk. Monseñor Urioste crossed himself as others around us vanished into alleys and shops. There was a stillness then and the truck peeled away with such a scream of tires that the sound seemed to stay in the air after it could no longer be seen.

"We must pray for that boy," Monseñor Urioste whispered.

This was the first and only time I witnessed an abduction, the moment when someone is made to disappear, to become *desaparecido*. Before and after this, I encountered the *desaparecidos* only in the body dumps, in the morgue, on the roadside, and along the beach, or I would study their faces in the photographs provided by their families and ask, sometimes aloud, *Where are you?* Over the years these faces have grown younger and younger.

WRITTEN IN PENCIL:

When someone joins a death squad he is in for life if you quit you might talk and no one wants to be fingered later for these crimes the first time such a man goes out on an operation he is tested by the others they tell him he must rape the victim in front of them then cut off certain pieces of the body they want to see if he has the stomach for this after that he is as guilty as the others and he is in his reward is usually money why isn't it enough to kill a victim why must each also suffer mutilation the death squad members must all be guilty of every murder so one rapes another strikes blows another uses the machete and so on until it would be impossible to determine which action had caused the death and the squad members are protected from each other by mutual guilt also when mere death no longer instills fear in the population the stakes must be raised the people must be made to see that not only will they die but die slowly and brutally.

I t was now the rainy season. It rained for a few hours every morning and also in the late day. At night, the death squads did their work. Morning came, and in front of a school, a corpse would be found with its shirt pecked open and its eyes gone. Margarita had to leave to visit her father in Ahuachapán, so it was decided that I would go with a woman they called Luisa to the house of her friend V, who lived in a quiet *colonia* shaded by the rustle of manaca palms.

By the time we arrived, the sun had already gone behind the city, and I remember worrying about the hour as it would mean having to drive back in the dark. When I mentioned this, Luisa nodded that yes, she agreed it would be dangerous to return at night.

"But what can we do?" she asked, then after a moment added: "We can probably sleep here."

"But I didn't bring anything."

"What do you need? You don't need anything to sleep. You close your eyes. Besides, it is better for the work if I have more time." She turned to face me, looking into my eyes for a long moment. I couldn't remember when the people around me had started to refer to "the work" or "working."

"You must be careful in this house, do you understand? We are just two women visiting a friend, something light and social. We are going to talk about unimportant things. Some men are going to come and then we will go upstairs and V will stay with the men. When they leave, if all goes well, we sleep."

"Does Leonel know we're here?"

"No. He just knows you're with me."

She reached under the driver's seat for a portable tape recorder, took the wrapper off a fresh cassette, inserted it, then pressed RECORD and PLAY.

"*Habla Colibrí. Habla Colibrí*," she whispered.

Hummingbird is speaking.

A maid opened the door and stood behind it to let us pass, as if to use the door as a shield, and then V came from somewhere, rushing toward Luisa, the women kissing on both cheeks, V reaching for me and kissing me too.

"Welcome, welcome."

She wore slender pants, high heels, bangle bracelets. Her dark blond hair fell in loose curls down her back. Her long nails were lacquered the color of the bougainvillea.

"Would you like something?"

Luisa said no, so I also said no.

V led us to the dining-room table. Clean ashtray. Bowl of fruit.

"Sit down, sit down. Please."

V's voice flitted like a delicate bat from this to that, something about friends they had in common, something about the beach, then laughter, a flame rising from her silver lighter. Luisa did seem to be V's friend, but was nothing like her. Luisa wore no makeup, her hair was pulled into a chignon, and she must once have been a dancer as she had a ballerina's carriage and floating walk. Luisa was calm and reserved while V seemed excited about everything. Everything was *precioso*. Yet there was something else going on, something I had learned to perceive here in the interactions between people. On the surface, they seemed lighthearted, but there were meaningful looks exchanged, whole sentences spoken through the eyes, and quick whispers having to do with other things. It was as if they were performing, for someone, but for whom? The truer conversation flowed in rivers of fear and caution beneath the music of what could openly be said.

V checked her watch, stubbed out her cigarette, and just then a buzzer sounded. Luisa caught my eye to say *Now,* to say *Be careful,* and I could tell that she was afraid but of what? The same little fountain of V's laughter and greetings splashed into the front hall, and the men Luisa had told me about came hurriedly into the dining room, one of them grabbing V affectionately around the waist and pulling her onto his lap. They set their guns on the table and asked the maid to bring them beer. I was introduced to each of them and I followed Luisa's lead, which was to smile the entire time and look pleased to meet them. These men weren't like campesinos, nor were they like the wealthy oligarchs. They were not thin, wore no straw hats, and didn't carry machetes on their belts, nor did they wear expensive suits and soft Italian shoes. Instead, they tucked guns into their waistbands, smiled with gold-rimmed teeth, wore their hair combed and wet, and smelled of aftershave.

One of them suddenly asked if I was an American, and what I was doing here. Luisa rushed to answer that I was from Miami and I had come to visit her. Isn't that wonderful? Tomorrow we were going on holiday to Playa El Tunco, the black sand beach. This seemed to satisfy him.

We said our good nights, and as instructed, I followed Luisa up the stairs, leaving V behind with the men, the one in whose lap she was sitting and the two others. In the upstairs room, Luisa motioned for me to lie down with her in the space on the floor between two single beds. She held her finger to her lips, and took the tape recorder out of her bag, then stretched out and with the tape recorder held close to her mouth, she pressed her ear to the gray tile floor to listen to the muffled conversation of the men.

The voices grew beer loud, then low, and every few minutes Luisa whispered what she heard into the machine. The voices were laced with V's laughter and then the voices died. A door closed.

V climbed the stairs to the bedroom door and Luisa went to her. They held each other for a moment, then broke away, nodding to each other that everything was all right. When V went back downstairs, Luisa patted the bed I was to sleep on and she lay down on the other one, turning toward me.

"D'Aubuisson's men," she whispered into the dark air. "Roberto D'Aubuisson."

I had heard him referred to as Blowtorch Bob because he used a blowtorch during torture sessions. They also called him Chele for his light skin.

"Was that man really V's boyfriend?" I whispered.

"No, but he wants to be. V helps us. You must never tell anyone what you saw here tonight."

———◆———

Now whenever Leonel pulled to the curb in front of a house where I'd spent a night, I would toss my rucksack in the back and climb in, no longer asking where we were going, as I thought I was now prepared for whatever might happen. He would hand me a weapon to hold for him, rolled into a magazine: usually a .357 Magnum or 9mm Smith and Wesson. Sometimes he would hand me another to cover with my sweater, and if, with a glance, I questioned him, his eyes would say *Wait*. We'd drive to the din of radio or wind, never the same route, never talking until we reached the open road. On this day, he said we were going to a special place. There was something he had long wanted to show me, but it had to wait until he felt that I understood how life was for most people in the *campo,* and until I had firmly in mind the fierce cold of night, the meager diet of salted tortillas and beans, the stench of waste in the ditches, the little sleep.

"This is something different," he said, "something possible."

Don't ask, I thought. Put your feet on the dashboard and don't ask. Eventually, he will talk. This "something possible" was, as it turned out, a long way from San Salvador. We were going to drive almost all the way to the coast, to a region where there weren't many roads.

Yes, I had my toilet paper, yes my flashlight, yes insect repellent, yes a change of clothes, a sweater, a poncho, a notebook. And he had his weapons, which, he insisted, wouldn't be needed once we were there, and he had his roll of white butcher paper, his drawing pencils, his pipe.

Not long before this journey to "something possible," he had begun taking me along with him some nights to the meetings of a rural labor union, usually held in a church assembly or a school, always in a room with a table and folding chairs, an easel with a large tablet of white paper, sometimes a chalkboard. The men arrived in guayaberas, trousers, and sandals, most of them holding or wearing straw hats, machetes dangling at their sides, and they sat waiting or stood along the back wall as opening speeches were made. When it was Leonel's turn, he would begin by pacing back and forth at the front, as if he were talking only to himself, turning to ask questions of the assembled without expecting answers in return. He asked: *So how has it come to this?* And *What do you think this means?* And then he would pick up a piece of chalk or a black-marker pen and begin to draw, just as he had at my kitchen table.

Apparently, some years ago, an official group from the United States had been expelled from the country for interfering in the affairs of a rural labor union, and this same group was now in the process of attempting, once again, to secure some control of the union by hiring one of its members as an "adviser" in exchange for a modest salary. But who among the union members should be selected for this somewhat lucrative position? And why should the union permit this? What, after all, would this mean? Two men were vying for the job, but other union members saw the danger in allowing anyone to work for an entity outside the membership. What to do?

Quickly, he drew at least twenty small figures on the white tablet, some wearing straw hats, others not, all standing together in a row, and on the other side of the paper, a single figure holding a bag with a dollar sign. He circled the group of twenty, talked a bit more, and sketched an arrow pointing at the stick figure holding the money.

"This is not how a cooperative works," he said. "The gringos know this. They want to control your leadership. Think about what it means to be controlled from the outside."

Leonel's illustrated lectures, followed by question-and-answer sessions, lasted into the nights until such time as it became too dangerous to leave any such meeting at a late hour, even in a large group.

The following day, he intended to make a similar presentation, he said, in this very "possible" place, and although the matter up for discussion was different, there would be ink drawings, speeches, and disagreement.

It was a long way to the "possible" place, and quite hot, as I remember, most of it along slow dirt roads, sometimes passing mule carts or men bent under the weight of bundles tied to their backs. Now it was Victor Jara's voice coming from the dashboard as we rocked in the deep holes and were knocked from side to side by the boulders just under the surface of the road—Victor Jara, the Chilean who had now been dead for five years but was still singing. Leonel was going over something aloud in his mind and I can see this in my memory, his laughter, the cold pipe held by the same hand that held the wheel, and I see myself too beside him, young, laughing at something he said, gripping the sidebar to steady myself. We are both relaxed. This is a part of the country where nothing has happened yet.

———◆———

"This parcel of land was in the family, but nothing had been done with it for a long time. As you can see, my dear, there are very few roads, and they are impassable in the rainy season, and therefore it isn't easy to make this land productive. So, my brother, he let me, shall we say, do something with this land. He never asked me what it was that I did."

We had stopped in front of a tree growing in the middle of the road, surrounded by a low wall of hand-stacked stones forming a protective ring around the tree. Leonel knelt, appearing to inspect the stones, and then rose to his feet and dusted himself off, laughing and shaking his head.

"What is it?"

"This road wasn't here last year."

"What do you mean wasn't here?"

"The people built this road by hand. With shovels and hand tools. And when they came to this tree, instead of cutting it down, they left it. But someone was thinking. Someone knew that a tree in the middle of the road would need protection. Wait until you see what I'm going to show you."

As we approached what I would have described as a *caserío*, children began running alongside us and then their mothers came out, holding other children, and soon there were men too, walking toward the road, one or two of them waving, and then they were calling out and Leonel was calling back to them. When he climbed from the Hiace they gathered around him and pulled him along toward a cluster of houses, and when I climbed down, they did the same with me.

"This is my friend, Papu. She's an American," he announced to the gathering, and a few of the women came toward me and the kids ran a little way off to study me from a safe distance.

That day we were taken from house to house, and in each we sat on low stools and talked while being given a sweet corn drink, some sorghum coffee, a small plate of black beans. There was much to report, it seemed, since Leonel's last visit. These houses were different from the others I had seen. Their mud walls had been whitewashed and someone had painted murals of flowers, birds, and trees on some of them. The artist might have been a child—everything bright and open.

The people wanted to show Leonel the playground they had built. There was also a school and a small clinic, but he had seen those before on other trips. From what I could gather, he visited this place only once a year, but he came without fail, and this time he brought me.

"Let them show you around," he said. "I have some business to do. It won't take long."

So we walked or, rather, I was pulled along, and finally wound up in someone's house in a hammock being rocked by children who took turns running off and returning with things to show me: a little sand pail and shovel, a drawing of a horse with five children on its back, a blond-haired doll without clothes. When Leonel returned from whatever business he was doing, I didn't want to leave, but of course "we had work to do" and "didn't have much time" to do it.

AFTER WE SAID OUR MANY GOOD-BYES, WE CLIMBED INTO THE HIACE AND SET off down the road again, around the protected tree and into what seemed a shore cloud of road dust.

"Well? What do you think?"

That village was like none of the others I had seen, and this had less to do with murals and playgrounds and more to do with the children's wanting to show off their things, with each house's opening itself, with little touches like stones stacked against trees and a swing set next to the school. I realized that I hadn't smoked in a few hours. I had forgotten to smoke.

"Let me give you a little history. Several years ago, some campesinos came to me and wanted to farm this land, which, as I have said, had been abandoned for lack of infrastructure in the area. Who wants to grow crops when there is no way to get them to market? So I said yes, and we settled on the percentage I would be paid. Fine. At the end of each harvest I would visit, make arrangements to collect my rent, and it went on like that. Soon, there were a number of families farming the land. One year, the crops failed. I don't know why. Maybe blight or drought or some such fucking thing—"

"You were charging people to farm your land?"

"This is the system here, but wait. That year, when I visited, I decided to cancel their debt because of the failure. Remember—I was learning something too. I told them that if they formed a cooperative, I would charge half what I had been charging. If they opted to stay on their own, the price would remain the same. The next year, I went back, and guess what? All but three had formed a cooperative. So I made good and charged the cooperative members half. The next year, everyone was a member. At that year's meeting, I suggested that they might want to do something for the children. I didn't say what. You decide, I said—but do something. That is how the school appeared. And as each year passed, the people became more secure. If the cooperative continued, it was always half price, if the crops failed, no charge, and each year when I visited, there was something else to show me: the clinic, the playground, the new road, and they then began to paint the houses. I realized that the one factor, the one difference, and maybe the only difference was this: The people felt secure. They made decisions together, they took risks together, they shared the risk, and, very important, they knew I wasn't going to kick them off the land."

The engine heaved and pulled and the sun bore down on us. We were off the dirt road now and onto the paved highway that led toward the coast. There was salt in the air. I was smoking again and drinking from the warm canteen.

"What?"

"That all sounds fine," I said, "but—" The water was almost hot.

"But what?"

"It's your land. You are the one who visits. You are the one who makes suggestions, and you are the one who collects the money. You make the rules. Why don't you just give them the land? They are the ones doing all the work." I crushed the butt into the ashtray and leaned back, folding my arms across myself. "That's what I think."

We drove, listening again to the engine.

"I can't give them the land."

"Why not? Of course you can. You're the *padrino*! This is paternalism, Leonel, pure and simple. You're the *jefe*. Well, good for you!"

I pressed my bare feet into the dash, leaned back, and closed my eyes. "Maybe that was a little harsh. I liked your village. But it's *yours*."

This sounded smug and self-righteous and I knew it, but I didn't know how to save the moment. The wind in the Hiace buffeted us because of how fast we were going on the paved road.

"I can't give it to them," he said again, flatly. "They have to take it from me."

That day, we ended our trip at the coast. It was the first time I saw the famous black sand beaches, the blond, foreign surfers bobbing in the water, the wooden fishing boats overturned, and this place, with its fluttering tablecloths protected by white paper upon which Leonel was certain to make drawings. He ordered *gambas a la plancha* for both of us: sweet white shrimp the size of a fist, turned twice over a fire, and he was in such a lighthearted mood that he even accepted the beer that the proprietor offered him. If I hadn't known better, this would have seemed like a rustic tropical resort, with hammocks strung between palms and drinks served in coconut shells.

"They have to take the land from me because if I give it to them it will not really be theirs."

"I don't understand. How would they take it?"

"For example," he said between mouthfuls of shrimp, "one year when I come they could refuse to pay me."

"Oh, right—they would never dare to do that."

"Well, they have to dare to do it."

"You are manipulating them."

"Yes, my dear, and so what? Remember, I have been learning too, all along. This has been a process for me too. Do you think any other small landholder in this fucking country would say to you what I just said? Do you know how long it took me to break through to this place? It all seems obvious now maybe, but there was a time when it wasn't so obvious."

"Do you think they'll demand the land from you? Ever?"

"Yes. They are getting close—next year or the year after that. They'll be nice about it, I think, but I hope they'll be firm. Several of them are emerging as leaders in the community and that interests me too. How is it that leaders emerge? What is the process of their formation? How is it that people begin to trust them enough to follow their lead? I'm interested in this because we'll have to begin replacing all the dead leaders in other parts of the country."

I pushed my chair a little away from the table.

"I'm glad you got a little angry with me back there," he said. "You were right."

"Well, I'm sorry I did. Who am I to accuse you of anything? I'm a gringa."

"Papu, listen to me. You have to be able to see the world as it is, to see how it is put together, and you have to be able to say what you see. And get angry."

AT THE TIME, I THOUGHT LEONEL KNEW EVERYTHING. HE COULD SHOOT A coconut open as it dropped to the ground. He could hear a faint whisper pass through a cinder-block wall. He was bulletproof, and because I was with him, nothing would happen to him or me. At the time that I thought this, he was thirty-seven years old.

The colonels and lieutenant colonels continued to ask to meet with me. One such meeting was to take place in the National Palace, in the offices of the ministry of defense. The building was next to the Metropolitan Cathedral, on one side of the Plaza Cívica. It was painted an ivory color that turned to gold when lit up at night. There were special ceremonial rooms within it, a red room, a yellow room, lit by chandeliers and as ornately decorated as some of the rooms at Versailles.

"I don't want you to go there," Margarita said flatly. "For what possible reason should you go alone into a place like that?"

"Some colonel Leonel wants me to meet with—I'm not sure. But there's always a reason."

"Well, if you are going to do it—and I don't think you should—I am going to go with you."

"You would do that? But, Margarita—"

"Yes," she said, always pronouncing it *Jess*.

By this time, I knew something of who she really was and something of what she was doing. I knew things that I don't think even Leonel knew, such as: One of the voices of the Church's radio station, YSAX, was a woman, and the death squads apparently thought this voice belonged to a nun. They were determined to find and kill her.

"And as long as they keep looking for a nun, I am safe," Margarita had said.

We were in her bedroom now, and she was dressing, tossing clothes and shoes on the bed for me to try on.

"When you do this work, you must always look like a bourgeois," she said, leaning close to her mirror to line her eyes with kohl. When I had chosen something, she turned me to face her and adjusted the dress.

"Don't be shy to show a little of your womanhood," she said, and then she handed me a different pair of shoes with a higher heel.

"So, we'll go then. You'll have this meeting or whatever it is, and then we will go to La UCA."

Margarita looked elegant. I looked like a stranger to myself. While I was with the colonel, she paced the corridor. This particular colonel was not at all friendly, and seemed not to know much more than I did about why we were meeting together. One could even say that he appeared to be nervous about it. He spoke in a clipped, insistent voice about the threat of communism's coming from all sides and expressed a barely concealed contempt for U.S. policy, particularly the withholding of military aid pending human rights certification. It occurred to me that I was here in order to be seen to be here. The colonel ended our meeting by warning me to be careful, in a voice that did not show concern for my safety or well-being.

One afternoon, while Margarita did some work at La UCA, I talked for a few hours with her friend Ricardo Stein, who was working to establish a "documentation center" there. Ricardo spoke mostly about the organized left but was conversant on a range of subjects. He explained things to me that Leonel hadn't bothered to explain, having to do with single-crop economies, fluctuations in commodity prices, the crisis within the plutocracy that was now split between those who thought it wise to industrialize and those who wished to remain agrarian. He also talked at length about the guerrilla factions and the differences among them.

For a short while, I also saw Father Ellacuría, who seemed rested and relaxed this time, which Margarita said was unusual, but he had just returned from a trip to his native country, Spain, so he had been able to breathe, she said, for a time. On that day, Ellacuría wanted to talk about "the unfolding of reality," and the ways in which individuals and societies inherit from the past, and bequeath to the future, in a continual unfolding into greater complexity. He introduced me to the word "praxis," which I understood to mean "human action to change reality" making possible "the liberation of liberty." I tried to follow his thought through the labyrinth of phenomenology and Marxist analysis and, most important, the thought of his greatest influence, the Basque philosopher Xavier Zubiri, who was interested in bridging epistemology and metaphysics, the distinction between the process of knowing and the object of knowing.

It was growing dark by the time we left the grounds, but we felt light-hearted as we walked to the car. Margarita playfully teased me about what I had understood and not understood about Ellacuría's ideas.

"He is a genius," she said. "No one understands him."

"Does Leonel know where we are?" I remember asking, but I don't remember what her answer was. I remember that she rolled the window down, lit two cigarettes, and handed one to me. Her lipstick was on the filter. We now felt that we were practically sisters.

That evening we'd planned to meet with some of Margarita's friends and a few European journalists who had arrived in the country several weeks earlier. We would listen to reports of what they had seen and we would tell them what we knew. There would be Coca-Cola and potato chips. We were still in the clothes we had chosen that morning, so yes, we did look bourgeois, but I would never have been able to run in those shoes. I could barely walk in them. Margarita pulled out of the parking lot onto what I would call a slip road—narrow and unlit, a road that wound around La UCA.

She was still laughing and teasing me when suddenly, and in a grave voice, she said my name, and the car was flooded with light. She pressed the accelerator to the floor. The vehicle behind us was following so closely that a person could have leaped from one roof to the other. Margarita sped into a tunnel of darkness ahead and the vehicle behind us sped too.

"*Escuadrón de la muerte*," she said, "it is the death squad, Carolyn. They are going to capture us—"

I turned around to watch the other car but couldn't see it for the light.

"Margarita," I remember calling out, "can you go faster?"

"No, Carolyn, I cannot. This is as fast as I can go. And I think I am lost."

"There's the city ahead of us. Drive toward the lights."

We sped. The other car sped too. This was going to be it, I thought, now when it wasn't expected, after a day of talking about philosophy and God and the practice of liberation. I wanted to be brave. I did not feel brave. I had no weapon; it would not have helped. There was no last chance to do anything over again. Are you afraid, Margarita? *Jess.*

They were still behind us when we reached a heavier-trafficked road, behind us when we got to the roundabout, and that was where the honking began, other cars whose drivers saw what was happening, other cars pulling into the roundabout, slowing down, blocking the way of those who followed us, and all the while horns honking and even some cars stopping and people getting out of the cars and then there was an opening and we took it. All the way to the house of the friends of Margarita we didn't breathe and then the door was opening, and we ran through it from the front of the house to the garden in the back where the journalists were standing around in the dark.

———◆———

I sank to the floor, pressing my back against the wall while trying to catch my breath. There was a bird of paradise growing there, where the terrace ended and the wet lawn began.

"Would you like to drink some water?" a woman asked. Everyone else was standing off to the side when she knelt and gave me the cold glass that slipped through my hands to the tiles and fell to pieces. Margarita lifted her arms in the air in a gesture of asking everyone to please leave us alone for just a minute. Just a minute while we catch our breath.

"They want to know what happened," she whispered, "tell them nothing happened. You can tell them this because nothing did. We are all right."

I nodded my head yes and tried to get to my feet without cutting myself. A young man came over and pulled me up and we were inside the house, now crowded with strangers. I think the journalists were from the Netherlands, one in denim overalls, I remember that. He had long hair and was a large man. Maybe some of the others were religious, I didn't know, but Margarita was comfortable with them and so I was too. Would I like some chips? No. Coke? Yes. Too much attention was being paid to us, too much kindness. These people knew that something had happened.

They didn't know what. They could see plainly, however, that Margarita and I had been terrified out of our minds by something. Had I followed the rules that Leonel had set down? Most. But it was night, we were driving on an unlit road, and that was the rule I broke.

The group turned toward me expectantly. Margarita had apparently just told them that I had been in the *campo* with Leonel that week.

"Tell them what you saw," she said, "this is what is important."

W RITTEN IN PENCIL:

On both sides of the road there was smoke it was blue and still rising when we passed although the fields were already black from being burned everything was burned they had shot the cattle yes even them and the pigs they had also shot so they were lying there already bloated and there was a smell of meat as well as death and a howling that couldn't actually have been heard but it was there the wattle in the houses was burned and the corn in the cribs we didn't stop we slowed down the turkey vultures were above us many also already on the ground they don't sing they hiss some things we saw through the field glasses some with naked eyes we couldn't tell how many people we didn't know how long it had been that's all I told them.

Leonel had driven as slowly as he could through the smoke.

"Look, Papu. Look at this. Remember this. Try to see."

WRITTEN IN PENCIL:

This is the village abandoned a pitted road stretches between burned shacks in the mud there is a saint's picture decorated with foil stars there is no smoke rising from cook fires where women would have turned the family's daily tortillas nor any from the fires that chewed through this village during a "search-and-destroy" operation the people returned here briefly and held orange rinds wrapped in cloth over their mouths as they gathered the dead listing their names and where this was possible sex and approximate age they poured lime over the assembled remains until the bodies seemed covered with hoarfrost a woman who had hid in the branches of a tree worked her skirt into knots as she told the story of what happened but she had so rubbed her eyes from grief that all she had seen could be seen in them in a different village a man told the story of having pretended to be dead in place of the cries of children for their parents a light rain ticks against the corrugated roofs that have slipped into the wet palms of the ravine. *In Salvador, death still patrols*, wrote Pablo Neruda in a poem. *The blood of dead peasants has not dried.*

Y es," Leonel said, "but Pablo Neruda also wrote *The poet gives us a gallery full of ghosts shaken by the fire and darkness of his time.*"

I was lying in the dark when the telephone rang. We had developed a signal to let each other know when all was well: two rings followed by silence. Now, after three rings, I picked up. He didn't say hello. He spoke as he had on the day he called to say that Colonel Chacón was dead.

"Remember Texas, Carolyn? Well, *ha habido un golpe*. You have your coup d'état."

Without a good-bye, the line went dead, the room dead. The *apertura* had been made.

W RITTEN IN PENCIL:

At first it was thought that the younger officers had taken control but there was too much shuffling within the military some officers could be cashiered yes but not others and there should be assurances that no senior officer would be prosecuted for his crimes however a blanket amnesty would mean that the butchers would remain in control and the kickbacks would continue and even though yes there could be a few civilians on the junta those civilians would have to resign for moral and political reasons to be replaced by others who were let us say more practical and so over the months the crack in the wall was repaired until it was almost impossible to see that an opening had ever appeared and yet use could be made of the fact that it had and so in hindsight all manner of explanations could be proffered as to how it happened and why it happened but rather than buying time for reforms from within rather than preventing all-out civil war rather than showing that change could come about through these means it was shown that the coming war was inevitable and this was the lesson taken from it.

W RITTEN IN PENCIL:

It is summer we are driving along a highway that turns into a mirage of water ahead of us there are now two weapons one of a caliber strong enough to stop a vehicle he had taken me finally to the coffee finca where he showed me how to breathe while shooting how to brace the weapon in both hands a bottle set upon the rock in the distance finally shattering and then it was time to take apart the weapon with eyes closed then put it back together rain ticking on the banana leaves and above the shimmery highway the birds almost too heavy to fly rising and falling from something on the side of the road it was a man lying facedown but the birds were also interested in something on the other side of the road and as we slowed we drove over what appeared to be a water hose but it was the man's entrails stretched out across the road maybe carried across by the carrion birds and I think I cried out *stop* but we couldn't stop he said not anymore and there was nothing we could do for that man and other things happened like that it was the time of the death squads the time of the devil's door where the bodies were dumped the time of "the beach" where they lay sprawled, skulls half-stripped flesh half-eaten torn clothes and nearly in each other's arms they lay the stench hanging there the ground giving off the whine of flies so we covered our mouths it was no use they are unrecognizable it is no use this is how the end will come if you are taken do not be taken make your own decisions Margarita said what he is doing is dangerous and he knows it and you should know too and learning to shoot won't help you are a poet there is the sound of gunfire at night near the garrison we can hear it as we lie on the floor talking between the beds a skirmish they said the guerrillas are training now in the mountains using sticks for rifles they have had enough do you know why it has come to this do you understand how innately cautious these people are what would get them to fight am I afraid yes will I continue yes will I die it is likely so tell me what better gift to give than one's life?

W RITTEN IN PENCIL:

Leonel has brought me to El Playon. We park and walk it is early morning and no one is here before stopping he had made sure there were no other vehicles we are alone but as he always cautioned: *don't be too sure* a loud hum of flies rose pulsing in the hot air Leonel passes a handkerchief to me take this take it turkey vultures hopped from corpse to corpse grunting and hissing they don't sing he said they lack vocal cords they have no predators they pull flesh in long strips from the corpses a ribbon of intestine hangs from a beak they are so fat with flesh they are unable to fly their name comes from the Latin *vulturius* for "tearer" it is almost a play on words isn't it and it is easier don't you think to talk about birds? the stench soaks the handkerchief but still I hold it to my mouth and almost trip on a broken bottle of Flor de Caña El Playon is a lava bed a skirt of black spongelike stone in the lap of the volcano there is a graveyard beside it El Playon "the beach" is a rock strewn with refuse and sea wrack a body a tin spoon bottle glass purple from the sun a paint can a skull with hair a shoelace trousers more bodies flocks of vultures fattening themselves on the ground a stripped spine a broken plate a palm open to the rain. El Playon is a body dump. *"Yo lo vi,"* Goya wrote beside his sketches. "I saw it, and this, and also this."

I awoke lying on a bed of ice like a fish or a corpse, the window flickering day, then night, then day. A few turkey vultures curled their talons around the bed rails, one of them hopping onto my stomach and even though I recognized their red masks and their hissing I knew they weren't actually there, these belching, oil-colored birds. They could not be. Saline dripped through a tube from a glass bottle inverted over the bed. Silver. My arm was taped to a splint, a spot of blood on the tape. My other wrist was fastened with gauze to the opposite bed rail. I had pulled the needle out more than once, as even I could remember. I had been *delirante* or whatever it was, crazy, unable to make myself understood, and I had nothing left, I knew that. Everything I had was in the toilet or in the basins but the fever was not out. My bones were still on fire and the fire was also in my head, burning behind my eyes. I couldn't think, and there was some confusion about who was in the room and who wasn't, how long it had been and why. In the darkness, Leonel had talked to me again about jaguars: Why there is a jaguar on my woven bag, why he had given me a small weaving of a jaguar on a torn piece of cloth. He sometimes also called them wildcats. "You are a wildcat, Papu," he said, "you just don't know it yet. That is why I gave you these things. The wildcat can camouflage itself. It can hide anywhere. It doesn't roar like the other great cats. It is solitary and nocturnal and can adapt to many environments. The Mayans call it *b'alam*. Certain humans have jaguar characteristics. They help with communication between the living and the dead. They are said to be extinct in El Salvador but they are not. Someday you will understand why I'm telling you this." A nurse laid a cold washcloth over my eyes. She put something else in the tube, something to help me sleep, she said, something for the pain, just lie quietly. Just rest. Again in my thoughts we run over the man's entrails with the car until there isn't anything left to think about. My dreams are a coffin with a small window cut into the lid over a girl's face. It is not my own. Someone had written on the glass *I will not forget you.* Many times I asked Leonel how it all began for him and finally he told me that when he was a young boy he had come upon a foreman beating a campesino. He went into the house, took his father's shotgun, aimed it at the foreman, and shouted *Strike him once more and I'll blow your balls off.* The foreman stopped beating the man. "And that is when I learned that something could be done," he said, "that there was not nothing we could do." It was quiet. A chance to ask him about the red horse. "It's really quite simple," he said. "The man you met in Guatemala told me several years ago that there would soon be war, and that I would have a lot of work to do, but I would not have to do it alone. Someone was coming who would help. A young person with a red horse. And I thought 'horse'? *Puchica,* I have no need of a goddamn horse. The young person who is coming will have to leave the horse behind—which, as it happened, you did." And then he asked if I could hear him. I nodded my head yes and the wet cloth slipped from my eyes. "It seems you have dengue fever, Papu, and also dysentery. You'll be here for a while." On the ground in front of me there is a skull with the lower half of the jaw missing and beside it an empty jug that once held cooking oil. There is a picked-clean skeleton splayed flat as if it were dancing with the ground. A shoe filled with blood. He's going to ask me if I know where I am. Yes, I do know. This is where they throw the bodies.

———◆———

They have taken blood again. The ceiling comes closer and the doorway shrinks to a smaller box of light. This will help me to sleep. "It is only a tremor," Leonel had said, when the sofa I had been sitting on galloped across the tile floor to the other side of the room. The tiles clattered like stones in a surf and settled into place again. "We have many tremors here," he said. "The earth is moving beneath us, sending fire through any volcanic *apertura* it can find and many of these volcanoes are asleep, but don't kid yourself. Izalco had been sleeping too until the night of the uprising. When I was a young man there was an earthquake in Ixcán not far from where my adviser lives, the man who predicted you. This is how we met. I had gone to Ixcán to offer help and what should happen but a city landed by helicopter in a remote place near a ruined village, a city made of heavy rubber balloons filled with air, balloon walls and roofs, everything pumped into place, balloon medical tent, balloon canteen, even the food rations the Americans sent were made of air. I helped, what else would I do, and that is how we met, the Mayan elder and I, and ever since he has allowed me to talk to him and even though he doesn't have a telephone he always seems to know when I will come to the day, almost to the hour and always he takes a nap then so I have to wait. I was never a patient man until then, I am still impatient. The reason they are taking your blood is that they have to monitor your platelet count. It can't go below a certain number or you will develop the hemorrhagic dengue. Your fever is high now, Papu, so you might see people who aren't here. They will come and go, so let them, it is normal."

All night I had heard cries of agony coming from somewhere close, a woman crying out as if she were being beaten, begging someone to stop, crying through the glass louvers all night like that as I lay awake and didn't move. In the morning, I learn that the cries were those of a parrot in a mango tree, like the parrot saying hello to me from the terrace of the colonel's house on the night I was called upon to answer for my country's new policy on human rights, the night the colonel drank, and I learned that what my former husband had told me was true: To prove a kill, *or for some other reason,* parts of the body were cut off, dried, and kept. I asked Leonel why bodies are mutilated both living and dead and he answered, "To show disrespect *or for some other reason.* Fingers, breasts, ears, genitals. They don't wipe the blood from the knife. Read your Eduardo Galeano, Papu. When the Portuguese captain Bartolomeu Bueno do Prado came back from Rio das Mortes in Brazil he had thirty-nine hundred pairs of ears in his saddlebags. And this was 1759. The Scythians collected skulls and drank from them. The Tibetans had a musical instrument made from a human thigh bone. In Vietnam, as your former husband could have told you, soldiers used to string the ears of the dead on their dog-tag chains. Why be sick about this night? It is something for your poetry, as the colonel said. You can write about this."

W

RITTEN IN PENCIL:

This was after they assembled the parts on the ground into a man it was the time when there were three choices: leave the country wait for them to come and kill you or go to the hills and fight I was given one choice and that was to write a dead woman cannot write we were sitting in the dark as we did then by that time the guerrillas were training in the hills but they were not killers he said they were farmers how far would they be able to take an armed struggle some had no guns they practiced with sticks they had no choice there was also a revolutionary group within the army yes they would come to think of themselves as guerrillas within the army they were behind the coup you saw what happened with that even Monseñor Romero's persuasion couldn't hold the first junta together it was the beginning of the counterinsurgency operation invented by your country wherein the people were seen as the enemy in the beginning they flew small helicopters with glass domes it was the time of flies above the blindfolded dead he said can you describe this? I said I didn't know he said well you have to describe it their throats were cut their eyes half open half closed the Guardia had practiced their beheading on coconuts their saying was *eyes and ears open mouth shut.*

WRITTEN IN PENCIL:

One morning I woke and everything had returned to normal: the door was the size of a door the ceiling where it should be no bottle above the bed a nurse tore the tape from my arm pulled the needle out and left a square of gauze where it had been you are going home she said the fever has broken your friend is coming here are your things get dressed do you need any help she asked everything was too bright.

When the call came, Margarita answered. I might have been reading or writing in the notebook, probably on the couch, from where I watched her pace as far from the wall as the cord would allow, turning until it was wrapped around her, then cupping the receiver to muffle her voice she said, "Carolina? Can you go to the seminary?"

Then, without waiting for my answer: *"Sí. Sí. Ella puede venir. Bueno. Ciao."* She was already reaching for her keys and her purse.

"Bring your camera," she said, "and your notebooks. You don't have to look nice. They just have to think you are *una periodista*. What you have on is fine. You have to hurry."

On the way to the seminary she told me that several hundred campesinos had fled the army and had been given sanctuary by the church. They needed medical attention, but mostly they needed a safe place.

"You must go there in this moment and be *una periodista*. The army might not attack if they see *una periodista* from the United States. If the army comes, be sure to let them see you."

"But I'm not a journalist."

"This is not important, Carolina, it is your presence that is needed."

———◆———

The people who had crowded into the courtyard were refugees from the combat areas in San Vincente and Cabañas, several hundred of them, many wounded, children with bloody bandages, women whose breasts had been slashed by machetes. There was no food for them yet and there were no medicines. I was giving a woman water when a child told me that someone was at the door and asked me to come. An American stood there, gaunt and exhausted, with two cameras hanging from his shoulders. He had been called here too. His Spanish was fluent, almost natively so. He was with *Time* magazine, was all he said, but "never mind that." We had been told that as soon as the people were given refuge, a rumor flew around that the soldiers were coming and they were going to kill everyone. That's why we had been called, the American photographer and me: to prevent an attack if this could be done by our mere presence. I don't remember that we exchanged another word. As one by one we heard the trucks pulling up near the entrance, engines thrumming, a seminarian who had been trying to calm someone down told me that it was time.

I left the water and stepped outside, as did the photographer, until we were visible to the open trucks where the soldiers rode standing, pointing their rifles at the clouds, the engines idling. I heard a *whir* and *click, whir* and *click. Click click click.* The American was taking photographs, so I opened my notebook and started to write nonsense, looking at the soldiers as if I were taking down names. You could hear the din of the courtyard from the street: crying, shouting. The soldiers seemed all to have mastered a certain demeanor: set mouths, hard eyes, helmet straps over their chins. The photographer was still photographing. I didn't want to go any closer, but they could plainly see me writing in the notebook. And then, just like that, one after another, the trucks wheezed into the road and drove away.

"Well, that was close," I heard the photographer say under his breath. He removed a film cartridge and pressed another into place, then gave me a look that said what couldn't be said. We went back inside the courtyard and by then more help had come: some food and also first aid supplies, basins and towels, carried by several nuns and women I thought might be nurses. The chaos had become more orderly. I thought I was going to be sick but there was no place to do that, so I was not sick. This was only from a nervousness that I would later outgrow. I was given something to do, I don't remember what, and when I looked for the photographer again he was gone.

W e moved to a place I will call Hotel X, as by then no one wanted to give any information about themselves or their whereabouts. Hotel X was under guard by government forces, who stood at its entrance, shouldering G3 assault rifles. They wore heavy black boots and olive uniforms, and often also flak jackets. Inside the lobby, private security guards in short-sleeved guayaberas, without flak jackets, would station themselves, their .357 Magnums holstered or tucked into belts. Two-way radios could be heard crackling before these men were seen, hissing in the potted palms. "Businessmen" in suits came to Hotel X, came and went from noon until late night, and they were more subtly armed, clustering in small groups before going into the restaurant or ordering something from the bar to be brought to the low tables in the lobby. Some ventured onto the patio to sit under rattling *palapas,* guns beside their drinks on the tables. Some appeared to have just stepped from a shower, slick haired and damp, barely concealing their nerves. If a woman was with them, she was most often not the wife but the mistress—younger and dressed for an evening, whose work was to smile, flirt, toss her hair from shoulder to shoulder. If one woman saw another she knew, they would take hands, kiss the air, and almost sing their greetings and, after breathless talk, would return to the men for the keys to the rooms rented for the next hours. The lobby was empty and at peace only in the morning: the hours of maids and busboys.

I had never wanted to stay in Hotel X, preferring almost anywhere else, but that was why, Leonel assured me, Hotel X was the best and safest place. Just try not to stand out, he'd say. Don't wear blue jeans. Fix your hair. Wear the dress Margarita gave you. If you hear something, pay attention, but don't get caught listening in on conversations. Be distant, he'd said—American.

◆

On this night, Luisa and I were sharing a room in Hotel X. We were on the fourth floor overlooking a ramp for delivery of hotel supplies. It was a beautiful night, as I remember, and so we were lying on the floor of our balcony, smoking and talking. From here we could see the full delivery zone through an opening below the concrete balcony wall. Luisa was still working for one of the militant groups, gathering information by various means, as she had done that night when we stayed at V's house. But since that night, Luisa had fallen in love, and so she wanted to talk about that rather than the political situation, rather than her clandestine activities, which she would not, in any case, have said much about. She seemed younger this night than I had perceived her to be in the past. Her love was leaving soon. He would go into exile as a member of the political wing of his organization and he would be assigned to represent the group somewhere else in the world. Any day now he would be quietly taken out of the country and Luisa would continue to watch, to listen, to whisper in the dark. I hadn't told Leonel about this work of hers. I don't think he knew that Luisa was operating clandestinely when he suggested that we room together.

"When will you see each other again?" I think I asked her.

"Who knows if we ever will," she said, tapping her cigarette until the ash fell. "This is not the time for a normal life. And what about you? Is there someone?"

Not now, no, I would have said, but just then two black Jeep Cherokees pulled into the delivery zone directly beneath us, and the doors were opening, and men in civilian clothes with military weapons were leaving the vehicles rapidly, decisively, slamming the doors behind them. Luisa pressed her forehead to the floor and whispered, *"Escuadrón de la muerte."* She was already moving backward into the room, still on the floor on her stomach. The room was dark. She rose and turned on the lights and began taking off her blue jeans.

"Carolina," she said, "we have to get dressed. Hurry."

I asked her if we were leaving.

"No. Get dressed. Good clothes, lipstick, hurry."

"Why aren't we leaving?"

"Carolina, what do you want? You want to run right into them in the hall? Get dressed."

She took the chain lock off the door and removed the deadbolt.

"Lie down. You lie on this bed, I'll lie on the other. In your clothes, yes."

"Why is the door unlocked?"

"So we won't have to wait during the time it takes for them to break it down. If they are coming for us, it will be quick. We will die looking like bourgeois women. Hold my hand."

She held hands with me across the space between the beds.

"Do you think they are coming for us?"

"It is possible. But it is also possible that they are here for someone else.

We are in this situation now together, Carolina. Would it help if I talked to you? You are afraid, and I also," she said.

"What are we going to do?" I heard myself ask.

"We are going to lie here until it is finished or until morning."

There was muffled machine-gun fire just then and she pointed at the ceiling to the floors above us. A short time after that, the vehicles below our balcony sped away, and then it was light. I bolted upright in the bed from a deep sleep and saw myself in the mirror as a different woman. Luisa and her things were gone. She had left a note: *Que le vaya bien.*

R ed and yellow banners unfurled in the streets, and over a hundred thousand people marched. A low-flying crop duster sprayed clouds of insecticide over them, and as the people arrived at the Plaza Libertad, shots were fired upon them from the roof of the National Palace. Security forces attacked and left 67 dead and 250 wounded. The following month, a bomb destroyed the transmitter for YSAX, the Church radio station that broadcast Monseñor Romero's Sunday homilies, the radio station that also carried Margarita's voice—the "nun" for whom the death squads mistakenly searched. On the same night, another bomb exploded in the library at the Catholic university, blowing the books from their shelves all at once and opening them in the air to land facedown among the scattered papers having to do with the mysterious ways God works among us on Earth.

Two months later, it was toward the end for me, but I didn't know it. I attended Mass in the basilica on Sunday, hoping once again to receive Communion from Monseñor, to feel the raindrops from his aspergillum land on me, even though I hadn't confessed the years I had been away from the sacraments, and even though I wasn't convinced that I would remain among the faithful. I took photographs of him at the altar, speaking into what appeared to be a telephone held by an altar boy whom I would meet decades later as a grown man attending school in the United States. Seated to the left of the altar is Father Ignacio Ellacuría, arms folded, not wearing his glasses, his eyes appearing to focus on Monseñor's raised hand.

After Mass, some young people from a popular organization asked to meet with me in one of the basilica's bell towers. They knelt, bandannas around their necks ready to be pulled over their faces, and whispered that their *compañeros* were among those in the coffins lined up along the Communion rail to be blessed, their faces visible through the windows cut into the coffin lids. I had gone close enough to look at the faces and they resembled photographs of children asleep. Strands of incense smoke still crawled through the gray air, and rock doves flapped their wings in the stone clerestory. As I left, I noticed a man wearing sunglasses who was, inexplicably, carrying an attaché case, which is maybe why I took note of him. He paused near one of the side altars as if offering a special prayer. The following day, a priest found an attaché case containing seventy-two sticks of dynamite behind that side altar. It had been set to detonate during a funeral Mass for a civilian member of the junta, scheduled for that afternoon, but the detonator had apparently failed. Later, I saw the man in the sunglasses standing in the lobby of Hotel X. I went up to him, said hello, introduced myself, and told him that I had seen him at Mass.

"You did not see me," he said stiffly, and he excused himself.

Leonel was skeptical when I told him the story of the man with the attaché case, because such a man "doesn't usually allow himself to be seen."

"Describe him again," he said, "you have to give me something more than sunglasses."

"He didn't look Salvadoran."

"You're telling me what? That he was a gringo?"

"I don't know."

"Well, you said you spoke with him. Was he a gringo?"

"I think so."

"You have to do more than think so. You have to be sure."

"Can we drop it, then? I'm not sure."

"*Mirá*, Papu, guard your credibility. This is something that cannot be recovered once lost. Remember the rumor that flew around about a young girl with a man's head stuffed into her stomach? Remember that? You know they found her that way. I know they found her that way. But it doesn't sound true."

"So?"

"So you can't say it. You can't write it. Even in a poem. If you had a photograph of the goddamn thing no one would believe you. As for your man in the basilica, your observations are imprecise. Next time pay closer attention. Someday you will be talking to your own people. Writing for your own people. I promise you that it is going to be difficult to get Americans to believe what is happening here. For one thing, this is outside the realm of their imaginations. For another, it isn't in their interests to believe you. For a third, it is possible that we are not human beings to them."

WRITTEN IN PENCIL:

The telescope is trained on the fly crawling the neighbor's roof tiles the AK is once again taken from beneath the blanket and set out of reach we are in the dark the Hiace is parked elsewhere there is only the loading and unloading of magazine clips as he did with the eyes closed did they ever tell you who killed the poet no I suppose they didn't it happened on Mother's Day and no it wasn't the military or the death squads it was the guerrillas themselves who accused him of spying for both the CIA and Cuba and why Cuba we will never know most people are accused of being CIA but back to Mother's Day as I was telling you they were holding him in a safe house and he left to visit his mother they said briefly and while he was gone another man also being held was executed they said and when Dalton returned to the safe house the man who is now in command of a large faction of the guerrillas the most proficient faction in military terms fired at Dalton and he missed you might ask how that is possible Dalton "threw himself on the bed" so they said and the poet shouted *No me mates* but this commander fired again and the second shot killed the poet so they said in my opinion it was a personal matter between them but also a conflict over strategy or so they said however this will tell you something about them and never take the safety off and never even if you think the clip is empty should you aim the weapon at your head.

L eonel was with Viera, the labor leader who took me with him in his truck that night from the compound where they asked about poetry. Viera and Leonel were now both involved in attempting to execute the agrarian reform that was to be part of the new junta's project, although few were more skeptical than they were about how the reforms would be carried out, who would truly benefit, and if this might be too little too late.

"If we succeed," Leonel had said, "we succeed, and if we fail? If we fail we are demonstrating this reform to be false, to be a matter of bad faith."

I went with them once or twice to listen to the speeches delivered by bullhorns in the *campo* to gatherings of weathered and skeptical men who nevertheless listened politely with arms folded and hats on as they were told the land would soon be theirs.

I would call this period the era of being my own person. I was spending more time with Margarita at the Catholic university and in the human rights office, and I was meeting on my own with people who were authorized to speak for the guerrillas in a more official way than the young people in the bell tower. One of these meetings took place in Margarita's living room and I remember how surprised I was by the appearance of this *guerrillero* spokesman: chubby, with thick-lensed glasses that kept falling down the bridge of his nose. His political analysis was impressive. I'm not sure who he thought I was. No one asked in those days. Someone had vouched for me, I was told, and from his tone he thought I was somehow someone worth his time. Also in those days, I worked closely with Margarita, which meant that I worked closely with the human rights office of the Church. I didn't always know what we were doing. There were lists and photographs and details about disappearances and always the steady presence of Monseñor moving among us.

That night I was to meet with a defecting member of the Christian Democratic Party whose name was given as "Alfredo." We were to have an interview on the eve of his exile, or a few days before. It didn't occur to me until later that this might be the man Luisa loved. I don't remember who made the arrangement or what was expected to come of it. I didn't tell Leonel because he seemed too busy. But Alfredo and Leonel knew each other, so I assumed everything would be all right.

I was to meet Alfredo in the lobby of Hotel X, swarming that night with heavily armed soldiers, private security guards with hidden weapons, foreigners (except journalists, who were at El Camino Real), the usual businessmen and mistresses, what Leonel called NGO types, a few prostitutes, but no kumbayas. The white noise and *cambios* of two-way radios could be heard, as usual, among the palms. Everyone was watching everyone else. A waiter tried to keep people happy with drinks. Empty bottles clustered in glass cities on the low tables. Outside, more soldiers patrolled, casting their armed shadows on the marble façade, as vehicle after vehicle pulled to the entrance to pick up or disgorge passengers as quickly as possible. I decided to wait outside, beside a nervous bellman. No one coming or going seemed to have any luggage for him.

Alfredo came in a loaned car, a businessman's car, something that wouldn't typically be driven by a man going into exile. He leaped out and opened the door for me, explaining that we couldn't stay here, that it would be better to meet at his house. Quieter. No people. I don't remember the drive there. It was dark. While in vehicles, I had begun to focus on the side mirrors, on the presence or absence of Jeep Cherokees, on breathing, on getting there, on being once again somewhere inside. I had already played with the tape recorder to be sure it worked, already said *Testing,*

testing, rewound, and listened. The recorder was borrowed from someone. Luisa, I think.

The little house was in a compound surrounded by a high brick wall. There was a grove of avocados, a few palms and other trees and, farther along the drive, a larger house, one story, wrapped by a veranda. There were no lights on inside that house. The swath of bare ground was bathed in the purplish light of a sodium lamp. Chickens skittered through the pool of light. Finally, we came to the place where Alfredo was staying and I could understand his choice of this house: a *casita* tucked deep into the property, hidden by foliage and overhung by a spreading cashew tree, its fruit hanging in glowing red bulbs.

He had been living here for a few months, and it was safe enough, he said, given the circumstances. There were shelves of books, a low table stacked with papers, something he was writing. There were cushions on the floor. A wool rug covered the earthen tile and little else. In the tiny kitchen, now lit by the open door of a small refrigerator, Alfredo was rummaging for something. Beyond the kitchen there was a bedroom not much larger than its bed and, beside it, a water closet.

Alfredo returned with two glasses of beer and seated himself opposite me on the other of the two cushions. We kept the lights off, as many people did in those days, but a silvery smear entered from outside. I wouldn't have to ask questions, as it turned out, or not many, or not yet. He would hold forth into the recorder, describing events up to this moment, events that had brought him to "take this decision," to go into exile and work for the opposition from abroad. This was, I soon realized, the last time he would give an account of this decision for himself. I asked him about the differences among the guerrilla factions, and why he chose to work for one rather than another. Alfredo could not then have been more than a few years older than I was, but I regarded him as more mature and sophisticated. He was handsome, well educated, and thoughtful, with the demeanor of a young professor of philosophy, albeit one whose name had been published in newspapers on a list of those targeted for assassination. Breaks in our conversation occurred when we used the toilet or I stopped to unwrap a fresh cassette. We finished a pack and a half of cigarettes be-tween us, and filled three sixty-minute tapes that night.

We talked for three hours then, but that didn't account for the drive from the hotel, the settling in, the beer pouring, the breaks, the retest of the machine. It was actually four that had passed. Alfredo realized this before I did, suddenly hiking his shirtsleeve to check the luminous num-bers on his watch. At first, I didn't know why he had gotten up so quickly, but I followed, gathering my woolen bag woven with jaguars, the tape machine that wasn't mine, the notebook in which nothing had been writ-ten that night.

"We have to leave now," he said, "*right now* we must go."

When I saw what time it was, I knew what we had done. We had stayed beyond the curfew during a state of siege.

lfredo opened the little door of the *casita* only a crack, enough to let a bit of night jasmine into the room, before closing again.

"We can't do this. It's too dangerous."

"Then I have to make a phone call."

"There is no phone here."

"What about in the other house? Is there a phone?"

"No, nothing."

"Then I have to go. They don't know where I am. They'll come looking. It's dangerous. It's against the rules."

"Whose rules is it against?"

"I promised Leonel—"

And then he conceded that yes, Leonel probably would come looking for me.

"All right, then, we'll go. But then I will also have to stay at the hotel."

He went into the bathroom, shut the door briefly, and returned, putting on a jacket.

The businessman's car was parked facing outward so we could coast down the long drive with the lights off, then out through the break in the walls. In slow motion I remember this: getting in, buckling the seat belt, rolling the window down halfway.

It was as if we had forgotten that people no longer did such things as talk all night.

Alfredo drove slowly, so close to the avocado trees that their branches brushed the roof. Just before pulling into the street we saw them, three men, hunched over a taxicab that was idling with its doors open, three men whose automatic weapons were aimed at our windshield. They wore black masks. Alfredo does not remember that part. He is already grinding the gears into reverse, whipping the car sideways against the wall, and calling me to get out and run back to the *casita*. I hear voices shouting underwater, the slamming of car doors, a long squeal of tires. Water silences the world. I'm running through the avocado trees, losing first one shoe and then the other, tree to tree until I reach the *casita* and push through the unlocked door. I didn't know where Alfredo was or what I would do if he didn't return. I didn't know if anyone was behind me among the trees, or whether the taxi in the road had been the vehicle to squeal away. In dreams to come, the windshield is shattered over and over in a spray of light, but now I'm in the *casita* and out of breath, wildly searching for a place to hide where there was none.

It was only minutes that I was alone before Alfredo arrived, ghost faced and leaning back against the door to close it behind him.

"Death squad," he whispered, catching his breath.

"Why didn't they shoot?"

"I'm not sure."

"Where are they?"

"Gone. They drove off."

"Why didn't they follow us here?"

"They think we have security guards and they didn't want to engage them would be my guess."

"Do we? Have security guards?"

"No. No one. Or they might think we have weapons."

"Do we?"

"No."

"So what now?"

"Now we wait. We have no choice. They might come back, but I don't think so, at least not tonight. In the morning, we'll get out of here."

We stretched out side by side on the bed, and as I remember we talked for a while, and then I heard his muffled breaths. It was utterly dark, as the sodium lamp outside had gone out. Not a gleam of light through the louvers and no buzzing. *Just because you can't see it doesn't mean it isn't there,* Leonel had said. Never believe anything until it is officially denied. I talk to everyone, he had said, I'm not pure or special. I would talk to the devil himself if it would make any difference, and come to think of it I have once or twice. He was in the guise of a gringo. We are all dying, Papu, there is no escape.

It was then that I heard the first rounds of machine-gun fire, coming from just above the little house. Ten, twenty rounds. Silence. Another ten.

"Alfredo," I called out, jostling him, "wake up!"

In his sleep he told me to go back to sleep. "Those are cashew fruits falling on the roof."

In the morning, he went to the main house, returning with a bullet-proof vest and my shoes retrieved from the grove. He put on the vest, we got into the car, and he drove through the opening in the wall. It was a bright morning and the street was empty. I slid down in the passenger seat as low as I could, keeping my head down. The back of the seat was my vest.

When we reached Hotel X, he told me to go upstairs and get my things quickly, taking only what I could bring down to the car in one trip.

"And don't stop at the desk, and don't speak to anyone."

I didn't have much with me, so this wasn't difficult. I only wanted my notebooks. Against his instructions, I left a note on my pillow: *With Alfredo. Am all right. Papu.*

When we reached the coast, I woke to the car door's opening, to people, to hands. I was led to a hammock tied to two trees behind an elegant house, all glass and sea, palms and bougainvillea, sea wind, and the cries of birds. I let one foot drop to the soft ground to rock the hammock. Someone brought me a fruit drink, and later a tortilla with a scoop of black beans and *crema*. It was mostly Alfredo's voice talking with the owners of this place, and it sounded as if they were his relatives, or close family friends. They wanted to know everything about the night before because it would now be necessary to move up the plans for his escape.

"Carolina?" A woman was tapping my arm. "Carolina, don't worry, Leonel is coming."

"Where am I?"

"You are in a safe house. You are safe."

When I woke again, it was because I felt the eyes of a child on my face, the way one can be awakened from sleep by the gaze of someone else. The child smiled, then ran away in the direction of a group of people, Leonel was among them. They were talking and he kept looking over at my hammock. I decided to roll myself out of it, half asleep as I still was from the heat. When I reached the group, he put his hand on my shoulder. It seemed that something had been decided. Alfredo was gone.

The Hiace had become an oven. "You're goddamn lucky to be alive, Papu."

He started the engine. He didn't have to say anything else. I realized that I wasn't crying and I wasn't shaking. I wasn't going to be sick. I rolled the window down and stuck my arm out. He passed me some water, I took a swig, recapped it, handed it back.

"Don't we have work to do?" I asked.

"You're all right, then?"

"Yes."

"You're sure?"

"Yes. Let's just go."

"You don't have to talk about it. Alfredo told me everything."

"I wasn't planning to talk about it. Let's go."

"Well. Now you know. I'm sorry."

I hadn't told him about being chased with Margarita, or about the night at the hotel with Luisa. I wouldn't have chosen to tell him about this ei-

ther, and until that moment I didn't know why I was withholding information from him.

"I think it's time for you to leave, Papu."

"I'm not ready yet. I still have to get those documents from the *coordinadora*."

"Never mind the documents. Lesson number six: Not everything is a matter for the individual to decide, and this decision especially will not be yours to make."

He then reached into the backseat to retrieve his woolen bag, and withdrew from it a piece of cloth folded up. It was a jaguar weaving on a torn piece of cloth, the same as the one he had given me before.

"But I already have this, Leonel," I said, unfolding the cloth. "How did you get it back?"

"This is another one. They are similar: two wildcats facing each other, standing on their hind legs, as if they were about to pounce. The funny thing is, I was given one of them years ago, and then when we were in Guatemala, I received the other. They came from different places, years apart. When you put them together, you will see. They were once the same cloth. They are yours now."

"But you can't," I protested. "Why are you doing this?"

"Oh, but I can, Papu. And someday you will know why."

—◆—

I spent that night and the next at Margarita's, lying on the gray tile floor between the twin beds, occasional headlights moving along the walls, pausing, moving again. There was gunfire in the distance from time to time, and Margarita would tell me where it was coming from and how far away it was. *Garrison. Power station. Do you want to keep my dress?* She asked. *You should take it.* I didn't want to go back to the United States and I gave her my reasons. She listened and seemed to consider them. The silver lighter sent its wavering flame from her hand to her face and then she held it to mine and admitted that she understood that it would be difficult for me to live in my country again without ever coming back. *But think of us who have to stay here with war coming.* You will be isolated, Carolina, yes, but you stand a good chance of surviving. For us—who knows? Our throats could be cut in a moment.

I would never again feel the fear that I felt in those days, even in other countries at war. In that place and at that time, there was a special quality to the fear.

That afternoon, Leonel made arrangements for me to spend time with Monseñor Romero at Divine Providence. A Venezuelan journalist was scheduled to interview the archbishop and I had been approved to join them. Monseñor arrived alone, walking under the flame trees and bougainvillea in his white cassock. It was five p.m. on March 14, the hour when the little parrots flock over the city so punctually that people set their watches by the passing. We sat at a table at one end of a community room, drinking water, with a fan turning back and forth, and Monseñor tapping lightly on the Bible he always carried. The Venezuelan journalist was there, and when he began asking questions, I turned on my little cassette recorder and preserved what I believe was Monseñor's final interview.

When asked whether peaceful means for finding a solution to the conflict had been exhausted, Monseñor replied, "No. For if that were true, we would already be in the midst of a full civil war."

The Carmelite Sisters of Divine Providence hurried in and out, carrying brief messages, bringing fresh water, and remaining at hand should Monseñor need anything. The journalist wanted a "story" from the archbishop, something new, controversial, and "newsworthy," and so he pressed him about his relationship with the popular organizations, which now had military wings. He wanted to know what Monseñor thought about the guerrillas.

"My relation with the organizations is one of a shepherd, a pastor with his people, knowing that a people has the right to organize itself and to defend its right of organization. And I also feel perfectly free to denounce those organizations when they abuse the power and turn in the direction of unnecessary violence. This is my role as pastor: to animate the just and the good, and to denounce that which is not good."

A wind rose in the palms, and the fan was unobtrusively silenced by one of the sisters. It was almost dark, but the lights in the room were not turned on. The sisters didn't want Monseñor to become tired; they wanted him to join them in the little convent kitchen for supper, and allow him a few hours of peace. The journalist, however, wanted Monseñor to clarify precisely his position, now that the people were beginning to take up arms.

"As I have told you, I do not have a political role in El Salvador, but rather a pastoral one. As a pastor, it is my duty to construct this Church, my community, the Church. That is what I am responsible for. And this Church, as a people, illuminated by God, has a mission too among the people in general."

The journalist had failed to elicit a condemnation of the organized opposition, and as the nuns were hovering nearby, he must have understood that his time was up. As delicately as he could, the journalist raised the issue of Monseñor's own safety.

"I have a great confidence in the protection of God," he said. "One does not need to feel fearful. We hear from Jesus Christ that one should not tempt God, but my pastoral duty obliges me to go out and be with the people, and I would not be a good pastor if I was hiding myself and giving testimonies of fear. I believe that if death encounters us in the path of our duty, that then is the moment in which we die in the way that God wills."

After the journalist left, we went to the kitchen, where Leonel also joined us. As the sisters hurried the food to the table, they joked with Monseñor and teased Leonel about something. The mood was light and unhurried. Over platters of *frijoles, plátanos,* cheese, and fruit, they talked about the day, recent developments, things that had happened to people they knew, and then Monseñor asked me about the night of my meeting with

Alfredo. Leonel nodded, so I told Monseñor a brief version of what happened, including the men holding machine guns over the roof of the taxicab. He listened with his eyes on the freshly wiped table, then nodded and said to Leonel, "It is for the best" that I leave the next day or something to that effect, that arrangements had been made, and I must have appeared surprised and resistant because Leonel suddenly chimed in firmly with "I agree."

"But, Monseñor," I said, "forgive me but it is so much more dangerous for you."

Monseñor now had his Bible on the table before him. He was tapping it with his fingertips again, and I saw the same soft light that I saw during the interview, silvery, coming from his eyes, his skin, even his fingernails, an emulsion of light, such as sanctity bestows.

"My child," he said, "my place is with my people, and now your place is with yours." That is what I remember verbatim, and the rest had to do with his wish that I speak about the sufferings of the poor, the repression, and the injustice, that I would say what I had seen, and when I told him that I didn't think I could do this, that I would have no opportunity, that I was only a poet and not a journalist or public figure, he assured me that the time would come for me to speak, and that I must prepare myself and I could do that best through prayer.

He rose from his chair and we all stood, and he made the sign of the cross in the air above us and we all crossed ourselves and then he was gone.

George Orwell writes of living in an atmosphere where certain things had dropped away and others had taken their place; I felt that now too—my life was all of a piece: My heart and intellect and soul were aligned with what I was doing in the world, and the people around me were also living and working in this way, and on behalf of each other were willing to live at risk. Many other writers and poets had also written works that expressed the feelings and thoughts I was having. Leonel had shown me, for example, this quote from Albert Camus: *It was in Spain that men learned that one can be right and still be beaten, that force can vanquish spirit, that there are times when courage is not its own reward.* He also kept this from Bertolt Brecht, folded into his wallet, and later, he passed this slip of paper to me: *Sink down in the slime, embrace the butcher,/If you could change this world, what would you not be willing to do?* But on the issue of what is to be done, things were not always so simple for him. He fell back on his Antonio Gramsci: *If you hit a nail with a wooden mallet with the same strength with which you would hit it with a steel hammer, the nail will go into the mallet instead of the wall.*

"You want to know what is revolutionary, Papu? To tell the truth. That is what you will do when you return to your country. That is all I'm asking of you. From the beginning this has been *your* journey, *your* coming to consciousness. All along I have only been responding to you. When you ask me a question, I try to place you in a situation in which you might find your answer. I do not have your answers, Papu. I am just a man."

———◆———

I didn't want my final view of the country to be from the air: white cattle grazing the field near the runways, haze wrapping the volcano, to leave Madre Luz, her hands on my shoulders, her eyes fixing upon me with the light that issued from them, did not wish to hear *Vaya con Dios*, embrace the younger sisters and go. I would stay with Margarita that night and early in the morning I would be driven to the new airport Comalapa Internacional that had replaced the dark shell of Ilopango, and after a brief layover in Guatemala City I would be on my way home and would not return for another twelve years, the years of the civil war that could not be prevented and would claim almost one hundred thousand lives, with eight thousand people disappeared, five hundred thousand internally displaced, and another five hundred thousand taking refuge in other countries. Leonel would remind me that history counts its casualties in round numbers. I would not return until "the signing of the peace" in 1992. Within a week of my departure, Monseñor Romero would be assassinated in the chapel of Divine Providence while celebrating Mass for the repose of a woman's soul. Madre Luz would reach him as he lay on the sanctuary floor and hold him as he gave his life. More than one hundred thousand people would fill the cathedral, the plaza, and the streets for his funeral, bishops from many nations, priests and nuns, but no government representatives from these nations. It was the poor who would attend the funeral for Monseñor Romero. When the first bomb went off in the plaza, the people would flee into the cathedral until it could contain no more, and with further explosions the cathedral itself would seem to shake, and there would be gunfire and panic. The American photographer from *Time* magazine would be there again, as he had been that day when the army prepared to attack those who had taken refuge in the seminary, and he would take photographs of the crush of people against the cathedral gates until he had to put down his camera to help them. His were the iconic photographs of the horror of that day.

On the day after Monseñor's assassination, hearings on El Salvador were held in the U.S. House of Representatives, as scheduled. In the morning, the intelligence agencies testified in closed session; in the afternoon, we were allowed into the room to hear the testimonies of human rights organizations and the religious community. The afternoon session was as compelling as the morning session was secret, but in the end, the committee voted to approve sending twelve military advisers (changing the name to "trainers" so as not to stir memories of the American war in Vietnam), and the first $5.5 million in military aid to the Salvadoran government. A short time later, Amnesty International invited me to join an ad hoc working group on El Salvador for a meeting at the United Nations.

The next few years involved turmoil in my personal life, a move to the East Coast, a brief period of teaching at two universities and in the old territorial prisons of Alaska, and the publication of my second book of poems, *The Country Between Us*. It was through this book, and as a poet, that I found myself at last speaking to people in the United States about the war in El Salvador, as Monseñor said I would. The travel of those years is a blur of dark auditoriums, church basements, blue-lit airport runways, late nights in the living rooms of activists who seemed always to bring tortillas and black beans to their potlucks. I spoke at colleges and universities, but also in bookstores, churches, synagogues, community centers, and even at

Rotary Club breakfasts, anywhere anyone would listen, and everywhere people seemed responsive, so there were at least some Americans who would take the word of a poet. We hoped to prevent U.S. military intervention, to provide sanctuary for refugees, and bring the war to an end, but every year U.S. military aid for the war increased exponentially, and so for most of that time, we believed ourselves to have failed, and I would remember that when our situation was particularly fraught, Leonel would turn to face me in the Hiace, paying no attention to the road ahead, and shout over the wind *Das Boot!*—the same thing he whispered in my ear on one of the last nights, when I embraced him and felt beneath his raincoat— something he otherwise never wore—an arsenal of holstered armaments. *I told you, Papu, that when it became truly dangerous, you would know.* Das Boot—*remember?* It was a film about a German submarine patrolling the Atlantic during World War II, whose crew is "beset by tension, boredom, despair, dwindling supplies, storms, and a sense of futility." *Das Boot* entered our dark lexicon. But I would also hear Monseñor's voice, coming from the convent kitchen: *We must hope without hoping. We must hope when we have no hope.*

My walls were covered with maps: The United States had pushpins marking every place I thought I should go, the isthmus of the Americas had *x*'s every place I had been. There were also photographs tacked to the walls, reports, newspaper clippings, Post-it notes with various reminders, lists of names of the *desaparecidos* and the dead: a paper war room, a paper cemetery, a paper command and control. When the windows were open, some of these items were lifted from the walls and rocked gently down to the floor, so there were often also papers scattered there as well, or stuffed into boxes and folders. I knew where everything was, I told myself. For the *desaparecidos*, I kept records of where everyone was last seen and what they were wearing at the time. Friends no longer asked what all of this was for, or what I was doing, and accepted that for a while at least, I would bore the dinner party with the latest news and trivia, such as how one high-ranking American in the foreign service was making a fortune airlifting illegally logged mahogany by helicopter out of Honduras. Things like that. One day—and I mention this now because it became important later—I saw a photograph in *Newsweek* of a photographer lying protectively over another photographer's wounded body in a street under fire. I tore it out and tacked it on the wall, most likely on top of something else. The photograph saddened me, but I thought nothing more about it at the time. Then another photographer sent word, asking if I would write a text for a book of photographs taken in El Salvador by thirty photographers from the United States and Europe. They had a text by a French writer already, but had decided that it wouldn't work. It was too *flowery* too *something* and *Harry didn't like it,* they said. When we talked about what sort of text it should be, every time I made a suggestion the response was *We'll have to check with Harry and get back to you.* Harry was in Beirut. Harry was in Paris. *We'll get back to you.* There was no Harry.

IT WAS DECIDED THAT I WOULD GO TO NEW YORK TO WRITE THE TEXT WHILE in the company of the editors, who would be at the table, moving photographs around within a mock-up of the book, changing their minds about the sequence again and again. Perhaps because it was a beautiful summer night, they all came to meet me at the airport and the first to greet me was a man who opened his arms and announced *See, Carolina? There really is a Harry.* He was driving an old purple Oldsmobile convertible then. The top was down, Ruben Blades was on the radio, and while crossing the Brooklyn Bridge, this Harry recited Hart Crane's poem "The Bridge" from memory. I was in the backseat, and I caught him looking at me in the rearview mirror as he made his recitation. It seemed that I was to stay in

Harry's loft on the Hudson River because the apartment the other editors shared was too small for guests. When we pulled into the parking lot that has since been replaced by a condominium building, he wrapped a chain around the steering wheel and padlocked it. His building had only a freight elevator with more chains, and as we rose on its dirty platform the six floors to his loft, I saw that the wallet in his back pocket was also chained to the loop on his jeans. Too many chains, I thought, and wondered if this neighborhood might require such security. The loft was without furniture except a bare kitchen table, hammocks slack against the support beams, and a mattress on the floor. I was familiar with that. He had rented an office typewriter for me and set it on a draftsman's desk. They would leave me to write there alone during the day while they gathered at the apartment to work on layout. Did I need anything else? Would I be all right? I should take the mattress; it was more comfortable than the hammock.

———◆———

By the second night, we both slept on the mattress in each other's arms, and when we weren't with the others we spent long hours talking about El Salvador, where he had gone after the revolution had triumphed in Nicaragua and he was no longer needed to document medical facilities for the new government in the aftermath of the war. I learned that he had come under aerial bombardment in Estelí, and because of the photos he took there, *Time* had given him a contract. We had overlapped in El Salvador but hadn't met there, and I explained that I didn't meet many journalists because I was doing other things. What other things I didn't at first say, but eventually I would tell him everything. One night I mentioned that I had, on one occasion, met a photographer in El Salvador, and I began describing the day at the seminary with the refugees. He was looking at me strangely.

"You were that nun? I remember you now. I thought you were a nun," he said, and he explained that it was because I dressed plainly, wore my hair short, and smoked like some of the other foreign nuns.

We were lying without clothes in the heat of the summer night.

"Obviously, I'm not a nun." And then I said, "I thought you were CIA."

"Why? I've been accused of that before. It's an accusation people like to make against Americans, but why?"

"I don't know. Your Spanish was too good. You showed up when no one else did. And I was suspicious of everyone then."

"That's understandable. But I'm not CIA, I can assure you."

In the next days, we talked, going through the photographs Harry had taken in El Salvador, some of which were included in the book. I kept returning to one in particular, a photograph of soldiers posing for his camera in the middle of a road, with mutilated bodies at their feet.

"You took this?"

He was quiet, then nodded.

"Tell me. Can you?"

"I don't usually talk about the pictures."

A quick cacophony of sirens and car horns rose from the street to his sixth floor.

"Okay, I'll tell you. This probably won't shock you as much as it would most people. I was driving north from San Salvador because I'd heard there was a major battle in Chalatenango province. There's a place there, a military installation or barracks—I think it's called El Paraíso—Paradise. The road was pretty much abandoned. The military had burned the fields on either side, so that there could be no cover for the guerrillas. They were trying to prevent ambushes, I suppose. There was an almost ozonelike tension in the air, like the prelude to a storm, and there seemed to be some . . . alteration in the atmosphere—a hot, dry wind, almost like near a desert. There was this haze in the road, the haze of heat, and I saw, about a hundred yards ahead of me, a group of men, so I started slowing down, and as I drew closer I saw that they were soldiers, and one of them was using a machete to chop up a corpse in the road. There were several corpses. Another soldier was sitting by the side of the road eating a melon, also opened by machete. There were several others standing over the dead with their rifles, and there was also an officer, also with a machete.

"At first, because I was tired and had seen a lot of combat in the past days, I thought maybe I was hallucinating. Was I seeing what I was seeing? Yes. I pulled the car within twenty feet of them, opened the door, got out, and as I walked toward them I started taking pictures, without too much conscious deliberation, without thinking, I just needed to take these pictures, and while doing so I began to engage the government soldiers—*Oh, what happened here?*—in a friendly manner. As I spoke to them, the officer moved behind the corpses and the others also moved behind them to pose. I remember the heat of the road and looking into the open chest cavities of some of the dead, and a leg that had been hacked off. I took ten frames in black and white and maybe three or four in color. Then there was a shift within me, and also perhaps within them, but whatever I had been doing was now over, and I was in danger myself, a danger I hadn't perceived in the beginning, but the soldiers who had done this could also do this to me, and they began acting a little strangely. This was the moment when I realized where I was and what had happened, and I remember asking about the battle up the road, and they said *Yes, it's dangerous, be careful,* or something like that. I got back in the car and drove around the bodies, because they were in the middle of the road, and I also drove around the soldiers, and pressed hard on the gas pedal—I wanted to get out of there. Within maybe ten minutes, I reached a firefight, and someone there turned, wheeling his weapon to point it at me, the weapon he had just been firing, and a sound came vomiting out of my mouth, the word *¡Firme! Attention!* given as a command to soldiers. It wasn't me speaking. But the soldier immediately came to attention. He might have thought I was an American military adviser, there were plenty of those. They had been arriving by helicopter in Gotera—those small bubble helicopters. Gringos. They were there to pay people off, they were intelligence officers—with some sort of folios under their arms. They were there for a few hours and then they were gone, but yes, I was the one who had given the command, yet it wasn't *me* speaking. In my memory, these two events are connected: this hallucination that was, in fact, real, and this language that was not my own. Perhaps that saved my life."

"Was there ever a time when you really thought *This is it?*"

"Many times. During the January offensive, I was on that same road in Gotera, going north toward Perquín, and I went up to El Carosal, a little town north of the Torola River. I stopped at a guerrilla roadblock. I knew these areas were often booby-trapped by the army or by the guerrillas, so it wasn't safe to pick up stones, or to move them, and while I was there, firing broke out, and I was no more than six or seven feet from the car, but because the bullets were so close, I knew that someone was aiming at me and not at something else, so I fell to the ground and crawled under the car and the car started taking rounds. I'm underneath the car. There's almost no clearance, maybe an inch. I've got the transmission in my face and I'm thinking *I don't want to get hit in the head.* Some people don't want to be hit in the genitals, some don't want to be hit in the butt, but I didn't want to be hit in the head. So I put my camera bag in back of my head. Each time a bullet hit the car, the car jumped, then fell back down again. At that point, I thought about getting out from under the car and crawling toward a ditch. I would have to slide myself maybe two or three feet to reach that lower position, but as soon as I started to move out there was a *ráfaga*—a burst of fire—that rippled through the macadam right there where I was going to move to. Then a helicopter flew over and sent a large round into the roof of the car. I wouldn't know that until later. The car had probably been shot eight to twelve times. But it still ran! Most of the bullets had gone through the door panels. There's a weird sound when a bullet goes through a door panel. A tearing and a suction sound, something unlike other bullet-impact sounds. When I started to pray under the car, I couldn't remember the Our Father, but I did remember the Hail Mary. Finally, the shooting stopped. I was bleeding from a cut. Flying stones? Then after about fifteen minutes, as I was getting ready to get back in the car, a military vehicle arrived—maybe it wasn't fifteen minutes—but the military vehicle pulled up and there were some soldiers on foot, and they patched me up and I got back in my car. Later I found this—rolling around inside my camera."

He placed a bullet on my palm that looked like a miniature, half-peeled banana. "My camera saved my life."

"Did you find out who had been shooting at you?"

"It's hard to say. There had to have been a military column, and there had to have been a guerrilla column, but I didn't see any of the guerrillas, and I didn't see the army until after it was over."

"How did you know it was safe to come out from under the car?"

"The firing had stopped—when you say 'safe,' what do you mean?"

A few hours later I accompanied him into the darkroom he had set up in the loft in the course of his ongoing project to transform one floor of this former spice warehouse that still smelled faintly of spices. He needed to develop some film and make a few prints. We stood together wordlessly in the safe light, while he swished the print stock through the trays of developer and fixative, and the images appeared, ghostly at first from white paper. When he flipped the light on, I saw the news clipping tacked to the wall among some other papers, with the photograph of the two journalists lying in the street.

"That was the worst. Olivier."

The prints were now hanging to dry, the trays empty of their chemicals, and he was washing his hands. I must have read the caption before, identifying the journalists, the two names, but I didn't remember, and didn't make the connection, when I first saw the story in *Newsweek,* with the man who had stood beside me at the seminary when the army trucks arrived.

"That was in Gotera too. San Francisco Gotera. The town was deserted. Olivier Rebbot, Benoît Gysembergh, and I had gone there together, I think we were in two cars. We knew it was a combat zone, but Olivier felt comfortable with me because I also spoke French. I was walking along a streambed and saw a corpse that had been eaten by dogs. His spine had been stripped of flesh but he still wore trousers."

"Did you photograph him?"

"No. There was no reason to do it. The man wasn't there any longer. I don't photograph corpses unless there are people nearby, living beings, unless the photograph can have some meaning.

"At a certain point, we came under fire. There was an army patrol, but I didn't see any other soldiers. We were south of the town, close to the road to San Miguel, I think the distance was thirty to forty kilometers, thirty to forty minutes of driving on that winding road. For some reason, we were walking on this side of town when a firefight broke out between the guerrillas and the army. We were not with either group."

"That's dangerous not to be behind the fighting of one side or the other, isn't it?" (Leonel had always told me that, among other things he taught about military engagements.)

"No kidding. Well, as you do in these situations, when the shooting started, I looked for cover. We were on an urban street, everyone hiding inside. They were adobe houses, painted in pastel colors. I pressed myself against the side of a building. Olivier crouched on the other side of the street near a stone wall. I began taking pictures of the army patrol moving up the street on foot. The guerrillas were about a hundred yards away, pinned down. I was watching the army, and then saw that Olivier had been hit. He was lying on the paving stones in the street. I got down on my hands and knees, crawled toward him, and turned him over. He'd been lying facedown. The shooting continued. I put my body over his because he was already wounded and I wanted to protect him from anything else. He was conscious but unable to speak. We weren't communicating verbally. We were pinned down in the crossfire. There were cracking sounds and I knew I couldn't raise my head. I thought we were both going to die, that we would be pummeled by bullets. I thought that if I could get low enough, if I could be eaten by the earth, if the earth could open up and make a space for us, we might be protected.

"When the firing stopped, a Red Cross vehicle came along, and I remember picking Olivier up and dragging him. One of the soldiers on the corner, who was in a firing position, came over and helped me drag him into the back of the Red Cross jeep. I got in, and they drove to the hospital in Gotera, eight blocks away. Olivier was convulsing, covered with blood. I was covered with his blood. He asked if he was going to die and I said no, you're not going to die. He had an open chest wound.

"I bashed through the doors of the hospital and there was nobody there. The place was empty. And I can remember running around in the halls of this small clinic, and finally finding two doctors who had been treating combat injuries for two days, and were trying to get some sleep. They came out, saw Olivier, set up the operating theater, and I watched them do the surgery. They put green drapes over him. There were no nurses, these doctors were in their midtwenties probably, and they managed to extract the bullet from his lung. They handed me the bullet, a little toxic mushroom in my palm. A NATO round. I still have it. One of them told me, as they do, that if Olivier made it through the night he might live. And then they pushed his gurney into a ward. The sun went down, and there was Olivier on an IV drip, feverish, delirious, and slipping in and out of consciousness. The ward was now filled with the wounded. I sat there all night with him, watching his chest rise and fall. Morning comes and there begins a flurry of communications, between the capital and New York and *Newsweek*—.

"The Associated Press publishes a photograph of Olivier wounded and me with him. Benoît Gysembergh does the same in France. So these images are out there in the world, unbeknownst to us. I'm getting calls from New York. I said: He's been wounded, he's been shot through the lung, it's extremely serious but he survived. They ask if I'll drive him to the capital and I say I don't think that's a safe thing to do, I don't think he'll make it, I think he'll bleed to death, and they say okay, we're going to send a private plane. So they chartered a small plane, which arrived either the next day or the day after. I flew in that small plane to San Salvador with Olivier and then somehow in another plane to Miami. I remember getting off the plane in Miami. My memory begins to weaken here but I believe that when we landed in Miami, I turned Olivier over to other people and I went back to El Salvador. I got back on the plane and was in Gotera again within forty-eight hours. The fighting continued for a week until the offensive was called off, and I received the news that Olivier had died of a massive hemorrhage. I had lied to him, telling him he was going to make it. I felt ashamed to have survived."

He had finished with the work in the darkroom, so we crawled through a low window and onto the roof of the adjacent building. The river wind came. There were doves and pigeons flying in and out of the windows of the warehouse across the street. The sirens and horns were far away now and it was almost possible to hear the wings of the birds and the river water slapping against the piers.

"A short time later," Harry said, "we went to the ocean to scatter Olivier's ashes, which were given to us in a metal can like a paint can. I held it in my hands, and we drove in a cortege of five or six cars to Sheepshead Bay in southern Brooklyn, and boarded a tugboat. It was one of those cold, sparkling winter days. The light was perfect. The crew of the boat were members of the Longshoremen's Association that had refused to load weapons onto ships bound for El Salvador. They understood who we were and what we were doing. They were people who understood in a country that didn't. Karen DeYoung was there, and Olivier's sister, Sylvie, Olivier's mother, and me. We were trying to pry the paint can open with a screwdriver. Karen finally managed to get the top off. I looked inside and there was this—bone meal—and we tossed it out over the water, along with flowers, and his mother said, *"Adieu, Olivier. Adieu."*

Early every morning Harry played a Nicaraguan revolutionary song on his cassette machine to rouse us to work, followed by serious Latin music or jazz. I told him my stories too, and he understood them. He had met Leonel in El Salvador on several occasions, he said, and thought well of him, but was also aware of the rumors regarding his possible affiliations, about which he "couldn't care less," except that he didn't want me to be involved any longer in such dangerous activities, even though he himself, of course, would continue to work as a war photographer. He bought a coffeepot for me and I taught him to drink coffee, surprised that he hadn't yet developed the habit. We shared a fondness for cigarettes. His refrigerator was filled with bricks of film, cigarettes, and Chuckles candy. I began to stock it with food. He figured out how to get the burners on the stove to work. Every night we went on the roof. Sometimes he cried out in his sleep (he said I did too), and several times called out to Olivier. I wrote during the day, attempting to produce a text that would please them, but one of the other editors thought that I wrote too much about the campesinos and not enough about the war. Harry defended me. He was restless and couldn't seem to sit still long, so he ran a lot of errands. By that time, I'd been traveling around the country for a while and was thin and jittery. Harry thought I should get off the road, but understood why that wasn't possible. I saw his El Salvador through his photographs. He saw mine through my poems.

As if he were going to stay in one place, and I was going to live with him, we bought dishes. After two weeks, I had finished the text, the photographs were in their proper order, and Harry had asked me to marry him, whereupon he left immediately for the war in Beirut.

———◆———

Years later, I would have long talks with one of the men who had leaped from the death squad vans and dragged people into them. His name was Alex. (Alex is a pseudonym, as even the death squad members had *seudónimos*.) I never learned his real name. All I have left is his photograph and several cassettes of the voice recordings he made and gave to me for safe-keeping. Harry photographed him, and it seemed at the time that he was looking into the camera quite normally, posing for the camera, resting his chin in his fisted hands. The film wasn't developed for a long time, until after Alex had left us. It was then, holding the image in his hands, that Harry remarked that the young man's eyes were dead.

He came to us when we were living in Washington, D.C., in a rented stucco house on a leafy street. The owners of the house, who were living abroad, had added a screened gazebo onto the back, perched high over a ravine planted with azaleas that blazed behind all our houses every spring. But this was November, so the azaleas were not in bloom, and the last of the yellow leaves were gusting to the streets, with the wine leaves of the Japanese maples still clinging to their gray branches. The weather that autumn was unusually beautiful, clear and crisp. On some days, it was warm enough to have lunch in the gazebo, especially if the winds were calm.

Our son, Sean, was three and a half years old that November, and the floors of the kitchen and living room were usually strewn with his "persons"—brightly colored plastic Lego figures wearing miniature construction hats, who had built their small cities on the coffee table and across the floor, leading from the oatmeal-colored sectional sofa, past the groaning shelves of books, and into the kitchen, where I was always stepping on them with bare feet. We were living a "normal life" by then. Harry was working as a documentary photographer in a housing project, and I was teaching aspiring poets at a nearby university. Our son was enrolled in a preschool that promised to teach him Spanish. We were among the few in our neighborhood not practicing law.

If a Salvadoran was to enter our house then, he or she would know we had something to do with their country. Our bath towels were printed with colorful villages from the paintings of Fernando Llort, who also painted a plaque on our wall, and the box in which we kept our *miniaturas*. There was also a photograph on the wall of Monseñor Romero celebrating one of his last Sunday Masses in the basilica. I took the photograph. It shows him behind the altar, smiling and raising one hand, with an altar boy in a surplice holding what appears to be a telephone receiver to the bishop's mouth, broadcasting his voice throughout the country. This altar boy will recognize himself in the photograph when he visits our house as a grown man. It is, historically speaking, the only important picture I have ever taken. Harry took many important ones, but now kept his work in archival storage boxes as they were not the sorts of images we wanted Sean to come upon, and Harry didn't want to look at them anymore himself.

We weren't so naïve as to assume that we had *moved on,* as our culture phrases it, or worse, that we had achieved *closure,* but we had created a home for our son that resembled those of his playmates, and they could come to our house for playdates without anything seeming amiss. Our kitchen was well stocked with juice boxes and packages of crackers shaped like little fish. There were alphabet magnets on the refrigerator that held Sean's drawings in place, and he could already count to ten in Spanish and knew the Spanish words for house, milk, chair, dog, and good night.

When the telephone rang one night that November, I recognized the voice as a friend of ours, a documentary filmmaker most known for his exposés on intelligence agencies and covert operations. Allan sounded jittery, but he always sounded that way, so I thought nothing of it. He spoke rapidly with interjections, talking to himself, and also as if someone else were listening in on his conversations. Most people would have thought him to be a bit paranoid, but we realized there was probably some basis for his caution. He told us that he needed help, he needed a favor, and could he come by for a few minutes to speak with us? He didn't want to talk on the phone, the matter was too sensitive, but in those days, many people hesitated to talk on the phone. I said yes, of course, come over, and then went around scooping up Legos from the floors and gathering Sean's "persons" into his toy hamper. I must have fed Sean his dinner and had most likely already tucked him into bed when the doorbell rang. Through the tiny peephole, I saw that Allan was with a woman who had been assisting him with some film editing. I don't remember her name. Maybe it was Andrea. She was quite thin and wore her hair upswept and wispy. Her black clothes seemed to flow about her, draped on her bones and held there by the clasp of her hand. She spoke and dressed like a New Yorker and wore many strands of pearls around her neck, which few women activists wore. It was she who explained to us who Alex was, and she who asked if we might allow him to stay with us for a short time. I mention this because it might have been her demeanor and graciousness rather than Allan's jittery, darting-eyed plea that made us imagine saying yes.

Alex had run away from a military unit in El Salvador that might or might not have been part of a certain brigade, the Atlacatl, but according to Alex, his unit had also functioned as a death squad and was responsible for many killings. He knew how the military death squads operated: who gave them their orders, who trained them. His life in the military was not as he had imagined it would be, however, and he had become afraid for his life. When he'd enlisted, it was promised that he would become an intelligence officer, someone important, and would wear his uniform with honor. This is what he wanted, this was all he wanted, but things had gone terribly wrong and by the time he realized how wrong, he felt himself to be trapped, so when the opportunity came, he ran away. He wouldn't tell us much about the journey, but it had taken him to Guatemala and Belize before he reached Mexico City by bus, where he knocked on the door of a human rights office, telling the people there that he wanted to confess his crimes, to tell the truth, to expose his commanding officers and their advisers, who, he insisted, were Americans.

The human rights office in Mexico didn't seem to know what to do, but they decided that Alex was a credible witness, and his testimony should really be heard in the United States. They made some phone calls, and that is how the matter landed with the filmmaker Allan, who recognized immediately how important such a person as Alex might be, given the rarity of death squad members' coming into the open. Alex had to be carefully handled, as the filmmaker put it. The matters of which he spoke were of vital importance, but to be in possession of such information was dangerous. Alex needed to talk to members of Congress and the media and also people who were well placed in the international community. None of this would be easy. There would certainly be those who wouldn't want Alex's story to be made public, especially regarding the alleged American advisers. This young, fleeing soldier had to have a place to stay while he was here, preferably a quiet place in a respectable neighborhood where he might feel safe. He also needed to be with people who would understand his situation and wouldn't look at him as if he were a monster. This more than anything. Not a monster.

It would be only for a few days, or a few weeks at most, and of course it went without saying that utmost care would be taken, whatever that might mean. I didn't ask Allan if we were his first choice for this, if others had turned him down, but I do remember that as he talked, Harry and I had one of our silent conversations, studying each other, and when Harry closed his eyes and brought his hand to his mouth, I knew he was in the past, and thinking as he had in the past. He needs, Allan said, to be with you. I told him who you are. He wants to talk.

At the time, giving Alex shelter seemed the right thing to do. It is what the Catholic activist Dorothy Day would have done, and what those in the hospitality house movement, who were feeding the hungry and homeless in American cities, would also have done. So later that night, the filmmaker returned with Alex, who had with him only one small bag of things that had apparently been given to him in Mexico. He wore a big green army jacket into which he seemed to disappear, offered by someone along the way to ward off the cold. I showed him to his room and gave him some Salvadoran towels, at which he smiled broadly. I showed him where the light switch was, and how to open the window, and when I turned, I saw that he was looking at himself in the mirror above the empty bureau, a bit surprised at seeing himself there. He leaned in, made a stern face, leaned out and smiled, ran his hands through his hair, and leaned in again. He was smooth cheeked and I guessed him to be in his midtwenties. His eyes were black, deep set, and they narrowed when he spoke as if he were skeptical or nearsighted. As he studied himself in the mirror, he caught my reflection and spun around, startled, facing me as if he'd been caught stealing something, and then he smiled again as he would were he having his picture taken, an odd grimace showing gold-rimmed front teeth.

"¿*Vale?*" I said. "Okay?"

"¿*Sí, como no?*"

So that is how I left him that first night, in the room by himself standing under a light fixture that I saw had become a trap of dust and moths.

———◆———

The next day began with coffee and the jangling phone, with getting Sean ready for preschool, packing his juice box and snacks, listening to the message machine's music of beeps and voices:

"Hi, Carolyn, this is Joan, I was hoping to touch base with you before . . ."

"Hey, if you're home, pick up."

"Yes, this is Robert's mother. I was wondering if you might be interested in . . ."

"This is Sarah. Are you there?"

And then Allan's voice: "We have to be on the Hill by nine." *Click.*

Alex looked like a soldier, even without a uniform, short and muscular and quiet, always seeming to take things in, giving the impression that he didn't miss much, despite his lack of English. He took what we gave him: iced tea, chicken, sliced papayas, an extra blanket, a glass of water at night, but he never asked for anything. When we slipped into English with each other, his eyes followed our conversation, as if somehow by listening well enough, he would understand. I showed him how to set the alarm on the clock radio and tried to explain the difference between the settings for music and the buzzing sound.

"You push this all the way for music," I said, "and halfway for the alarm." But he wasn't looking at the clock. I felt, even then, that he was studying me.

Every morning he went with Allan to Capitol Hill. Sometimes Harry went with them, and a few times I did too, but mostly I stayed home, taking care of our normal house or grading student papers. When Alex returned, usually in the late afternoons, I would ask him how things went, and he would shrug and smile and shake his head. *"Vale."* So I taught him to say *Fine.*

At night, I would hear him talking into the tape recorder we gave him. He suffered from insomnia, and whenever I woke, which was often to check on Sean, to comfort him from a dream or cover him with the blanket he had kicked off, I heard Alex murmuring downstairs. Sometimes I watched him from the landing, in his circle of lamplight as he sat on the couch, leaning over the coffee table with his notes, and what he called his charts, talking to himself or into the machine. Sometimes I went all the way down the stairs and sat beside him to see if he wanted to talk, but usually he said that he preferred to tell the machine everything, and then we could listen later.

On one tape, he tried to talk a bit about himself rather than other people, but he found this difficult because he was genuinely bewildered by who he had become, and found it almost impossible to connect his boyhood self with himself in the present.

On this tape, he kept starting over: "Hello. My name is Alex." PAUSE. "This is Alex speaking." PAUSE. CLICK. "This is Alex. When I was seven years old, I was a normal child of that place, without ideas and without a future." CLICK. He never said the name of his country. It was always "that place."

"What am I trying to say with these declarations? What can be done with the truth of one person?" he said into the machine.

—◆—

CLICK. "I was born on the 21st of September 1962. My pseudonym is Alex. I'm from a middle-class family, and because of the times, I took refuge in military service. They promised me a special training for special work. I was to join an elite group, they said, and I was proud because of it, proud before my father and proud of what my intelligence had made possible for me. The training we received was very precise, very specific. At first it was about codes and code breaking, and then about surveillance techniques, and by the time it was about interrogations and disposing of people, it was too late." CLICK.

Alex said he would take people into the back of a van, tie them up, and bludgeon them to instill fear, not bludgeon to death, or even to loss of consciousness, and all the while the interrogator, or the intelligence officer or the adviser who was with him, would ask questions, and through their swollen mouths, broken teeth, and blood these people would try to answer, and often the answer, according to Alex, was "I don't know." And, in fact, Alex said, he believes now that this was true, that they didn't know, and so, shaking his head sadly at this new realization, he whispered into the machine, "so they were telling the truth." Nevertheless, when the questioner had had enough, Alex was told to dispose of the person, which he understood to mean killing.

CLICK. "Our unit was ordered to dispose of people after their interrogations were finished. I always looked at the faces of the interrogators: the face of Corporal Alvarez, the face of Subsergeant [unintelligible], codenamed Eduardo, for the sign."

The youngest victim in Alex's memory was a boy of fifteen, the oldest an old woman, old enough to be a grandmother, he said.

"How did you do it?" I asked, pretending that I didn't know, that I had not seen the bodies such teams as his threw onto the roads or left at the so-called body dumps, stripped and hacked apart, eyes gouged or pecked by vultures, that I hadn't seen the machete marks, the open mouths stuffed with genitals, swollen bodies in putrefaction, that I hadn't taken the smell of corpses into myself so deeply that for the rest of my life I would know that smell and not mistake it for anything else.

"Well, in my case," he said, "I would take my knife to their throat and look them in the eyes so that I could see their fear and helplessness, which interested me, and I would start cutting. The air would create bubbles in the blood from the throat, and there would be a deep gurgling noise. Sometimes they were still looking at me, terrified and helpless, as this happened. That bubbling and gurgling is a distinct sound. Sometimes I dream of the bubbles."

"Alex, who did you think those people were that you were killing?"

"I was told they were persons of interest, and also that they were Communists and subversives and so on. You know, *subversivos*. They were all *subversivos*. But I had no idea."

"And then what?"

"And then we left them somewhere, sometimes in front of a specific house in order to send a signal, and at other times this seemed not to matter, so we took them, as I told you, to the beach or to the dump or we just tossed them out along the road. Some corpses were thrown into the lakes. And I know that several living people were pushed into the sea from helicopters. In some disposals we took them to the beach and tied them to dynamite so their bodies would explode and scatter on the rocks near the sea. There were all sorts of ways of doing things."

———◆———

After preschool one afternoon, Sean brought his chess set to Alex and asked if he would play with him. Sean didn't yet know how to play chess, but he enjoyed moving the pieces around, which he also called "persons." I might have asked Sean not to bother Alex, but to my surprise, Alex seemed pleased and began setting up the board.

"I know this game," he said. "I know this! ¡Ajedrez! This is the game they taught us during our training to help us understand strategy. Sí. I used to play against myself, both sides of the board. Either way I won, either way I beat myself."

He shook his head and laughed for perhaps the first time during his stay with us, and somehow, that afternoon, he taught Sean what the pieces were and how they moved—¡el rey, la reina, el caballo, el torre, el alfil, el peón, y muchos peones!—and somehow Sean learned to play, although he made his moves impulsively, while Alex studied the board for a long time between moves. Alex was a patient teacher, but he also took every game seriously, even those played against a child, and that is how I glimpsed that he was at least in small measure a child himself, he was still the boy he was on the day he entered military service. During their games, I brought them juice and Goldfish crackers or milk and bread with jam, and the birch fire rose behind them in the fireplace as night fell and the early winter windows blackened. It seemed all right then. Harry was coming home earlier and earlier, which was nice too, but I didn't ask him why. I assumed that his work in the housing project was going well and, of course, he liked best to make photographs when the light was good, and the light faded early in November.

———◆———

By the second week or so, Alex seemed to be growing weary of telling his story over and over, and was beginning to feel that no one understood what he was trying to say, or else they didn't care, which was a source of great frustration. One night he said to me: "People think that what happens to someone else has nothing to do with them. They think that what happens in one place doesn't matter anyplace else."

This reminded me of something I had read years earlier—a single sentence from *The Captive Mind* by the poet Czesław Miłosz, written when he was also young: *If a thing exists in one place, it will exist everywhere.* That sentence had lodged within me, glinting in the darkness of my unformed thoughts, and what it meant to me was that every evil permitted anywhere in the world could spread to the whole of the world. I quoted Miłosz to Alex, who seemed pleased that his observation was reflected in the writings of an important Polish poet.

"What else does he say?"

"Well, there's a passage where he describes a village in Europe during the war, the villagers going about their business, a man bicycling to his office, buying bread I think it was, and the next day, this same man is searching through the smoking ruins of this village for a potato. Or something like that. I think the chapter began with Miłosz's trying to explain why people in the West, Americans, seemed like large children to the Europeans. Miłosz thought it was because they had never experienced this kind of loss: a bustling village one day, and ruins the next."

"Like children?"

"I think that's what he thought, yes, as I remember."

"This is interesting, thank you," Alex said.

———◆———

Toward the end of his time in El Salvador, Alex had started to dream about the killings, and despite all his training, these nightmares took away the peace of his sleep, and he woke, more and more often, drenched and crying out, having gazed into his own eyes in the dream as a knife wielded by his doppelgänger sawed away at his throat.

"I was killing myself," he said, "using my own technique—I had to get out."

This was more than he had ever said. We were sitting on the oatmeal-colored sofa. It was well after midnight.

"I realized what they had done to me," he said after a long silence.

"What who had done?"

"My superior officers. They had taken my soul away and made me into a monster. This wasn't me doing these things. It was the man who was trying to kill me in my sleep."

"Why didn't you quit?"

He looked at me with patient incredulity.

"You *can't* quit," he said. "If they think you are even slightly pulling away or having doubts, they do something to you. And they *know.* You can't hide doubts from them. They give an order and if you hesitate, that's it. For a while I knew I had to get out but I also had to wait for my chance, because I would have only one chance, and if I didn't make it that would be it. You can't tell anyone. You can't confide in anyone. You have to have a plan. My plan was to take a bus to Mexico City and find some group, human rights or Green Cross, and tell them everything and ask for protection."

"So what happened?"

"I'm here, talking to you. I'm not going to say how I did it. Someone else might want to get out too, using the same method."

"These men who were going to kill you, Alex, who are they? Who did you run away from?"

"*Mirá,* this is what I have been trying to tell you, all of you. Here you live happily. Children live happily, with a great sense of tranquillity. I come from a country where there is only misery, and I've been thinking . . ."

The logs hissed from the wetness of the unseasoned wood, and a blackened split of oak fell into the ash.

"Thinking what?"

"The risk I'm taking is very great. Someone said to me—Allan said—why don't you tell the Americans this and why don't you tell the Americans that? Tell them where their money is going. But the man who is suggesting that I talk doesn't know what it's like to come out of a military—*concentration camp*. I've been making these declarations in the offices on Capitol Hill, and I have realized something. The Americans already *know* what's going on, and have known for a long time. What's going on is *fine* with the Americans, so what am I doing here? Yes, I tell them, we introduced civilians into the black-windowed vans. Yes, we were out of uniform when we did this. The people were hooded and bound and had no chance whatsoever to save themselves. We were under orders. So now the Americans know the truth. I told them who Orlando Zepeda is, the vice minister of defense. I told them about the commander of the Belloso Battalion. They know. So it doesn't matter now if they put me in prison. I feel much more tranquil. The information is released. I feel tranquil. And I don't care whether the tape recorder is on or off."

———◆———

Some nights later, Allan brought a police artist to the house who carried with him a book of faces: a catalogue of noses, eyes, lips, chins, beards and mustaches, foreheads with their hairlines, the hair itself, and this artist sat beside Alex, asking him to choose a nose from among the noses that most clearly resembled the nose of the man Alex had been calling William, the American adviser who taught his unit techniques of interrogation and methods of disposal. They were to make police sketches of two men, William and another American who never gave his name but who spoke Spanish well and Alex believed him to be originally from elsewhere. This nameless, quieter American seemed to be there always to observe William, as if he were an apprentice, but he was also there, Alex thought, because he was the only person who spoke both languages.

"He used to interpret for us."

"Interpret interrogations?"

"No. Interpret William to everyone else."

Such sketches were then done by hand, and the artist patiently redrew Alex's changes of mind until there were two sketches before us, his final version of both faces, drawn to Alex's satisfaction. He marveled at the accuracy of the depictions and, after the artist left, kept lifting the sketches from the coffee table and gazing into them, his face clouded with anger.

I don't remember quite what these sketches were for, nor to whom they were to be shown. Allan wanted them, perhaps for a film he was making about all of this, or for the television news, hoping someone would come forward to identify these Americans, and, of course, the significance of having to depict them in this way was not lost on anyone.

———◆———

Every dawn I heard the shower running down the hall, a door opening and closing, and then footsteps hurrying down the stairs. Before everyone else was up, Alex was usually seated at the table, hair slicked back, dressed in the crisp new clothes Allan had brought to him: khakis and a dress shirt buttoned all the way up, no tie, waiting patiently for coffee. On this particular morning, I woke earlier for some reason and was already busy in the kitchen when he came down. *Buenas.*

On this morning, a light snow drifted like ash from the clouds. According to the radio, there was a blizzard in Nebraska, with gusting winds and temperatures as cold as 25 degrees below zero. In Michigan, where my parents still lived, it was also snowing. Outside now there were only flurries, ticking like coarse salt against the windows, with here and there a dry brown leaf rattling on a branch.

Alex had his own radio now, a portable Grundig shortwave, and he had been spinning through the frequencies that morning. I remember vaguely listening to the high whines of his signals, intermittent voices, and white noise coming from his direction, when I noticed that he'd gotten up and crossed the room, turned on the television set, and was kneeling before it, watching with his eyes close to the screen. There was footage from El Salvador with the breaking news that six Jesuit priests at the Catholic university had been murdered, along with their housekeeper and her daughter. Among them was Father Ellacuría. Alex was studying the footage: soldiers milling about, and although it was not yet reported that these murders had been committed by the Salvadoran military, Alex was convinced that he recognized members of his own unit in the footage.

———◆———

A few nights later, I was sitting with him again. Harry and Sean were both asleep. The refrigerator hummed but otherwise the house was quiet. It was still snowing. Something had changed in Alex since the Jesuit murders were reported. He was armored again, much as he had been that first night, and he was nervous too. I offered him a glass of water, and he said no but then took it. There was something he wanted to ask me.

"Do you think I killed some of your friends?"

"What do you mean?"

"You're looking at me as if you think I killed some of your friends."

He was leaning toward me, reading me, narrowing his eyes, and then, satisfied, leaned back into the couch and smiled, as if he were teasing or joking.

"I'm tired," I remember saying. "I'm going upstairs." And I asked if he wanted an extra blanket.

"No, thank you. I don't sleep."

The next day, Allan brought Alex's "girlfriend" to the house to "calm him down," and she stayed with us too, for about a week, mostly in the guest room with the door shut. I began to make telephone calls on the advice of a human rights lawyer in San Francisco, but it seemed there was no provision in international law to protect such men as Alex. No country would provide asylum to a confessed perpetrator of crimes against humanity, no matter how contrite, no matter how valuable his testimony. If such a man emerged from the darkness of the abattoirs to give evidence of state crimes, there was simply no place for him to go. I realized that Alex now knew he was trapped.

Harry had also noticed a shift in Alex's demeanor and by now had seen the dead eyes in his photograph. Sometimes, he told me, the camera sees things we don't. It was time for Alex to go.

When they left, I gave him a packed lunch and a carton of cigarettes. He wouldn't look at me at first, and then smiled sheepishly.

"You did the right thing, coming here," I told him. "I hope you find peace." *Que le vaya bien*—

A few weeks later we were told that twenty-seven federal agents had surrounded the apartment where Alex was staying in Los Angeles, had apprehended him, and summarily deported him to the custody of the Salvadoran government, whereupon he was immediately imprisoned. Some years later, Sean would tell me that he didn't remember the man called Alex, who had once stayed with us, but he had always wondered how he had learned to play chess.

The photographs of the people Alex and the others killed were collected by Salvadoran human rights workers into those plastic photo albums with peel-away plastic pages: the high school faces of the dead, some of them still students, others social workers or teachers, labor organizers, activists, lay church workers. There were doctors and lawyers among them. But most seemed oddly to be the same age, about eighteen, posing in the last photograph taken as they were about to finish school. Yes, there were some who were younger and some older in these pictures, those who had looked into a camera at a wedding or family gathering, but still they comprised a graduating class of the dead. We didn't, of course, think of them as dead yet but as disappeared, and until one of them was found at a body dump or on the beach or in the morgue, and the swollen or mutilated face somehow matched to the smiling face in the book, we thought of them as missing. When a body was found that matched, it would be placed in a coffin, sometimes with a window cut over the face so that the mourners could see that yes, this was indeed that brother or friend, and the coffin would be taken to the altar for Sunday Mass, where Monseñor Romero welcomed them and recited their names into microphones, so the names would be heard throughout the basilica or the cathedral, and also on the radio and in the streets. It didn't matter how many names. He called out all of them.

A ll we had in the beginning was one table in a shack with primitive tools and no saws to break up the bodies. We were going to have difficulties here, the doctor told me, but it doesn't matter. We can do it with one knife. That is how they began to perform autopsies on the butchered dead. Later the forensic specialists from Argentina would excavate the mass graves at sites such as El Mozote in Morazán, where hundreds of civilians were massacred by the Atlacatl battalion trained in counterinsurgency by the Americans. El Mozote had declared itself neutral, aligned with neither the guerrillas nor the army. El Mozote had twenty houses, a church, and a convent. In the days before the massacre, people from the surrounding countryside had taken refuge there. When the soldiers arrived, they made the people lie facedown while they searched and questioned them. Then the villagers were told to lock themselves in their houses overnight. Anyone seen leaving would be shot. The soldiers spent the night there too, and in the morning the villagers were gathered together again: men separated from women and women from children. First the men were taken, then the women and girls were raped and machine-gunned. They cut the throats of the children and hung them in the trees. When everyone was dead they set fire to the buildings. The single surviving witness had hidden herself in a tree. Over a month later, journalists reported blackened bones and rotting human flesh beneath the ruins, but these reports were denied by the governments of El

Salvador and the United States, and the journalists accused of "gross exaggerations." Such massacres also happened at that time in La Joya canton and the villages of Jocote Amarillo and Los Toriles and also in Cerro Pando canton. Eventually the forensic specialists gathered and stored the remains in a one-story white building. Shoeboxes held the skeletons of infants.

S mall things can always be carried. Miniature clay figures broken into many pieces. I have a small collection from the war years, and I had always planned to repair them, but for that I would need patience and time, a magnifying glass, the tiniest of tools, and whatever glue would hold together pieces of unfired clay. My sight is not what it was, nor my memory. It would require days of sorting: a pile of limbs, plantains, hats, mangoes, *cántaros* for drawn water, market baskets, another basket of shoes, heads, and roofless huts, the man and the woman broken while making love under the clay dome, one or the other crying out. I have kept the pieces, so it wouldn't be impossible, just as certain thoughts have kept their broken moments in my forgetfulness: the abandoned road, the still-smoking crib of blackened corn, the blue smoke rising from ruined fields.

T here were eight attempts to assassinate Leonel, and finally the military sent a unit of sixty soldiers to apprehend him. He received an advance warning and managed to hide himself in a large pile of garbage against a building on his street. He had to stay in the garbage for hours. "The dogs knew I was there," he said, "the children knew I was there, everyone knew I was there except the army. I was very moved that no one gave me away."

He arrived in Washington, D.C., and was eventually granted political asylum. During much of the war, he worked tirelessly to inform individual congressmen and senators about El Salvador, particularly those who had committee assignments that gave them power over such matters as certification of respect for human rights. Sometimes I worked with him, but I also spent some of the war years in Lebanon, South Africa, and France, and when I returned to the United States, I continued to give readings and talks, but was mostly taken up with keeping a household and raising our son. When the Chapultepec Peace Accords were signed in 1992, I returned to El Salvador to attend the celebrations of the peace at the invitation of Resistencia Nacional and my friends in the Catholic Church. I also went back several times during the 1990s to help Leonel with various projects, mostly investigations of political assassinations and corruption, so we did work together during stretches of time, and I was able to see Margarita too, who also visited me once in the United States. We have stayed in touch with each other. In 2009, I was invited to attend the twentieth-anniversary commemoration of the murders of the six Jesuit priests, their housekeeper, and her daughter. That was a very moving week and included visits with Leonel, who now lived with a dog named Rupert who appeared to be a husky, and a mean parrot who tormented the dog. One afternoon then, I was sitting in Leonel's *casita,* watching the parrot pull on the dog's coat and run away, and talking with Leonel about gold-mining operations in Cabañas, when John Taylor, the Peace Corps volunteer who had picked me up that first night at Ilopango International Airport all those years ago, walked in unexpectedly. We were pleasantly surprised to see each other but, in hindsight, it was a bit strange that we reunited just then after thirty years. We sat for an hour or so and talked. Leonel was happy that we were there. Like old times.

I t isn't the risk of death and fear of danger that prevent people from rising up," Leonel once said, "it is numbness, acquiescence, and the defeat of the mind. Resistance to oppression begins when people realize deeply within themselves that something better is possible." He also said that what destroys a society, a state, a government, is corruption—that, and the use of force, which is always applied against those who have not been convinced or included. He was always talking about corruption: trying to prevent it, expose it, eradicate it. He was dedicated to the task of *bringing the sin to the eye.*

"This is the stage of denunciation," he said, "which precedes the revolutionary moment." He did not believe in war as a solution. There is no instance, he said, of a country's having benefited from long warfare. But if the armed struggle begins, it must not fail or the poor will suffer for another two hundred years. He said he hoped that the leadership of the various guerrilla factions were not imagining more than they could achieve. It wasn't that he was either for or against them.

"I have no doctrinal allegiances. I'm interested in critique of ideology rather than its promulgation. But we will see," he said, "as your poet Bertolt Brecht suggested, the power of the poor to change the course of history is the world's one hope." (When he quoted poets, they were somehow almost always referred to as *my* poets.)

"What I have been doing is something like three-dimensional chess.

When you are playing chess with oppressors, you must think twelve moves ahead. Must not let your guard down. Must stay focused, as the Vietnamese were, must have patience as they did, must study and know the enemy better than they know themselves." Eventually, he would tell me that he had gone to Vietnam, and I was never clear whether this was at the end of the American war or just after, but he had met General Võ Nguyên Giáp, who commanded their forces against the Americans and was considered one of the greatest military strategists of the twentieth century, according to Leonel. Did I remember the photograph I had seen in the *casita*? The man with whom he was shaking hands? That was General Giáp.

In Vietnam, Leonel had studied how the war had been fought, but he'd not had much time, which is why he kept reading anything published on this subject. Later I was told, by someone in a position to know, that some of the Salvadoran guerrilla fighters had received their training from Vietnam, not Cuba, so they fought like the Vietnamese. One night, after one of the peace talks, Leonel took a friend out to see the flickering of flashlights in the surrounding hills.

"They keep moving on the perimeter," he'd said, "they don't rest or slow down. They can fight with fewer this way, fast and mobile but fewer, light on their feet, without the need for massive supply lines. They can discharge their weapons and run ahead, firing from another place, so that it seems they are greater in number, forcing the enemy to use up its ammunition."

It was Leonel, working tirelessly for years, who "put the peace talks together," as they said, and brought about the end of the war.

"It was like putting a massive jigsaw puzzle together and it took him years. He did it with friendships, contacts, connections. We were only some of the pieces of this puzzle," the person in a position to know said.

I asked this person, whom I will call David, many questions, and here is some of what he said: "Leonel was invited to join the Resistencia Nacional faction of the guerrilla forces but he declined, saying he could do more good on the outside. He was in touch with their commander, Fermán Cienfuegos, who called Leonel *Gordo*—you can guess why. It was Leonel who arranged the first peace talks between the FMLN [Farabundo Martí National Liberation Front] and the military. The representative of the FMLN was, as it turned out, the "Alfredo" of the night of the cashews raining on the roof of the little *casita*. Alfredo had long had Cienfuegos's permission to talk to Leonel, and Leonel had given him good information throughout the war. Leonel had talked to everyone, as he always insisted, but because that included the Americans in those days, he came under suspicion.

"It was the commander of another faction who put out the word that Leonel worked for the CIA," said David, "the same commander who, it is alleged, killed the poet Roque Dalton. But you know, Carolyn, at that time the CIA operatives in Central America were old Cold War anti-Communists and Leonel despised them. He would talk to them, but that's all it was. Talk."

I wanted to know about Leonel's collection of miniature ships, which had grown to the size of several fleets. Leonel had first shown a few of them to me when he was drawing his first mural in California. They were made by Wiking-Modellbau in Germany.

"I don't know about that," David said. "I wasn't involved with the ships."

Early in his exile in the United States, when asked about himself, Leonel answered that he was a coffee farmer, and later, when they took his coffee farm away, he would describe himself as a social critic and political exile and, finally, an investigator of crimes against humanity. He would not say that he had also been a champion marksman and motorcycle racer, a painter, an expert on Formula One cars, a historian of military strategy, a part-time inventor, a collector of miniature ship models, and an adviser to politicians, Catholic priests, Carmelite nuns, diplomats, labor leaders, and at least one guerrilla commander. He would never tell anyone that the handmade AK-47 awarded to him in competition, which he kept in a glass display case, was fully loaded and always had been. We were mistaken to think that the sign affixed to the case that read IN CASE OF EMERGENCY BREAK GLASS was a little joke.

During those winters of exile, he wore an old army jacket but never a hat. He loved dogs and called them all *Chucho* (Mutt). Once I found him making plastic boots out of sandwich baggies for a small dog put in his charge so as to keep the ice and snow from its paws. For himself, he acquired good hiking boots, camping gear, fine pipe tobacco, and a Swiss Army knife with multiple gadgets. In answer to many people's questions, he would reply: I'm not an American, but I *like* Americans; he would also add: except assholes and sons of bitches. To solve problems, he would fall asleep for a little while and often wake up with an answer. He was sensitive to the moods of others except when utterly oblivious. The obliviousness was always deliberate. He would go over and over everything he worked on and thought about, playing the reel of his recall, rewinding, playing again, listening for what he might have missed, asking the same questions over and over, repeating his stories again and again, almost word for word until some detail stopped him, something that seemed right the first twenty times but wasn't. Let me show you something, he would say, and then take me to a barracks, a village, a *maquiladora,* and ask me to tell him what I saw and then what else I saw. He would eventually point out what it was that I had missed. You daydream too much, Papu, you don't pay attention. I once asked him what it would take to make the United States a good country. Well for one thing, you could green the hemisphere, he said. You have the resources and the capacity. You won't do this, unfortunately, but you could. You believe yourselves to be apart from others and therefore have little awareness of your interdependencies and the needs of the whole. Other times he said that he admired Americans for their philanthropic generosity, not highly developed elsewhere. He also admired German engineering and Swedish aid projects. He was critical of Marxists but not of Karl Marx. One of the times I angered him most, I remembered, was when I disparaged the Soviet Union, and he reminded me of their loss of twenty million souls during the war. You Americans wouldn't begin to understand, he said, and do you know what happened to Soviet Russia only four years after their revolution? That isn't in your textbooks, is it? I think not. And Cuba? What *about* Cuba? They're Latins. The goddamn Soviets tried to get them to sit down and play chess. When it came to El Salvador, however, he brought everything back to the campesino. What about the campesino? he always asked, no matter what was under discussion. When I first met him, he was trying to prevent a war he knew was coming, that in fact had already begun, and later devoted himself to bringing that war to an end. *I don't have much time,* he often said. Or: *I'm running out of time.* Or *we* are running out of time, and I wondered to whom this *we* referred, and felt best when I imagined that he somehow included me in his efforts.

Cuando me hiciste otro, te dejé conmigo.
When you made me into another, I left
you with me.

—**Antonio Porchia**

Ｗe climbed the slope of the Guazapa volcano with the box of his ashes, taking turns as we carried it, having left the vehicles behind on the stony road. His were finer and grayer than the ashes of others, and I wondered why this was, thinking that the fire in which they burned him must have been hotter—but mercifully the vision of him in flames died out, and I returned to the work of making my way over the stones behind the men from La Mora: Luis and Candelario. The mayor of the nearest town was to be next in our convoy, but his jeep gave out when its undercarriage struck a boulder loosened in the rainy season. So now the mayor, too, walked, but only we carried the box, although nothing was ever said about this, that we should be the only ones to carry it: Leonel's two daughters, their mother, and I.

Sunlight broke through the canopy of jacaranda, cedar, and bamboo, filtering down to the saplings that had already grown to my height in the deepest crater dug here during the war, when the blast was heard in the surrounding hills and seen as black smoke rising to the clouds from where it came—trees yanked out by their roots, boulders sprayed into the air, and earth blasted away, taken up, never to rain back down. Nothing was ever found of that earth again. It remained in the clouds.

None of us had expected that he would die in a hospital bed. Even toward the end, when he fell asleep as he talked but no longer slept through the night, we didn't expect this way of death. We feared that he would be assassinated, or that one night, our telephones would ring and we would be told that he was disappeared, and in the days that followed we would search through the body dumps and along the black sand beaches of the coast for his corpse.

From the peak of the volcano, city and sea are visible, and the whole of the country as it shrinks to its place on the maps, small and poor beneath us—a country that had for a time grown large under the gaze of the world. Before the war, tapirs lived in the mountain's folds, monkeys and iguanas, coyotes and even jaguars, the wildcat of his prescient dreams. Hundreds of species of birds alighted here, a thousand of butterflies, and the streams ran clear through Guazapa's ridges to the river. No longer. Thousands of pounds of bombs rained into this forest during the war. White phosphorus and napalm also rained. So that might have been the reason he had brought me here just before the war began, and why he was silent all afternoon more than thirty-five years ago. He had said that he wanted to show me a beautiful place, to take a rest from the work we were doing, to climb, to see as far as we could. But I now know that we were here for a different reason: here so that he could steady the far hills in his field glasses and read the terrain of a future free-fire zone, here to commit the mountain to paper and then to say good-bye. I still have the paper on which he drew the mountain.

Ahuachapán prison, too, remains with me. When I hear the word "Ahuachapán" there is a wind rising out of a smoking village, and processions of campesinos on the roadside, my husband is holding Olivier in his arms, and along the banks of the Río Sumpul, vultures rise and fall over the dead, and so thick is this flock that the banks seem to be rippling like the river. Ahuachapán gives me the last time I saw the labor leader José Rodolfo Viera alive, and he is waving to me from the back of a truck before it rolls into a white cloud of road toward his future assassin. Margarita and I are walking along the beach, trying to find the corpse of a missing Danish woman, and we don't find her but someone else does—she had been shot through the forehead after watching her young husband be tortured to death. I can show you their photographs and give the details; there are reports on everything. Ahuachapán.

In this country named for the savior, its cities and villages for the saints, people throw flowers into the lakes to calm the volcanoes and prevent the disappearance of fish. They paint their lives on *copinol* seeds they call the seeds of God. The children follow behind the coffins of the dead and sing, tossing little gifts into the graves.

This morning, we're expected to leave Leonel here in the skirt of the sleeping volcano. Luis and Candelario have a place in mind and we follow them toward it as though we were in a *guinda,* walking single file up the volcano, but there is no army pursuing us. The men know what they're looking for: a spot high on the slope with a view of the hills, not for him but for those who will come here in the future to pay their respects. And they will come. Light soaks through the bamboo stands and palm fronds, a whirring light, and moments of the past arrive, hovering like the dragonflies above us. Our photographs are taken in the bomb crater among the saplings that have grown almost to our shoulders since the war, and beside the truck that will now be given to Padre Walter Guerra. Despite the solemnity of the occasion we laugh over the decision to divide his ashes between the volcano and the *jocote* tree that grew behind the clinic in La Mora so that he will always have *jocote* to eat and the people will have a place to bring flowers and questions to him. The girls who had once played with rabbits on my floor are now grown, and they concur with the decision. From the *jocote,* he will have a view of the mango tree that gave shelter to the first peace talks, which wouldn't have happened so soon or perhaps at all without him. There are plenty of his ashes to go around.

Over the years, I have been asked why, as a twenty-seven-year-old American poet who spoke Spanish brokenly and knew nothing about the isthmus of the Americas, I would accept the invitation of a man I barely knew to spend time in a country on the verge of war. And why would this stranger, said to be a lone wolf, a Communist, a CIA operative, a world-class marksman, and a small-time coffee farmer, take any interest in a naïve North American poet? As one man put it, what does poetry have to do with anything?

We reach the chosen place and open the box, and before digging my hand into his remains, I ask him quietly within myself if I might tell the story now. Everything. Or almost everything. Of course! he bellows. Write! Write and do not waste time! Why do you think I brought you to Salvador in the first place? So you could eat papayas? You're a goddamn poet, Papu. You must write.

People ask me now what it was like to work with him in the early days before the war. Some still want to know who he really was, of course, but that is now becoming apparent to friends and also to enemies, as he knew it might one day. This is what I tell people now:

It was as if he had stood me squarely before the world, removed the blindfold, and ordered me to open my eyes.

Acknowledgments

T his book was written from memory over a period of fifteen years, with help from notebooks and photographs, reminiscences with those who shared in these lived moments, and research to confirm the facts inlaid in the recollections. I am not a historian or journalist but a poet, and although this might be called a memoir, it is not about myself but about others living and dead to whom I owe a debt of immense gratitude, especially to the mentor who guided this journey, Leonel Gómez Vides. He died before I could finish this book, but I hope I have at last fulfilled his only request: that I write about what happened. This story includes some events in my earlier life, a summer in Mallorca, and seven extended stays in El Salvador between early January 1978 and March 1980. There are passages about the war and its aftermath, and several return visits ending in 2009. Many men, women, and children in El Salvador helped me toward awareness, receiving and educating me with immense patience and generosity, most especially St. Oscar Romero of the Americas, who was then our Monseñor Romero. I'm deeply grateful to my friend and sister Margarita Herrera, and also to Padre Walter Guerra, Dr. Vicky Guzmán, the late José Rodolfo Viera, Ricardo Stein (Guatemala), Padre Ignacio Ellacuría (Spain), Monseñor Ricardo Urioste, and Madre Luz and her religious community of the Congregation of the Carmelite Missionary Sisters of St. Therese. My gratitude also to those who were not known by their birth names then or have wished to retain their pseudonyms now for reasons of privacy: "Luisa," "V," "Fina," "Ana," "Ricardo," "Alfredo," "Porfirio," "Chencho," "Bartolomé," and, for his testimony, "Alex." Thank you, Bruce Forché, for so generously sharing war memories, and Katharine Anderson for giving permission to quote extensively from a letter written by her late father, Tom Anderson. I also thank Teresa Gómez Koudjeti, Gene Palumbo, Joselito Acosta Alvarez, Salvador Sanabria, and Alexander Renderos; the people of the Empalizada and Conchagua fincas and the communities of Santa Marta and La Mora. For that first inspiring summer in Deià, I thank Maya Flakoll Gross and her mother, the late Claribel Alegría; her late husband, Bud Flakoll; and their other daughters, Patricia Alegría and Karen Fauché. For patient guidance and friendship during my earlier years, I thank the late Teles Reyna and Ya-kwana Goodmorning of Taos Pueblo, and John Chaske Rouillard, Santee Dakota Sioux.

Among those from the United Sates, I wish to acknowledge John Taylor, Peace Corps volunteer; the late congressman Joe Moakley of Massachusetts; Congressman James McGovern of Massachusetts; Tim Rieser, senior foreign policy aide to Senator Patrick Leahy of Vermont; and also Richard McCall, Tim Phillips, Leslie Bumstead, and her husband, Doug Farah, then of *The Washington Post*. For support from the beginning, I thank Laurel Blossom, John Teeter, the late Josephine Crum; Rose Styron and Robert Maurer of Amnesty International; for certain confirmations of fact, the late Robert Parry of Consortium News; for background on the disappearance of James Ronald Richardson, former ambassador William Walker; for courage and tenacity in the cause of justice, Carolyn Patty Blum, clinical professor of law emeritus at the University of California, Berkeley, and senior legal adviser of the Center for Justice and Accountability.

For the gift of peace, solitude, and time, thank you, Hedgebrook, where much of this was written, and especially its founder, Nancy Nordhoff; the Civitella Ranieri Foundation in Umbria and its director, Dana Prescott; the Atlantic Center for the Arts; and the Fine Arts Work Center in Provincetown. I'm grateful to the Benedictine monks of Glenstal Abbey, and to Fanny Howe for sharing contemplative time with me there; Honor Moore for many readings of this work during those autumns at Otterbrook; and my dear extended family, Ashley and Maryam Ashford-Brown of Le Bois Valet in Normandy and Scott Cairns and Marcia Vanderlip of Tacoma. For much needed encouragement and support, I thank J. Patrick Lannan and the Lannan Foundation; Fr. David Ungerleider, S.J.; Robert and Peg Boyers and Patricia Rubio of Skidmore College; Daniele Struppa, Anna Leahy, and Richard Bausch of Chapman University; the faculty of Newcastle University in Newcastle upon Tyne; the Sierra Nevada College MFA program; and President John J. DeGioia and my colleagues at Georgetown University. Thank you to James Silk of Yale University's Law School, to the Divinity School, and to the Beinecke Rare Book and Manuscript Library for the Windham-Campbell Prize. I'm grateful to those who honor the work of St. Oscar Romero, most especially the Rothko Chapel and the Romero Center Ministries of Camden, New Jersey, particularly the late Lawrence DiPaul.

Many writers, poets, and friends have discussed this work with me along the way and helped me toward clarity, among them Linda Anderson, Connie Braun, Barbara Cully, Chard deNiord, Joanna Eleftheriou, Nick Flynn, Aminatta Forna, Andrea Gilats, Lise Goett, Garth Greenwell, Patricia Guzmán, Kaaren Kitchell, Elee Kraljii Gardiner, Susan Landgraf, Jen Marlowe, Glen Retief, Suzanne Roberts, Kaia Sand, Mona Sfeir, Gloria Steinem, Penn Szittya, and Duncan Wu; and for helping me to the finish, Lars Gustaf Andersson of Lund University, Sweden; Robin Flicker of New York City; and Francisco Larios of Nicaragua, living in the United States. For encouragement at the beginning, I thank Margaret Atwood and my first agent, the late Virginia Barber. Her successor, Bill Clegg, found the best possible publisher. Thank you, Ann Godoff, and everyone else at Penguin Press. My editor, Christopher Richards, has been exemplary. Thanks also to Sarah Hutson and to Juliana Kiyan for publicity and to Bruce Giffords for editorial production.

Fifteen years ago, this book began at the behest of poet Ilya Kaminsky, who said it was time. Over the years, young people from El Salvador who were brought to the United States by their parents because of the war and its aftermath have come to me wanting to know more about their birth country. This is for them. It is also for my son, Sean Christophe, so he will know this part of his parents' past, and for my father, Michael Joseph Sidlosky, and in memory of my mother, Louise Blackford Sidlosky. Finally, I thank my husband, Harry Mattison, my first and always reader, for sharing this with me, his memories, his photographs, the life and its testimony, always with love.